Politics Ancient and Modern

For Benedetto Bravo

Politics Ancient and Modern

Pierre Vidal-Naquet, 1930-

Translated by Janet Lloyd

Polity Press

This translation first published 1995 by Polity Press in association with
Blackwell Publishers.

Published with the assistance of the French Ministry of Culture.

Editorial office:
Polity Press
65 Bridge Street
Cambridge CB2 1UR, UK

Marketing and production:
Blackwell Publishers Ltd
108 Cowley Road
Oxford OX4 1JF, UK

Basil Blackwell Inc.
238 Main Street
Cambridge, MA 02142, USA

ISBN 0 7456 1080 3

A CIP catalogue record for this book is available from the British Library and
the Library of Congress.

Typeset in 10.5 on 12pt Times
by Graphicraft Typesetters Ltd., Hong Kong.
Printed in Great Britain by Hartnolls, Bodmin, Cornwall.

This book is printed on acid-free paper.

Contents

───◦◦◦◦◉┤◄◄◄►►►▷│◉◦◦◦◦───

Translator's Note

I have used the following translations of classical texts:

Chicago University Press, Chicago and London:
Aeschylus, *The Suppliant Maidens*, tr. Seth G. Benardete, 1956.
Sophocles, *Antigone*, tr. Elizabeth Wyckoff, 1954.

Loeb Classical Library, London and Cambridge, Mass.:
Diogenes Laertius, tr. R. D. Hicks, 1979.
Plato, *Apology, Phaedrus*, tr. Harold North Fowler, 1967.
    Epistles, tr. R. G. Bury, 1981.
    Gorgias, tr. W. R. M. Lamb, 1953.
    Protagoras, tr. W. R. M. Lamb, 1967.
Plutarch, *Moralia*, tr. Frank Cole Babbit, 1968.
Thucydides, tr. Charles Forster Smith, 1969.
Xenophon, *Memorabilia*, tr. E. C. Marchant, 1965.
    Hellenica, tr. Carleton L. Brownson, 1968.
Pseudo-Xenophon, *The Constitution of the Athenians* in *Scripta Minora*,
    tr. G. W. Bowersock, 1968.

Acknowledgement

Chapter 2 is reprinted from *Critical Inquiry* 18, Winter 1992, pp. 300–6,
© Chicago University Press 1992, by kind permission.

Introduction:

Athenian Democracy in 1788

Politics Ancient and Modern is the title that Polity Press has chosen, with my full approval, for this collection of seven studies all but one of which[1] have already appeared, in French, in a book entitled *La Démocratie grecque vue d'ailleurs* (Flammarion, 1990).

I believe the English title succeeds in conveying what the pages that follow are about. What they set out to do is not so much to 'compare', in the sense in which, in social anthropology, comparisons are made between different societies or contrasts are drawn between societies once known as primitive and our own society. Their purpose, rather, is to 'reflect' upon a twofold register that is both 'ancient' and 'modern', remaining mindful of the fact that, on the one hand, the temporal element itself plays a by no means indifferent role and, on the other, the past of the ancient societies in question is not just any old past: it cannot, for instance, be set on the same level as the Indian or the Chinese past – a fact for which we should be both thankful and sorry. Sorry because comparisons between the Greek past and the Chinese past certainly can contribute most fruitfully to an understanding and interpretation of our own societies;[2] and thankful because there is no way of getting around the fact that the Graeco-Roman past is our own closest past and that it was upon the basis of that past and in relation to it that certain of our own still flourishing disciplines, such as philology and classical archaeology, were established.[3]

What I set out to do in the present work, then, is to operate against two different backgrounds in the context of a number of different subjects: Plato, for instance, and the question of when philosophy, as such, entered into our historical consciousness; the question of what, between 1750 and 1890, became of representations of the political institutions of the Greek city-state and of others too which, even today, still go by their Greek or

Latin names, for example 'democracy', 'republic'; and, last but not least, how certain myths much used in our own society fared in that period. One of my studies is devoted to an example that made and continues to make an exceptionally resounding impact, the myth of Atlantis, which, in the course of three centuries, has been used to promote various forms of modern nationalism despite the fact that it was for essentially pedagogical and philosophical purposes that Plato originally invented it. A recent collection of essays in which many parallel examples may be found bears the subtitle 'Is Antiquity modern?'[4]

That is a question one might assume to have been long since settled. One of the central themes of the present work is that of the distance separating the moderns from the ancients. As early as 1764, Jean Jacques Rousseau, in the ninth of his *Lettres écrites de la montagne* was warning the citizens of Geneva: 'you are not Romans or Spartans, you are not even Athenians'. And it was a warning which, after the Revolution, was re-peated by Benjamin Constant and then again in 1864 by Fustel de Coulanges in *The Ancient City*, not to mention the later admonishments of a revolutionary such as Karl Marx. However, that warning from Rousseau, whom plenty of revolutionaries claimed as their inspiration, had failed to prevent many of them – Robespierre and Saint-Just to name but two – identifying the destiny of the young French Republic with the Sparta that 'blazed like a flash of lightning amid the vast shadows'. And despite the fact that, in the nineteenth century, Athens settled down and became respectably bourgeois for the French and the English, as opposed to the Sparta to which many German intellectuals claimed allegiance, it was yet to undergo some astonishing and radical revivals in later years – as in 1968, for example.

It so happened that exactly five years after that now rather forgotten Parisian spring, Moses I. Finley sent me his little book *Democracy An-cient and Modern*,[5] which again set the democracy of the present day and its real or imaginary supporters alongside Athenian democracy, not over-looking the latter's activist aspect that had come under such critical fire ever since Plato or indeed Thucydides and Xenophon. There was a po-lemical dimension to Finley's book. Is it true that, as Anglo-Saxon theorists such as Seymour Lipset and W. H. Morris have suggested, what we call apathy is a factor that is favourable to the exercise of democracy, or does apathy, on the contrary, destroy democracy's very bases? Protagoras of Abdera, the only Greek theorist of Athenian democracy, believed, as did Finley, that every citizen could, in fact should, take pride in the exercise of the *techne politiké* that Zeus allotted to man.[6] That kind of political activism certainly involved risks, as Socrates' execution, following the vote of the *heliaea*, clearly shows; but it also made possible a fantastic social evolution, which even today continues to command our admiration and arouse our envy.

When his book was translated into French, in 1976, Finley asked me to set the polemical references in a French context. I did so in a long introductory essay[7] in which, using the example provided by the French Revolution, I tried to show how the Athenian concept of democracy had been transmitted – or, more likely, not transmitted – by the philosophers and actors of the great movement that marked the entry of France and Europe as a whole into our modern world.

The reason I mention this, a tiny point in itself, is that it marked my own personal entry into a new field, that of historical studies in historiography.

Such studies were certainly not alien to the thoughts and works of Finley, who in 1975 had published a collection of papers entitled *The Use and Abuse of History*, one of them a reprint of 'Utopianism ancient and modern', an essay originally written in honour of Herbert Marcuse.[8] Now that volume was, precisely, dedicated to Arnaldo Momigliano, the undisputed master of historiographical studies. Of course, when I in my turn ventured onto this path, one then relatively untrodden by French scholars, I inevitably did so as a disciple of Momigliano, whose *Studies in Historiography*[9] became one of my bedside books. Upon deeper reflection, Finley and Momigliano turn out to have more in common than simply their esteem for each other: both were exiles. In 1952, at the peak of the McCarthy crisis, Finley had been obliged to abandon his students at Rutgers, to whom he later dedicated the lectures that marked his return there in 1972. All his essays on historiography were written after his exile to England. As for Momigliano, who left Italy when Mussolini adopted a body of racial laws imitated from those of Nuremberg, his intellectual clash with fascism quite clearly played an important role in his early work as a historian of history,[10] the field in which he produced his masterpieces following his exile to England.

Having recalled the above facts, let us now ask ourselves why we do study the history of history. What do these enquiries in the 'ancient and modern' field contribute to our studies, in the most general sense of that word? I immediately detect two fundamental yet antagonistic motivations, both of which stem from what may, since Plato, be called the dialectic between the same and the other.

The first is a quest for axioms, a reaching back to origins, a return to sources. Since when have we been studying Roman and Greek history? Or, to be more precise, when was it that we stopped believing that Athenian history began in exactly 1581 BC, with Cecrops' reign in Attica, as is stated in the inscription (the Arundel Marble or Parian Marble) that

Nicolas Fabri de Pieresc found in Smyrna in the early seventeenth century and that may now be examined in the Ashmolean Museum in Oxford? The answer to that question is: since the publication, beginning in 1846, of George Grote's *Greek History*,[11] a work that set out to establish a radical separation between the time of myth and the time of history, tackling a problem that the entire Age of Enlightenment had confronted but not managed to resolve. It is true that the discovery of the Mycenaean world has, in its turn, once more called the whole matter into question without, however, making it possible to re-establish the chronology of those long-lost times.

The second approach that is favoured focuses systematically upon, not 'the same', but 'the other'. It seeks to trace epistemological cut-off points or breaks. It sets out to arouse unease rather than confidence. It reminds us that 'Thucydides is no colleague of ours'[12] and that we are the contemporaries of neither Xenophon nor even Voltaire.

There are disadvantages as well as advantages to both approaches. The danger of the search for what is the same is that it tends to obscure whatever is different. Is George Grote, the mid-nineteenth-century English liberal, really so close to us? We are accustomed to organize our bibliographies making a distinction between direct sources and scholarly research. The danger here is that we may be entering upon a *regressio ad infinitum*. Conversely, if one overemphasizes the 'epistemological breaks', one may cease to see that, despite all their disagreements, successive generations of scholars *have* understood one another.

As well as these two contrasting methodological approaches, another source of conflicts rates a mention. A specialist in ancient history who studies the history of his own discipline by, for example, tracking back to the eighteenth century will not reason in quite the same way as an eighteenth-century specialist for whom ancient history represents simply one particular dimension of his general field of study.[13] The first of these two scholar models will more or less automatically set the greatest value upon vertical relations, specific connections with sources, while the second will swear by horizontal relations. For example, the former will see Gibbon as a reader of the *Historia Augusta*, while the latter will regard him as a contemporary of Voltaire and the enlightened despots.

Throughout his vast *oeuvre*, Arnaldo Momigliano emphasized how very much an eighteenth-century historian was caught in a vortex of problems. It was not he who had invented them, nor did he resolve them, but it was certainly in the Age of Enlightenment that they were posed with the greatest intensity. And what were they? First, there was the problem of the contrast between two different kinds of historian, on the one hand the kind who told of the events of the past, on the other the antiquarians who specialized in indefinite exegeses on documents from the past.[14] It is tempting, with hindsight, to say that it was this split, which began in the seventeenth century and continued into the nineteenth, that produced two well-established disciplines that are still very much alive today: that of the scholarly historical narrative, for which the first model was Gibbon's *The Decline and Fall of the Roman Empire* (1776),[15] and the archaeological study, that is to say the history of mankind pieced together from material traces left over the centuries.[16]

Furthermore, the scholarly historical account itself presupposed a new hierarchical assessment of the sources. Should we set Herodotus' account of the Persian Wars on the same level as Plato's, in Books III and IV of the *Laws*? Whom should we take the more seriously, Herodian or the *Historia Augusta*? Gibbon himself is not always a trustworthy model in this respect. It was George Grote who tried to introduce a measure of necessary discrimination.

But the major split in the literary genre, the category to which the historical account still belongs today, is the move away from the ancient version. In 1976, on the occasion of the bicentenary of *The Decline and Fall*, in Lausanne, two specialists expressed their contrasting views on this subject. Sir Ronald Syme presented Gibbon as continuing in the tradition of the historians of Antiquity, pointing out that, like the *Historia Augusta*, he asserts that Emperor Gordian concurrently possessed twenty-two concubines and 62,000 books, despite the fact that any sane critic is bound to disbelieve both those claims. For Momigliano, in contrast, in conformity with views that he had already expressed in 1954, Gibbon's integration of erudition within the historical account had marked a break with the ancient historical tradition.[17]

Let me be so bold as to venture two remarks in this connection. The first, which relates to the break with the ancient historical tradition, is to suggest not Gibbon, but another name, that of the chevalier Louis de Beaufort, yet another exile, a French protestant who found refuge in Holland.[18] In mentioning Beaufort, what I have in mind is not so much his *Dissertation sur l'incertitude des cinq premiers siècles de l'histoire romaine*, published in Utrecht in 1738, which by and large continues in the line of the scepticism of the classical and even pre-classical periods.[19] Rather, it is his *République romaine ou plan général de l'ancien gouvernement de Rome*, published in The Hague in 1766, ten years before the appearance of the first volume of Gibbon's work. Why this choice? Because no later than in the introduction to this book, in which he repairs what he had demolished in 1738, he produces the following truly innovative statement: 'Everything combines to prove to us that the Romans were virtually strangers in their own history. This people, so devoted to ensuring its liberty at home and extending its conquests abroad, paid scarcely any attention to the transmission of memorable events to posterity.' His point here is not whether or not ancient texts have been correctly transmitted, nor even whether they purveyed truth or falsehood, but rather whether they could even bear any relation at all to reality.

Secondly, I would suggest that it is important to recognize that, in this domain as in others, any notion of progress *ad infinitum* must be rejected. More than three centuries after Louis de Beaufort, a great debate has arisen over *Black Athena*,[20] a book that seems to me to raise two fundamental questions. The first is whether the establishment of classical Greece as the ideal historical model, as opposed to an Egyptian or Semitic East, owed anything to racism or, to put that more mildly, to the Euro-centricity of scholarship in the late eighteenth and the nineteenth centuries. I believe that it is possible to answer this question in the affirmative, albeit with many qualifications. The second is whether an ancient account, in particular that of Herodotus, which represents Greece as some Egyptian or Babylonian colony, can be re-established today. In this case, to reply in the affirmative, as Martin Bernal so forcefully does, seems to me to be to dismiss two whole centuries of historical criticism, which I for my part am not prepared to dump on the rubbish heap.[21] The idea that Athena was black is one that elicits populist sympathy on some American campuses. It is a twentieth-century extravagance that may perhaps encourage us to relativize the indignation that we feel as we analyse the hypotheses of the Swedish scholar Olof Rudbeck, who believed he had proved that Plato's Atlantis was none other than Sweden, with its capital at Uppsala, the seat of the university of which he himself was Rector.[22]

Finally, let me point out that, incomplete though it was, this break with the historical discourse of the Greeks and the Romans merely foreshadowed another, much more fundamental one, to wit the break with the biblical discourse that was later, sometimes more, sometimes less clumsily, tacked on to the Graeco-Roman discourse. From the point of view of classical studies, the eighteenth century is no doubt not a very great period. It is easy to express many reservations about the quality of the classical culture of the generation that produced the French Revolution.[23] However, there can be no doubt that, as Peter Gay has shown,[24] the cult of Antiquity was one, among others, of the instruments that made it possible to break with the Christian tradition. To speak of 'neo-paganism' would perhaps be excessive but, as I see it, the historical traditions borrowed from the ancient republics and empires undoubtedly did serve that end.

All the same, it is a strange problem. Whatever relation can there be between, on the one hand, the France of the last Bourbon kings, Hanoverian

England and the Prussia of Frederick II and, on the other, those little city-states that achieved the peak of their glory around the middle of the first millennium? The very idea of such a link provokes an astonishment that is only dispelled when we reflect seriously upon the phenomenon of cultural survival, the possibility of ideological cross-fertilization in which everything becomes grist to the mill and, above all, the process of identification that is one of the keys to ideological systems generally. Consider, for example, the way in which the seventeenth-century English revolutionaries identified simultaneously with both the people of the Old Testament and the citizens of the Roman Republic.[25]

But the strangest thing of all in this matter is the choice that the French Revolution made, faced with the double legacy bequeathed by the classical tradition and the philosophy of the Enlightenment, a tradition and a philosophy that seem a far cry from the activist democracy rehabilitated by M. I. Finley.

It was a tradition bequeathed, not by the fifth century, the age of tragedy, Protagoras, Democritus and even the funeral oration that Thucydides ascribed to Pericles, but rather by the fourth century, the age of the 'moderates', whose shared ideas Jacqueline de Romilly has recorded with such zest.[26] The 'tradition' means Isocrates, revised and corrected by Plutarch. It means, not an instituting democracy, but an instituted one, a regime of 'notables' that, by the fourth century already, was claiming descent, not from Cleisthenes, but from a mainly mythified Solon.[27] Nobody would seek to deny that the spirit and even the nature of Athenian democracy changed with the 'Restoration' of 403 BC.[28] But the choice made by the French *philosophes* and scholars – in particular Rollin (1661–1741) for example, the most influential professor of the age of Louis XV, whose *Histoire ancienne* began appearing in 1730 and continued to be reprinted until the mid-nineteenth century – is, notwithstanding, quite clear. For them the great man was not Pericles and certainly not Cleisthenes, whose founding role was completely discounted, but Solon or, better still, Phocion, one of Plutarch's heroes, an Athenian *strategos* particularly active in the second half of the fourth century and installed by the Macedonian Antipatros as the leader of an Athens by then delivered from democracy (322 BC). What was true of France was also true of England. According to the Tory Mitford, one of Grote's predecessors, 'Cleisthenes was at this time not less tyrant of Athens than Peisistratus had been. His power was equal, but his moderation was not equal'.[29] At least hatred made for lucidity in Mitford's case, for it certainly was Cleisthenes as the founder of democracy whom he hated.

A great debate did take place amongst the intellectuals of the Age of Enlightenment, between the partisans of Athens and the admirers of Sparta, a debate that was of concern to the whole of eighteenth-century Europe.[30] What did Athens stand for? Not so much for democracy as a power system as for free enterprise, consumer freedom and free trade, an ideal that anglophiles like Voltaire strove to promote in France. And what did Sparta symbolize? Austerity certainly, the pure civic virtues dear above all to Rousseau, a transposition of an idealized Geneva,[31] equality amongst *homoioi* and perhaps also that particularly pitiless brand of authority that the Jacobins were to wield.[32] There were sometimes strange slippages between the two cities. Thus, according to Mably, the 'radical' thinker retrospectively considered one of the intellectual authorities who moulded the generation of the French Revolution: 'Phocion, in corrupt Athens, retained the simple and frugal manners of ancient Sparta.'[33]

But it was not just a matter of Greece. One reason why, in France, the 'Republic' was followed by the 'Empire' was that the image of Rome proved more formative than that of Athens or even that of Sparta.[34] Of course things change, and in the eighteenth century direct contact with the architectural splendours of the Greek East was made. The English dilettanti discovered Athens and the French and the English gradually entered into competition there.[35] Nevertheless, the book which, in 1764, revolutionized the history of ancient art, Winckelmann's *Geschichte der Kunst des Altertums*, was the work of a man who had set eyes on not a single authentic Greek sculpture, only Roman copies. Perhaps that adequately makes the point that the Greek mantle in which a number of the orators of the Revolution draped themselves was a costume that was doubly borrowed.

There is no need to dwell at this point upon the debate on imaginary representations of Greece that was sustained by the actors in this great French crisis, the Revolution, for the subject is amply treated in several chapters of this book. But let us now, albeit in asymptotic fashion, approach that fateful date, 1789.

Between 1787 and 1789 Charles Garnier, a publisher also known for having produced the *Cabinet des Fées*, published thirty-nine volumes of a series entitled *Voyages imaginaires, romanesques, merveilleux, allégoriques, amusants, comiques et critiques*. It was thus possible to read the last series of these 'imaginary voyages and marvellous dreams' simultaneously with the earliest of the revolutionary pamphlets, 'those dreams and invitations to a voyage of a different kind', at the precise moment when history itself was embarking upon a journey that was to put any imaginary voyage in the shade.[36] I should perhaps add, virtuously, with B. Baczko:

> However, the coincidence was purely fortuitous. It was just one of
> those conjuring tricks that history plays when it suggests symbolisms

and interconnections that are as facile as they are misleading. The interplay between the social imagination and reality is far more complex: those 'imaginary voyages' were in no way prophesying the Revolution, in no sense were they premonitory signs of it. The Garnier series merely offered its readers some interesting literature that allowed them to venture into the domain of the imaginary and the impossible.[37]

But is that altogether true? In this series,[38] which starts with a reprint of *Robinson Crusoe*, Antiquity is under-represented, but one of the foremost traits of Utopian literature, ever since Plato, the Plato of the *Laws* even more than the Plato of the *Republic*, has always been a passion for regulation, for laying down every last detail of the mode of life to be enjoyed by the inhabitants of the ideal city. It was from classical, particularly Greek, Antiquity that thinkers of the Age of Enlightenment borrowed the crucial figure of the lawgiver – Solon and Lycurgus for example, whose busts were to ornament the meeting hall of the National Convention; and the determination to legislate, to transform through the law and abolish through the law, was to be one of the most important phenomena of the Revolution and even of the Bonapartist period (the Code Napoléon, etc.). It was, to be sure, no longer a matter of a Utopia. Indeed, as J.-M. Goulemot has pointed out, during Year II, 'Utopia deserted written texts and began instead to haunt the clubs, the various tribunes, the assemblies and the revolutionary festivals. It had a timid rebirth in 1795, at the end of the Thermidorean crisis.'[39] In this sense, it is perhaps after all fair to say that this series of Imaginary Voyages did constitute a premonitory sign.

But now let us turn to another, much clearer, sign. December 1788 saw the publication, in Paris, of *Le Voyage du jeune Anacharsis en Grèce vers le milieu du quatrième siècle avant l'ère vulgaire* by Abbé Jean-Jacques Barthélemy (1716–1795).[40] This is an astonishing work that calls for a careful reading and has in fact been read on a number of different levels. Barthélemy was a by no means negligible scholar; he occupies a definitely front-rank position in the gallery of eighteenth-century 'antiquarians'. He was an orientalist who had mastered both Hebrew and Arabic and also a numismatist, the curator of the Cabinet des Médailles, even one of its creators in its present-day form, who had expanded its collections considerably and reorganized their display. His greatest achievement as a scholar was deciphering Palmyrenian and identifying the Phoenician alphabet. However, this orientalist, who paid a long visit to Rome, never travelled either to Greece or to the East. In southern Italy, he laboured over the deciphering of a number of papyri from Herculaneum but never

ventured beyond the site at Paestum, where he was at least vouchsafed the
sight of some authentic Greek temples, which, however, it never occurred
to him to mention in his *Voyage*.

On 15 October 1764, on the Capitol, Edward Gibbon, an English gen-
tleman with a Vaudois education who was, in a way, yet another exile,
was visited by an intuition from which *The Decline and Fall*, the masterpiece of Enlightenment historiography, later sprang. In 1757, Barthélemy
had likewise been visited by a Roman intuition. Gibbon's first idea had
been to write the (eminently republican) history of the cantons of Switzerland. As for Barthélemy, his first idea had been to describe the Renaissance Rome of Leo X in all its great splendour. 'But from that idea
another was born: it became clear to him that a similar work might set
within the grasp of all and sundry the thousands of documents pertaining
to the history and life of ancient Greece, documents that it occurred to no-
one to seek out in the in-folios of Gronovius and Meursius.'[41] The reader
successfully targeted was the man of the world who had scant interest in
Phoenician, even the Palmyrian variety. Barthélemy was supported on the
one hand by a scholarly member of the nobility, the comte de Caylus,[42]
a fellow member of the Académie des Inscriptions, and on the other by
another nobleman, who was first a minister, then an ex-minister, the duc
de Choiseul, whose exile Barthélemy shared at Chanteloup in Touraine.
Here he wrote what was in effect a Hellenic encyclopaedia, a treatise that
collected together all the information that a man of his period could glean
from every category of the sources available. There was not a single
scholion he had not read, not a monument he did not know by description,
not a city he did not visit in his imagination, with the paradoxical exception of the cities of Magna Graecia for, in his eyes, Western Greece
stopped at Syracuse, to which Plato had come, so his hero Anacharsis
never displayed the zeal to push as far as Marseilles, close though it was
to Barthélemy's own birthplace, Aubagne.

But, encyclopaedic though Barthélemy's erudition was, he did not write
the *Encyclopédie*, a fighting text if ever there was one. Nor was what he
wrote a history book in the sense that Gibbon's and Grote's works were.
When giving an account, as for example in Parts I and II of the Introduction to his work, where he writes in his own name, without the mediation
of his hero, recounting the history of Athens and Greece from the 'beginnings', that is to say from Cecrops down to the end of the Peloponnesian
War, his intention is simply to set the sequence of ancient writings in
order; he is not concerned to assume a critical distance from them.[43]
Consider, for example, the following evocation of the beginnings of the
Trojan War: 'Paris passed into Greece and repaired to the court of
Menelaus, where the beauty of Helen attracted every eye'. The critical

level here is dramatically lower than in Thucydides' 'archaeology', despite the fact that unlike most 'gentlemen' of his time, most of whom only read Herodotus, Barthélemy was not unacquainted with Thucydides – whom, however, he was incapable of using when it came to reflecting upon the past as opposed to simply recounting what the sources said.

The scholarly discourse, supported by thousands of reference notes and an appendix composed of a number of mini-dissertations, is one aspect of this work, and the one that has attracted the most attention. Another is its worldly tone, which also struck its contemporary readers, who all reckoned Barthélemy's Athens was remarkably like Paris. For instance, in a detailed review dated May 1789 Grimm wrote: 'One singularity by which the reader of *Le Voyage* cannot fail to be struck, is the prodigious similarity between the *mores* of Paris and those of Athens.'[44] The tone is that of 'conversation, that moribund daughter of leisured aristocracies and absolute monarchies', as the nineteenth-century Jules Barbey d'Aurevilly put it.[45]

The name of Barthélemy's main character comes from Herodotus, who had recounted the adventures of a distinguished Scythian by this name who had tried to introduce Greek customs and the Greek religion in his own country, paying with his life for the attempt.[46] This at a stroke made Anacharsis the prototype of the 'noble savage' or even, I would venture to suggest, a supernumerary candidate for inclusion in the list of the Seven Sages.[47] It was not at all a bad idea to make one of his descendants a traveller in Greece in the period between the battles of Leuctra (371 BC) and Chaeronea (338 BC). Nor was it in itself absurd to make him an honorary citizen of Athens, even if, in the West, no one had yet devoted any thought at all to the gold of the Scythians.[48]

As well as being a kind of encyclopaedia of classical Greece, Barthélemy's work was, then, an imaginary voyage, a Utopia altogether comparable to those that were published or republished by Charles Garnier. And, as in those accounts of fabulous travels, it was systematically made to take place on two levels, that of the imagined society and that of the contemporary society, except that in this case the 'imagined' society was understood to have once been 'real'.

How did Barthélemy and his hero stand in relation to the great ideological debates of the time? Was Anacharsis Athenian or Spartan? He did his best to avoid answering that question. He began his trip in Byzantium and it was in Thebes that he met the man whom he considered the greatest of his time, Epaminondas, the victor of first Leuctra, then Mantinea, who 'was no less devoted to his country than Leonidas, and perhaps more just even than Aristides'.[49] Through a remarkable oversight, Barthélemy even made this Theban general one of 'the great men of Athens'.[50]

Barthélemy devotes eleven of his eighty-two chapters to Sparta and Laconia – quite apart from a trip to Messenia, which had by now regained its independence. The tone is scarcely at all critical where the past is concerned, although the author does remark, as Xenophon once did,[51] that the laws of Lycurgus are no longer applied.[52] He even asserts that there are 'more domestic slaves in Lacedaemon than in any town in Greece', regarding this as a sign of decadence.[53] When he speaks of 'the vices for which the philosophers of Athens reproach the laws of Lycurgus' (chapter 51), this is, of course, an allusion to the *philosophes* of Paris. He devotes one whole note to exonerating the Spartan leaders accused of having secretly assassinated the best of the helots.[54]

He is thus only partially beguiled by the 'Spartan mirage'. In Sparta, one of his characters reports, but does not personally confirm, that there are people in Athens who regard the Spartans as demi-gods (chapter 51). But that is clearly not the opinion of Barthélemy himself, nor of his principal character.

That said, however, is the comparison between Athens and Sparta, which it would after all have been hard to avoid, a comparison between an oligarchy and a democracy? Not really. Certainly Lysander, at the end of the Peloponnesian War, had 'everywhere abolished the democratical government'. But strangely enough, although in line with Spartan tradition, that crime, in the excessive form that it took, was 'considered in Sparta as an "atrocity" that must be borne in silence' (chapter 51).

Barthélemy was a no more than moderate Spartophile and it is to Athens and Athens' institutions, philosophers, orators, art forms and, above all, theatre that he devotes most of his chapters. He analyses and describes democracy and shows how it functions, writing its history in the mode of what I have called 'the tradition'. For Barthélemy, Athenian democracy is above all the work of Solon, Athens' answer to Lycurgus:

> Nothing resembles less the genius of Lycurgus than the talents of Solon nor the vigorous mind of the former less than the mild and circumspect character of the latter. There was nothing common to them but the ardour with which they laboured, though by different means, to procure the happiness of nations. Should we suppose them to have changed places, Solon would not have effected things so great and sublime as Lycurgus; we may doubt whether Lycurgus would have performed such beautiful things as Solon.[55]

Beauty thus falls to the side of Athens in politics as in everything else. However, Solon's democracy was destined to become corrupt. It was Cleisthenes and, even more, Pericles who were responsible for the decadence that Athens' victories in the Persian Wars had made inevitable.[56] Is the Athens that the younger Anacharsis visits still a democracy? It would seem that it is, since its institutions are those of a democracy. Yet, in this book so crammed with discussions about religion, philosophy, art and literature, you could seek in vain for a single debate on politics. Aeschines rubs shoulders peaceably with Demosthenes and Phocion, just as Plato dines with Isocrates and his friends Ephorus and Theopompus (chapters 7 and 8). Plato and Aristotle set out their theories without ever treading directly on political ground. At the most, Aristotle explains his principle of democracy, yet without eliciting a word of either approval or condemnation from his interlocutor: 'Liberty, say the fanatic favourers of the popular power can only be found in a democracy: it is the principle of that government, it infuses into each citizen the will to obey, and the ability to command; it renders him master of himself, the equal of others, and valuable to the state of which he makes a part.'[57] The adjective 'fanatic' (not one used by Aristotle himself) says plenty about the feelings of the *Voyage*'s author, who, like his hero, felt scant sympathy for anyone who mingled 'fanaticism with his virtue',[58] However, opinions are one thing, the matching of an account to the political reality – a compound of tensions and conflicts – quite another; and it is that reality that one scarcely comes across in the *Voyage*, despite the fact that Barthélemy had certainly studied Book V of the *Politics*.

What about the social reality that set some individuals above others according to whether they were *homoioi* or helots, citizens, metics or slaves, a reality that struck a vibrant chord in the troubled France of 1788? Strangely enough, that reality, in the form described by Cournot in a famous passage in his recollections, where he calls the society of the *ancien régime* 'a cascade of scorn' (*'une cascade de mépris'*), *is* conveyed in Barthélemy's *Voyage*. But we glimpse it in an evocation not of Greece but of Persia (Montesquieu, the author of *Les Lettres Persanes* is not far away), into which the narrator launches himself for the entertainment of Aristotle. I cannot resist the pleasure of citing this passage:[59]

We passed whole days with Aristotle, and gave him an exact account of our travels. The following particulars appeared to engage his attention. I told him that, when we were in Phoenicia, we were invited to dinner with some Persian noblemen, at the home of the satrap of the province. The conversation, as usual, only turned on *the great king*. You know, said I, that the authority of the Persian monarch is much less respected in the distant provinces than in the capital of the empire. Many instances were given of his haughtiness and despotism. It must be granted, said the satrap, that kings believe themselves to be of a totally distinct species from us. Some days after, being in the company of several subaltern officers of the same province, they complained to us of the ill-treatment and injustice which they had suffered from the satrap. It appears manifest to me, said one of them, that a satrap thinks himself of a quite different nature from his inferior officers. I afterwards interrogated their slaves, who all lamented the rigour of their fate and agreed that their masters must certainly think themselves a race of mortals of a superior kind to them.

This is one of the few passages in Barthélemy's 'imaginary travels' in which one senses the approach of the Revolution. As for that word itself, it appears in the following sentence: 'Greece was close to the moment of revolution.'[60] But the moment in question is that of the great turmoil that marked Greece at the time of the battle of Mantinea (362 BC), described by Xenophon at the end of the *Hellenica*.

Barthélemy's Greece thus functions as a land visited in the course of travels in Utopia and, like all Utopias, it is destined – by history as Barthélemy understands it – for a sudden eclipse. Chaeronea and the constitution of the League of Corinth (338 BC) marked the end of this particular story: 'The liberty of Greece then expired.'[61] It was only at this decisive point that Phocion and Demosthenes, both dear to Barthélemy's heart, clashed politically. They 'negotiated' together, but without reaching agreement. 'Two men of different kinds of genius but equal obstinacy engaged in a battle that attracted all eyes in Greece'[62] – 'in Greece', not 'in the city'. Barthélemy was torn between the tradition, as championed by Phocion, and Utopia. His hero, no longer so young after thirty years of travel, returned, dispirited, to his native Scythia, where he possessed adequate means.

This 'negative' break represented by Chaeronea, which the author of the *Voyage* emphasizes so strongly, deserves an extra word. To me it seems the creation of, not so much the contemporaries of Demosthenes and Philip, but rather the ideologues of the 'second Sophistic', those Greek intellectuals who, under the domination of Imperial Rome, attempted to resuscitate the glory of Athens – and sometimes also that of Sparta – with the aid of copious reading of Demosthenes.[63] The historiography of Barthélemy's day recognized the reality of that break but by and large took the part of Philip, the 'enlightened despot' who seemed so much like Frederick II of Prussia. The Englishman John Gillies, for example, regarded Philip's victory as a victory for civilization over 'barbarians' who had quite a lot in common with the American 'insurgents'.[64]

Closer to Barthélemy's position was that adopted by his own pupil, the baron de Sainte-Croix (1746–1809), who was to publish or republish much of his master's work, after the death of the latter. In the first edition of his *Examen critique des anciens historiens d'Alexandre le Grand* (1775), Sainte-Croix observed, in the style of Barthélemy, that 'these republican brothers of ours [the Greeks] were soon no more than a herd of lowly slaves' and that 'the total subversion of democracy brought in its wake the decadence of all letters, in particular the historical genre'. In 1804 he produced a new, much modified edition of his book, in which he renounced that opinion. He himself never discovered Hellenistic culture, but he at least paved the way for the German J.-G. Droysen, whose *Geschichte Alexanders des Grossen*, much influenced by the figure of Napoleon, appeared in 1833.[65] In any event, whether seen as positive or as negative, that break marked by Chaeronea was destined to a fine future . . .

Such, then, was Barthélemy's discourse; and, in the last analysis, it really was not very political. As frequently happens, its reception was very different from what its author expected. It was greeted with both enthusiasm and alarm, the alarm being caused by precisely what also elicited the enthusiasm, in those peculiarly explosive days. Let us take a look at the *Correspondance littéraire* of Baron Grimm, Diderot's friend, possibly the best official representative of the 'philosophical' party, which in 1789 by no means identified itself with the 'patriotic' or 'national' party. In 1790, Grimm discontinued this collection of letters for the most part addressed to German princes, and emigrated. He commented briefly on the *Voyage* when it first appeared, in December 1788, then returned to it at greater length, in May 1789, in the wake of a description of the inaugural sitting of the Estates General.

The work had certainly provoked a sensation, but Grimm forcefully warned its readers that it might prove dangerous:

Just because once, five or six thousand years ago, at the very tip of a small peninsula, in one of the kindest climes in Europe, for a few centuries a democratic government was beheld to combine the elements of the stormiest ever system of liberty with the highest ever degree of culture, along with great wealth and power and every kind of ambition and glory, is that any reason to think that it would be easy to reproduce the feat of such a moral and political phenomenon elsewhere?[66]

Grimm then proceeded to point out that the citizens were in a minority in Athens, which was a republic for which the term 'aristocracy' would be more apt than 'democracy'.

Another German baron, Jean-Baptiste Cloots, the nephew of Cornelius de Pauw,[67] took Barthélemy's book very seriously. He himself assumed the name Anacharsis, declared himself to be 'the orator of the human race' and became a representative in the National Convention. But things went badly for him and he was guillotined along with Hébert on 24 March 1794. On 26 December 1793, the Convention had decreed that citizens born in foreign countries be expelled from its midst.[68] The modern dialectic between citizen and metic was just beginning. The affirmation of a nation within its frontiers created some liberties but also some exclusions. This was what has recently been described as *La Tyrannie du national*.[69]

As for Barthélemy, who was himself imprisoned for a few hours in August 1793, he had little affection for a republic which nevertheless believed it owed him something. He lived long enough for the Thermidorians, having shaken free from the Spartan dream, to restore all his honours to him.[70]

The Greek words that he had helped to diffuse in Western societies are still at work there, where they continue to undergo transformations and to transform us. In the 1830s, for instance, the 'proletarians' became 'helots' whom some believed therefore needed to be freed, while others regarded them quite simply as 'barbarians'.[71] And on 2 May 1990, Marie-France Stirbois, representative for the 'Front national' spoke at length in support of an ideology of exclusion, basing her argument on the example of Athens.[72] Surely we should do better to emulate Baron Anacharsis Cloots's attitude to the human race.

Pierre Vidal-Naquet

Notes

1 Namely, the chapter entitled 'The Enlightenment in the Greek City-state'.
2 Cf. G. E. R. Lloyd, *Demystifying Mentalities*, Cambridge University Press, 1990.
3 Cf. G. Pucci, *Il passato prossimo: la scienza dell'antichità alle origini della cultura moderna*, La Nuova Italia Scientifica, Rome, 1993, and, with indispensable qualifications, A. Schnapp, *La Conquête du passé: aux origines de l'archéologie*, Carré, Paris, 1993.
4 R.-P. Droit (ed.), *Les Grecs, les Romains et nous: l'antiquité est-elle moderne?*, Le Monde Editions, Paris, 1991; cf. also, for example, G. Cambiano, *Il ritorno degli antichi*, Laterza, Bari, 1988.
5 Rutgers University Press and Chatto and Windus, 1973.
6 Cf. *Protagoras*, 320c–322d.
7 'Tradition de la démocratie grecque', Foreword to the translation, by Monique Alexandre, of *Democracy Ancient and Modern*, Payot, Paris, 1976.

8 M. I. Finley, *The Use and Abuse of History*, Chatto and Windus, London, 1975; see pp. 178–92 for the essay dedicated to Marcuse.
9 Weidenfeld and Nicolson, Worcester and London, 1966.
10 On the early days of Momigliano as a historian, see the irreplaceable record by C. Dionisotti, *Ricordo di Arnaldo Momigliano*, Il Mulino, Bologna, 1989.
11 Cf. A. Momigliano, 'George Grote and the Study of Greek History', *Studies*, pp. 56–74.
12 The title of an article by Nicole Loraux, *Quaderni di storia* 12 (July–December 1980), pp. 55–81 ('Thucydide n'est pas un collègue').
13 Here is a concrete example. I have recently been involved in examining two very different French theses: that of Mouza Raskolnikoff, *Histoire romaine et critique historique dans l'Europe des Lumières*, École française de Rome, 1992, and that of Chantal Grell, *Le XVIIIe siècle et l'Antiquité en France: étude sur les représentations sociales et politiques, littéraires et esthétiques de la Grèce et de la Rome païennes*, Studies on Voltaire, Oxford, 1994. The two works, both of a very high standard, the one by an antiquarian, the other by an eighteenth-century specialist, are methodologically very different.
14 The basic study, which appeared in 1950, is 'Ancient history and the antiquarian', in A. Momigliano, *Studies*, pp. 1–39. The question is studied in detail in Chantal Grell's thesis (see n. 13) and also in the very full work by Blandine Barret-Kriegel, *Les historiens et la monarchie*, 4 vols., PUF, Paris, 1988–9; see also Chantal Grell, *L'Histoire entre érudition et philosophie: étude sur la connaissance historique à l'âge des Lumières*, PUF, Paris, 1993.
15 Cf. A. Momigliano, 'Gibbon's contribution to historical method', *Studies*, 1954, pp. 40–56.
16 On this point, see the synthesis by A. Schnapp, op. cit., pp. 179–219.
17 These two studies may be found in P. Ducrey (ed.), *Gibbon et Rome à la lumière de l'historiographie moderne*, Droz, Geneva, 1977, pp. 57–72.
18 The work by Mouza Raskolnikoff cited above is centred upon this figure.
19 Cf. R. H. Popkin, *The History of Scepticism from Erasmus to Descartes*, rev. ed., University of California Press, 1979.
20 Martin Bernal, *Black Athena: The Afroasiatic Roots of Classical Civilization*, 2 vols. so far, Free Association Books, London, 1987 and 1991.
21 The special number of *Arethusa* (Autumn 1989) devoted to Martin Bernal's thesis strikes me as on the whole insufficiently critical, to put it mildly. For a forceful comment, see Mary Lefkowitz, 'The Afrocentric Myth', *New Republic*, 10 February 1992, pp. 29–36, and 'Ethnocentric History from Aristobulus to Bernal', *Academic Questions*, 6–2 (1993), pp. 12–20.
22 Cf. below, chapter 2.
23 Cf. below, chapter 5; Chantal Grell's above-cited thesis provides much useful information on this point.
24 P. Gay, *The Enlightenment: An Interpretation*, I. *The Rise of Modern Paganism*, London, Weidenfeld and Nicolson, 1967.
25 Cf. Z. S. Fink, *The Classical Republicans: An Essay on the Recovery of the Pattern of Thought in Seventeenth-Century England*, Evanston, 1945.

26 'Les modérés athéniens vers le milieu du IVe siècle, échos et concordances', *Revue des études grecques*, LXVII, 1954, pp. 327–54.
27 Cf. M. I. Finley, 'The Ancestral Constitution', 1971, in *The Use and Abuse*, pp. 34–59, which draws important comparisons with 'modern politics'.
28 For a general study, cf. M. H. Hansen, *The Athenian Democracy in the Age of Demosthenes*, Blackwell, Oxford, 1991, and, for a close study of the transition, cf. M. Ostwald, *From Popular Sovereignty to the Sovereignty of the Law: Law, Society and Politics in Fifth-century Athens*, University of California Press, 1986.
29 W. Mitford, *History of Greece*, I, London, 1784, p. 284. For a similar assimilation between Cleisthenes and Pisistratus, the 'peaceful tyrant', cf. the *Supplément à l'Encyclopédie*, Amsterdam, 1776, I, pp. 673–4.
30 Two crucial references: E. Rawson, *The Spartan Tradition in European Thought*, 1969, paperback ed., Clarendon Press, Oxford, 1991; L. Guerci, *Libertà degli Antichi e libertà dei Moderni: Sparta, Atene e i 'philosophes' nella Francia del 700*, Guida, Naples, 1979.
31 See the forthcoming admirable thesis by Yves Touchefeu, *L'Antiquité et le Christianisme dans la pensée de Jean-Jacques Rousseau*, EHESS, Paris, 1992.
32 This is the well-argued suggestion made by Chantal Grell in her above-mentioned thesis.
33 *Entretiens de Phocion sur le rapport de la morale avec la politique*, translated (fictitiously) from the Greek by Nicocles, Amsterdam, 1763. On the so-called 'radicalism' of Mably, see the reservations expressed by J.-M. Goulemot in his fine study 'Du républicanisme et de l'idée républicaine au XVIIIe siècle', in F. Furet and M. Ozouf (eds), *Le Siècle de l'avènement républicain*, Gallimard, Paris, 1993, pp. 25–56; on Mably, cf. pp. 53–5.
34 The ancient hero revered above all others by the Revolution was Brutus; cf., as well as the information provided below in 'La place . . .', A. and J. Ehrard, 'Brutus et les lecteurs', *Revue européenne des sciences sociales (Essays in honour of B. Baczko)*, XXVII, 1989, no. 85, pp. 103–114.
35 Apart from all the information provided by the above-cited works of C. Grell and A. Schnapp, see M. McCarthy, 'The Image of Greek Architecture 1748–1768', in P. Boutry et al., *La Grecia antica: mito e simbolo per l'età della grande rivoluzione*, Guerini e assoc., Milan, 1991, pp. 159–71, along with F. Hartog's study, 'Liberté des anciens, liberté des modernes: la Révolution française et l'antiquité', in R.-P. Droit (ed.), op. cit., pp. 119–41; on the Revolution itself, see the bibliography cited below, 'The place . . .'.
36 B. Baczko, *Lumière de l'Utopie*, Payot, Paris, 1978, p. 43. On the publication of Utopian texts in the eighteenth century, see the comments of J.-M. Goulemot, in R. Chartier and H.-J. Martin, *Histoire de l'édition française*, II, 2nd ed., Fayard/Promodis, Paris, 1990, pp. 285–97.
37 Ibid.
38 It does, however, include translations of Apuleius and, of course, of Lucian's *True History*.
39 Loc. cit. (see n. 33) p. 291; I have also learned much from another study by J.-M. Goulemot, 'Utopies pré-révolutionnaires et discours réglementaires', *Essays in honour of B. Baczko* (cited above), pp. 93–102.

40 The work enjoyed a huge success which lasted well into the nineteenth century. Given the very many editions, adaptations and translations, I have settled for simply giving the chapter numbers (from 1 to 82). The English translation used here is *Travels of Anacharsis the Younger in Greece during the Middle of the Fourth Century before the Christian Era*, London and Dublin, 1794 (2nd ed.). On Barthélemy, see M. Badolle, *L'abbé Jean-Jacques Barthélemy et l'hellénisme en France dans la seconde moitié du XVIIIe siècle*, PUF, Paris, n.d. (1926).

41 Cf. M. Badolle, op. cit., p. 228. On the Roman scene and its crucial role in the resurrection of Greece, see the special number, edited by Joselita Raspi Serra, of *Eutopia*, 1993, II, 1, *Idea e scienza dell'Antichità. Roma nel primo' 700*.

42 The above-cited books by Mouza Raskolnikoff and Alain Schnapp provide much information on the comte de Caylus.

43 See M. Badolle, op. cit., p. 274, who cites the following characteristic remark from n. II to Pt II of the Introduction (devoted to the period of Solon), apropos the supposed visits of the Cretan Epimenides to Athens: 'It is indeed possible that this may be true; but it is still more so that Plato was mistaken.' Are two journeys by one man 110 years apart really a possibility?

44 *Correspondance littéraire*, 14, p. 350 (1831 edition).

45 In a short story in *Les Diaboliques*, 'Le dessous de cartes d'une partie de whist'.

46 Herodotus, IV, 46, 76–7; cf. F. Hartog, *The Mirror of Herodotus*, University of California Press, Berkeley, 1988, ch. 3.

47 Diogenes Laertius, *Vit. Ph.* I, 12; cf. J. Ferguson, *Utopias of the Classical World*, Cornell University Press, 1975, pp. 16–22 and 40.

48 Barthélemy knew nothing at all of the collections being acquired by the sovereigns of Russia in his own day; cf. V. Schiltz, *Histoires de Kourganes: la redécouverte de l'or des Scythes*, Gallimard, Paris, 1991.

49 Ch. 5.

50 Ch. 24.

51 In the last but one chapter (or last, depending on the edition) of his *Constitution of the Lacedaemonians*.

52 This is the theme of ch. 51.

53 Ch. 42.

54 N. XI to ch. 42; cf. Thucydides, IV, 80 and the last essay in my book *Assassins of Memory*, Columbia University Press, New York, 1992.

55 Introduction, II, 1.

56 A theme taken over recently by H. Van Effenterre, *La Cité grecque: des origines à la défaite de Marathon*, Hachette, Paris, 1985.

57 Ch. 62; for Barthélemy's source, see *Politics*, 6, 1317a40f. The *demotikoi* mentioned by Aristotle are clearly not 'fanatics'.

58 An expression used in connection with a Theban in ch. 78.

59 Ch. 62. As usual, Barthélemy refers to a whole series of texts. As anyone who checks them out (Aelian, *Varia Historia* 8, 15 and 9, 41, and Quintus Curtius 7, 8, and fragment 31 Kassel-Austin, of the comic poet Philemon) will see, this is a pure fabrication on Barthélemy's part.

60 Ch. 12. The word is used in the same sense as in Abbé Raynal, who is an exceptionally rich 'lexical witness' according to Alain Rey, *'Révolution': histoire*

d'un mot, Gallimard, Paris, 1988, p. 55. The sense is that of political disturbance, change, novelty, but not necessarily change of a positive nature.

61 Ch. 82.

62 Ibid.

63 Cf. my essay 'Flavius Arrien entre deux mondes', postface to Arrian's *Anabasis*, Editions de Minuit, Paris, 1984, pp. 326–8.

64 Cf. Momigliano, *Studies*, pp. 58–9.

65 See my essay cited above, 'Flavius Arrien entre deux mondes', pp. 374–6.

66 *Correspondance littéraire*, 14, p. 355.

67 Cornelius de Pauw is mentioned several times in chapter 4.

68 Cf. the monograph by Madeleine Rebérioux, 'Anacharsis Cloots, l'autre citoyen du monde', in G. Kantin (ed.), *Thomas Paine, citoyen du monde*, Éditions Creaphis, Paris, 1990, pp. 31–41, and also the bibliography.

69 The title of a book by Gérard Noiriel, Calmann-Lévy, Paris, 1991.

70 Cf. M. Badolle, op. cit., pp. 134–42.

71 Cf. P. Rosenvallon, *Le Sacre du citoyen: histoire du suffrage universel en France*, Gallimard, Paris, 1992, pp. 253–67.

72 Cf. N. Loraux, 'La démocratie à l'épreuve de l'étranger (Athènes-Paris)', in R.-P. Droit, op. cit., pp. 164–90.

1

Plato, History and Historians

The title that I have chosen for this study is so general that it calls for at least a few preliminary comments. I am a historian, not a philosopher. This means that when I study Plato's thought, I do not consider it as a timeless doctrine, even if it has indisputably survived long after the conditions in which it was produced.[1] In my student days, Louis Lavelle's maxim 'one philosophizes in so far as one Platonizes' was very fashionable. But I am not interested in that kind of Platonism. The Plato with whom I am concerned is the one who was a witness to the changes, or what some would call the crisis, that affected the Greek city in the fourth century BC, a witness who would have liked to be more of an actor but was, essentially, disappointed in that respect.

That seems obvious enough. But what is not so obvious is the nature of my Platonic *corpus*. Which are the Platonic texts on which I, as a historian of the Greek world, will base what I hardly presume to call my analyses but from which I shall at least draw my examples?

What better way to answer that question than to start by seeing how those before me have answered it? Let us turn to a book that presents a full picture of the cultural conflicts of the fourth century and was one of the earliest works of a very great historian of our times: Arnaldo Momigliano's *Filippo il Macedone*.[2] We shall find, no doubt to our surprise, that while Isocrates 'rates' nineteen references, some of which run to several pages, in the index of this book, Plato is mentioned only four times.[3]

The first reference, in truth, is not to Plato himself but to the unknown author of Epistle V, which is addressed to Perdiccas of Macedonia: 'Plato

This study first appeared in Jacques Brunschwig, Claude Imbert and Alain Roger (eds), *Histoire et structure, à la mémoire de Victor Goldschmidt*, Vrin, Paris 1985.

was born late in the history of his country, and he found the *demos* already old and habituated by previous statesmen to do many things at variance with his own counsel.'[4]

The second example: when speaking of Archelaus of Macedonia, who reigned from 413 to 339, Momigliano repeats a tradition recorded by Karystios of Pergamum, according to which Plato (born 428–427) was in his youth in contact with Archelaus.[5]

The third reference is to the famous letter which Speusippus, Plato's nephew and successor as head of the Academy, is supposed to have sent to Philip of Macedon. If authentic, this is truly a text of capital importance, given the light that it sheds on the question of the social function of philosophers and historians in the fourth century:[6] in it, Speusippus explains that it was Plato, rather than Isocrates, who helped Philip to establish the legitimacy of his possession of Amphipolis. Even if not authentic, the text is important at least for an understanding of how the relations between a philosopher and the royal court were represented.[7] Momigliano's last reference to Plato is also to this text. And that is the lot.

If I have taken as my starting point *Filippo il Macedone* and the relatively small space that it affords Plato, it is certainly not for what would be the somewhat perverted pleasure of catching out a very great contemporary scholar, and in one of his youthful works at that. Rather, it is because, throughout his *oeuvre*, Momigliano has taught us to reflect upon the modern historiography of Antiquity in relation to the ancient historiography and therein, precisely, lies my problem.

Recently Nicole Loraux has, in her turn, reopened a similar debate, declaring that 'Thucydides is not a colleague'.[8] 'In France, . . . in the field of Greek studies, historians and literary scholars share, without frontier disputes, the terrain in the forbidden zone where boundaries are blurred.' Of course, Thucydides is read by both groups. But, apart from editors of texts, what literary scholar ever reads Diodorus or Polybius? And what historian reads Erinna, the poets of the Anthology, or even the tragic texts? Moreover, as soon as one turns to philosophical texts, the situation is even worse, that is to say the division is even more clear-cut. Consider the edition of Plato in the collection produced under the aegis of the Association Guillaume Budé. There is one Plato for the literary scholars, the Plato of the Socratic dialogues, who is translated by the Croiset brothers and by L. Méridier; and there is another Plato for the philosophers, edited by A. Diès and L. Robin. As for the historians, they do not get a look in, unless one annexes Louis Gernet, who was a sociologist, jurist and philologist as well as the author of an admirable comparativist introduction to the text of the *Laws*. Are we to believe that the divisions between university departments correspond to epistemological frontiers?

Surely experience shows that a discipline such as ours can make progress only by abolishing frontiers. In our field, intellectual transformations
come about not so much through the discovery of new documents such
as the *Constitution of Athens* or the archives of Zeno, but rather through
reforming the hierarchy of sources. Of that there can be no doubt, as soon
as one steps back a little to examine how a particular period was treated
a century or two ago. Today, to bring philosophy as such into history may
be a new way of helping ancient history to progress. It is advisedly that
I say 'philosophy as such'. In the Age of Enlightenment, many Platonic
texts – starting with the *Critias* – were considered 'historical' sources, on
a par with Herodotus, Thucydides, Diodorus and Polybius, although
admittedly this did cause a certain amount of confusion.[9]

But before returning to the history of today, let us try to see how the
Ancients themselves tackled this intellectual obstacle represented by the
presence of philosophers and philosophy in history.

Let us open a history book produced in the fourth century BC, which is
the very first of its kind to have come down to us intact. Xenophon's
Hellenica. One hardly expects to come across the name of Plato,
Xenophon's rival in the Socratic tradition. But what about Socrates? Even
his name appears once only.[10] The passage concerns the Arginusae affair
of 406 and Callixenus' famous proposal that the *strategoi* should be judged
by a summary procedure, the *diapsephisis*, a block vote going for a 'yes'
or a 'no':

When some of the Prytanes refused to put the question to the vote
in violation of the law, Callixenus again mounted the platform and
urged the same charge against them; and the crowd cried out to
summon to court those who refused. Then the Prytanes, stricken with
fear, agreed to put the question – all of them except Socrates, the son
of Sophroniscus; and he said that in no case would he act except in
accordance with the law.

Why does Socrates intervene *in Xenophon's text* at this point? (And I
insist on that italicized expression.) The exact form taken by Socrates'
intervention in the meeting of the *Prytanes* we shall never know. Who
spoke just before him, who spoke immediately after, what manoeuvres
were employed by the various parties in the no doubt unruly session are
all questions that we have absolutely no way of answering. Once again it
is Xenophon, the Xenophon of the *Hellenica*, who is far and away our
best source. If Socrates intervenes *in the text*, it is not as a philosopher,
nor because he is Xenophon's own teacher; because for Xenophon history

is inconceivable unless it is strictly civic. The reason why Socrates intervenes here is because, as a *prytanis*, he is one of the fifty who represent public power in the *prytaneum*, the 'common hearth'.

This single mention of Socrates' political role, in the *Hellenica*, raises a number of overlapping questions. The episode in question is not mentioned solely in this text in the *Hellenica*. Plato himself alludes to it several times. He does so in the *Apology*, that is to say the only Platonic text, apart from the *Epistles* (if any of those are authentic), which is neither a Socratic nor an extra-Socratic dialogue. Socrates is said to have spoken as follows: 'I, men of Athens, never held any other office in the State, but I was a member of the Council'.[11] He goes on to say that it happened to be the turn of the Antiochis tribe, his own, to hold the presidency 'when you wished to judge collectively, not severally, the ten generals who had failed to gather up the slain after the naval battle'. What follows is identical to Xenophon's account. Socrates is the only one to resist, risking imprisonment or death.

An *Apology* such as Plato writes for Socrates is not a work that derives from history, history as written by Thucydides or Xenophon, a work based on a radical distinction between the *private* and the *public* spheres, between the philosopher thinking in his study and the citizen at the assembly. In this domain, as often happens with disciples, Xenophon went even further than his Thucydidean model. If there was one man who, for Thucydides, played a role somewhat analogous to the one that Socrates played for Xenophon, it was the famous sophist and *rhetor* Antiphon. Thucydides devotes an extraordinary eulogy to him, explaining that he never spoke before the people or in any debate (*agôn*) unless compelled to. So how was it possible to record the public action of this man who did not wish to be a public figure? Thucydides solves the problem – in connection with the oligarchic putsch of 411 – by explaining that, although Antiphon was not the proposer of the decree which abolished the democracy, he was nevertheless the man who 'set the whole thing up' (ὁ μέντοι ἅπαν τὸ πρᾶγμα ξυνθείς). And Thucydides makes use of another technique too, when he has an Athenian ambassador to Sparta say that, along with Pisander, Antiphon was one of the leaders of the oligarchy.[12]

But let us return to the *Apology*, a text whose function clearly is not to provide us with lists of the public actions of public figures. There is one extremely striking detail in this account. The proposal concerning the *strategoi* of the battle of Arginusae that is put to the Assembly's vote is summarized by Plato as follows: 'You wished to judge collectively, not severally, the ten generals who had failed to gather up the slain after the naval battle; this was illegal' (ὑμεῖς τοὺς δέκα στρατηγοὺς τοὺς οὐκ ἀνελομένους τοὺς ἐκ τῆς ναυμαχίας ἐβούλεσθε ἀθρόους κρίνειν παρανόμως). Now let us consult Xenophon's account. It presents a few difficulties, it is true, but it is easy enough to see that Xenophon takes care to make it clear who is condemned and who is not. Only eight *strategoi* took part in the battle. Conon, one of the two who did not, was absent because he was blockaded in the harbour of Mytilene. Of those eight who were present, only six returned to Athens and were condemned and executed. Conon, naturally, was not among them.[13]

So why that Platonic adjustment? Because, while it may be true that no account is entirely innocent, accuracy is certainly not what mattered in an apologia for Socrates.[14] Whether or not Plato knew the truth of the matter, we certainly do not, ἀθρόοις, 'collectively' is probably the critical word in his account. And that expression inevitably suggests the normal, regular number for *strategoi*, namely ten, without bothering Plato in the slightest. Thus what is in question as a whole is an institution of Cleisthenes' Athens, the city of ten tribes. Remarkably enough, Aristotle repeated that number of ten *strategoi*, at the same time producing an absurd explanation to account for why not all were present (*Constitution of Athens*, 34, 1). But any historian who hesitated between believing Plato and Aristotle on the one hand or Xenophon on the other would indeed be a very strange historian.

However, that is not all, for Plato returns to this affair, this time in a dialogue, the *Gorgias*.[15] Socrates ironically explains to Polos that he is not one of those people known as politicians: 'Last year (*perusi*), when I was elected a member of the Council, and, as my tribe held the "presidency", I had to put a question to the vote, I got laughed at for not understanding the procedure' (καὶ οὐκ ἠπιστάμην ἐπιψηφίζειν).' In this text there is no allusion at all to Socrates' stand for legality. What has happened? In comparison not only to the text of the *Hellenica* but also, in part, to the text of the *Apology*, a double shift has taken place. First, an institutional shift: Socrates passes from the condition of an ordinary *prytanis* to that of the *epistates* of the *prytaneum*, for technically the *epistates* of the *prytaneum* was the man responsible for putting matters to the vote;[16] secondly, a personal shift, one that was already suggested in the Apology, a text in which Plato insists on the exceptional nature of Socrates' political experience – a shift from political activity to non-activity, which Plato was later to illustrate by the famous episode of Thales falling into a well because he was looking up at the stars instead of where he was going.[17] It is precisely because Socrates is not a political man that it is possible, at the end of the *Gorgias*, to describe him as the only man who is truly political. But there is yet more to this matter. In Plato, Socratic dialogue is explicitly set in opposition to democratic debate. Plato's Socrates has been described as 'the antidote to the funeral oration';[18] and the dialogue is surely the antidote to the assembly debate. Let us read the lines immediately preceding our text in the *Gorgias* and also those following. 'You have only to ask anyone of the company here', says Polos. Socrates pretends to understand by this something that Polos has not said at all, namely that he has been asked to get those present to vote. 'Do not call upon me again to take the votes of the company now . . . For I know how to produce [only] one witness in support of my statements, and that is the man himself with whom I find myself arguing.'[19] The collective debate is replaced by a conversation between two individuals, which, although certainly presented as though the two are on an equal footing, really stems from a master–disciple relationship. Nor is the democratic debate the only victim in this operation. Also confidently swept aside is the historical account in the manner of Thucydides and Xenophon, the account based on a succession of years and magistracies. For Socrates tells us that this episode took place 'last year'; and that automatically establishes the fictional date of the dialogue: 405. Yet elsewhere in this same dialogue,[20] we are told that Pericles has died just recently (*neôsti*). Since Pericles died in 429, the fictional date must clearly be 427, the time of Gorgias' embassy to Athens. Yet, still in the *Gorgias*,[21] Archelaus of Macedonia is mentioned as though he were a living king; and he reigned from 413 to 399, so that means pushing the fictional date of the text even further back.[22] Just a whim on the part of the philosopher? As slight yet as significant as his whim to have Socrates and Aspasia converse together in the *Menexenus* long after both were dead.[23] I believe that Plato quite deliberately decided to break out of the chronological framework which was that of the city. A man became a *strategos*, a *bouleutes* or an *archon* for the duration of one civic year, and civic time, the time of the *prytany*, was fundamental to the city reformed by Cleisthenes. But what a Platonic dialogue does, precisely, is blur time, just as it also blurs the outline of the city.

What exactly is going on in the *Gorgias*? What is the point of these chronological fantasies? One constant feature of Plato's thought is that he thinks of the fifth century as a whole, without emphasizing details and making no attempt to distinguish Themistocles from Miltiades or Pericles, or Pericles from Hyperbolus. Indeed, Plato refuses to acknowledge any difference between the great age, so dear to the orators of the fourth century and the historians of his own day, and the time of decadence. Plato is quite specific on this point in the *Gorgias*.[24] Pericles and Cimon, Miltiades and Themistocles – and Plato deliberately chooses politically antagonistic figures – were no doubt better servants (*diakonoi*) of the city than their successors, to the extent that they were more skilful than the men of the fourth century in providing the city with ships, ramparts and arsenals, all things that Plato objects to and rejects for his own city. But if what really matters is to do what politics – according to Plato – is supposed to do, that is to say modify the city's desires (μεταβιβάζειν τὰς ἐπιθυμίας), resist them and improve it by means of persuasion and constraints,[25] then, as he sees it, there really is no difference between yesterday and today. Indeed there is a rather astonishing text, still in the *Gorgias*, which explains why it is only in a strange digression that Socrates recalls his role in the Arginusae affair. Speaking of the political leaders of the fifth century – although admittedly with one significant omission: Aristides – he points out that all of them were condemned by the Athenians. Miltiades, the man of Marathon, was supposed to be put to death and hurled into the *barathron*, the ravine for those condemned to death, and would have suffered that fate had it not been for the opposition of the leader of the *prytany*.[26] Socrates certainly does not say that such a decision would have been just. But he does think that it was to be expected. What is being challenged here is the way the democratic city functioned as a single entity. Socrates, or his homologue who prevented Miltiades' death, was an exception; it was the rule that was dangerous.

Is that a maxim propounded solely by the Socratic dialogue as written by Plato? Not at all. Let us return to Xenophon, so scrupulous and accurate even if, in the *Hellenica*, he did sometimes make mistakes. In the *Memorabilia*, Xenophon twice explains his view of the Arginusae affair and the role Socrates played in it. First, in the preface:[27]

> For instance when he was on the Council and had taken the councillor's oath by which he bound himself to give counsel in accordance with the laws, it fell to his lot to preside in the Assembly when the people wanted to condemn Thrasyllus and Erasinides and their [nine] colleagues to death by a single vote. That was illegal and he refused the motion in spite of popular rancour and the threats of many powerful persons.

Where, in this passage, is the shift away from the basic account, that of the *Hellenica*? There is, of course, the problem of the numbers: nine *strategoi* instead of the six who were present. But, more importantly, on the level of a historical account, an account of a succession of events linked together in accordance with certain rules which, in this instance, are of an institutional nature, this version, like the one in the *Apology* and the one in the *Gorgias*, is quite simply absurd. If Socrates had been the president of the Assembly and had refused to put the illegal proposition to the vote, it would never have been carried. There is a shift of emphasis from the collective to the individual.

And here is the other text: 'When chairman in the Assemblies, he would not permit the people to record an illegal vote.'[28] This time the reading of the historical event is practically monarchical. It is centred on the figure of Socrates, not Socrates the public man, in so far as he was one, but Socrates concentrating the transparency of public life upon himself: 'Concerning Justice, he did not hide his opinion but proclaimed it by his actions (ἔργῳ). All his private (ἰδίᾳ) conduct was lawful and helpful: to public authority he rendered such scrupulous obedience in all that the laws required, both in civil life and in military service, that he was a pattern (διάδηλος) of good discipline to all.'[29]

But let us now return to our dialogue between the historiography of yesterday and that of today. Were there any historians of Antiquity who were capable of stepping outside the strict chronological framework of seasons, magistracies and eponymous magistracies? It is a complex question and the reply to it is bound to be so too.

In a whole series of domains, the permanency of separate literary genres is very noticeable. The philosopher, not philosophy, was a figure in comedy long before becoming one in history. Socrates appeared as a philosopher in Aristophanes, not in Thucydides, whom it would be hard to imagine breaking off to say: 'In those days, there was a certain Socrates . . .', as Flavius Josephus is said to have broken off in his *Jewish Antiquities* to write, 'In those days, Jesus . . .'.[30]

Plato was a figure in middle comedy[31] before becoming a figure in history. Aristotle, to the confusion of many generations, paradoxically in a way created the history of philosophy in Book I of his *Metaphysics*, but it did not occur to him to include that so-called history in his account of the history of Athens, which is preserved in the only one of his *Politeiai* to have come down to us. But then it is true that Aristotle did not consider history a serious discipline.

So to the extent that the historical account continued to be modelled on those of Xenophon and Thucydides, themselves largely influenced by Herodotus,[32] the same exclusions operated. For example, so far as we know Theopompus respected them in his *Hellenica*. Yet it was with this historian, born in 378–377 and slightly better known than the rest of his contemporaries, especially since the appearance of W. Robert Connor's fine book,[33] that the situation seems to have begun to change. Speaking of Theopompus and his grounding as a historian, Dionysius of Halicarnassus has this to say:[34] 'He was the eye-witness (*autoptès*) of many events, and when composing his history, he cultivated the acquaintance of the principal figures of his day: military and political leaders as well as philosophers (στρατηγοῖς δημαγωγοῖς τε καὶ φιλοσόφοις).' Unfortunately, that is a text from Dionysius, not an extract from an autobiography of Theopompus. But this historian from Chios was certainly the first historian of whom such a thing was said.

Now this particular comment by Dionysius is by no means absurd. As we know from both Athenaeus and an inscription from Rhodes, Theopompus engaged in a polemic against Plato, accusing him of lying and plagiary.[35] His own *Meropia*, a narrative on the theme of two rival mythical cities, placed in the mouth of Silenus, is clearly a pastiche of Plato's account of the clash between Athens and Atlantis.[36] Rather more interesting is the fact, which seems to bear out Dionysius' comment, that Theopompus establishes a connection between the lives of Plato and Philip. It is through him that we know that Plato, who died in the thirteenth year of Philip's reign, was posthumously honoured by the latter.[37] And that piece of information indicates that philosophers were public figures, just as kings and *strategoi* were. It is even tempting to suggest that philosophers and kings increasingly found a place amongst the figures in whom historians took an interest, as the traditional magistrates failed to occupy their former position there.

But the life of a philosopher is not the same thing as his philosophy. In the third century a man such as Philochorus, one of the founders of 'antiquarian' history,[38] included the history of the Academy as an interesting aspect of Athenian Antiquity. A fragment of Philochorus is known to us through the 'Herculaneum index', and we also know that he had drawn a contrast between Aristotle the metic and Plato the Athenian, who was a friend of Chabrias and Timotheus.[39] Philochorus was also interested in Speusippus,[40] but it cannot be claimed that information such as this means that the history of philosophy had made deep inroads into history *tout court*. Even Polybius, who declares in Book VI of his history[41] that he himself is inspired by the Platonic historical method, is far from being a historian of philosophy.

The 'Paros marble' was to integrate into the chronicle of Athens all the victories of the various comic and tragic writers, but it made no mention of philosophers. Of course philosophers won no competitions, a fact which, in an agonistic historiography such as Greek historiography, was bound to make a difference.

We are no longer historians of the third century BC. As historians of the second half of the twentieth century, we are the grandchildren of Vico, Hegel and Marx and the children of Bloch, Febvre, Christopher Hill, Braudel and Vilar. Is the book by Momigliano that provided me with my introductory text in this enquiry into Plato and the historians any more than a youthful mistake which, given another chance, its author would no longer have written in the same way? Maybe, but let us look closer to home. Claude Mossé's *La Fin de la démocratie athénienne* is a doctoral thesis which was published in 1962. The book contains an index of sources that indicates the texts the author considered important for her subject, although it clearly mentions many others too. Twenty-four of them are texts from Plato: fewer than the references to Aristotle (fifty) but comparable to those to Isocrates (twenty-nine). Plato is frequently used in this book for factual information, but most of what Claude Mossé has to say about Plato is obviously to be found in the chapter entitled 'The theorists and the political crisis',[42] the conclusion of which is determinedly pessimistic: 'Their criticisms [those of the philosophers] and the remedies that they suggest had no real effect. The destiny of Athens and the Greek city was played out away from them. Their contribution to the elaboration of a new form of civilization was only to become effective once the Athenian democracy had been militarily and politically defeated.'[43] I am not fundamentally in disagreement with that view, but it seems to me that, even if it did not resolve the crisis, a philosophy such as Plato's at least tells us something about that crisis.[44] It seems to me that what a historian should do in this matter is take the entire body of data into consideration. Now, of the twenty-four textual references to Plato, fourteen come from the *Republic*, three from the *Laws*, three from the *Politicus*, two from *Epistle* VII, one from the first *Alcibiades*, and one from the *Gorgias*. This means that all the great metaphysical dialogues of Plato's last years (the *Parmenides*, the *Theaetetus*, the *Sophist*) are absent. Also absent are the *Timaeus* and the *Critias*. Also absent the great dialogues of Plato's maturity, the *Phaedo*, the *Phaedrus*, the *Symposium*. Also, with one exception, the dialogues known as 'Socratic'. And despite all the *Menexenus* tells us about, precisely, the philosophic critique of the city,[45] this text is absent too.[46] Who would dare claim that even the *Parmenides* is of no interest at all to a historian of the 'crisis' of the fourth century BC?[47]

Here is an even more recent example. In 1981, G. E. M. de Sainte-Croix published his long-awaited study on the class struggle in the ancient Greek world.[48] His Platonic corpus, which is easy to identify thanks to a most efficient index, is not fundamentally different from Claude Mossé's: the *Republic* (mainly Books VIII and IX) and the *Laws* account for most of it.[49] Sainte-Croix's merit is that he is clear both about his own mind and about his deliberate choice of sources:

> My concentration on Aristotle as the great figure in ancient social and political thought and my relative neglect of Plato will surprise only those who know little or nothing of the source material for fourth-century Greek history and have acquired such knowledge as

they possess from modern books – nearly always very deferential to Plato.[50] Aristotle, in the *Politics*, usually keeps very close to actual historical processes, whereas Plato, throughout his works, is largely unconcerned with historical reality, with 'what happened in history', except for certain matters which happened to catch his attention, inward-looking as it generally was.[51]

So this accidental realist of a Plato in whom Sainte-Croix is interested is above all the Plato who stressed the opposition between the city of the rich and the city of the poor.[52]

These seemingly clear remarks call for a few comments and a number of reflections, which, in the present context, I can do no more than sketch in. Sainte-Croix, a historian of the class struggle, sets Plato in opposition to Aristotle. H.-I. Marrou, a historian of education and culture, was careful to keep a balance between Plato and Isocrates, the masters of two rival models of eduction that were to continue to compete until the Late Empire.[53] But Sainte-Croix contrasts Aristotle and Plato, seeing the former as a writer who tells us of the true historical process and the latter as one whose writing has nothing to do with historical reality. Aristotle, like Marx, is supposed to reveal to us historical truth as opposed to appearance. Yet Aristotle had been the pupil of Plato, the philosopher who had drawn precisely that contrast between appearance and reality. Did he 'turn Plato upside down', just as Marx claimed to have 'straightened out' Hegel?[54]

Can thought, even abstract thought, be alien to historical reality? Can anything be alien to historical reality? To be sure, there are different levels of reality, different degrees of reality, you might say, but it is hard to see how thought, even reactionary thought, can be alien to historical reality.

In studying the relations between intellectual works and social realities, must we restrict ourselves to what those works say explicitly? Is it not risky, for example, to assume that Aristotle is expressing the *hidden* reality of his time directly, with no intellectual mediation on our part? May one not, on the contrary, seek in Plato, just as Lucien Goldmann sought in Racine, Pascal and the Jansenist movement, for an ideological expression of the social tensions of his age?[55] In such an undertaking, can one really afford not to read *all* the dialogues?

Finally, there is a whole current of historiography, which admittedly is not representative of *all* modern historical research, that is nevertheless very much alive and active, that constantly reflects upon history as discourse, on the interplay of the signifiers and the signified, on the multiple facets of historical language. And in this domain, Plato is surely a master

whom it is difficult to ignore.[56] However that may be though, the Plato
limited essentially to the *Republic* and the *Laws* is certainly the Plato of
most of today's historians.[57] For them, the rest of his work is *terra
incognita*. The strange thing is that a similar dichotomy is detectable, if
less marked, in the work of a sociologist, A. Gouldner, whose chosen task
is, precisely, to draw a contrast between the Greek world and Plato, Plato
seen as the founder of social science in a particular context.[58] His book
falls into two parts: 'The Hellenic world' and 'Enter Plato'. Plato is
virtually absent from the first part.[59] In the second part, the *Republic* and
the *Laws* take up most of the room. A Greek world quite separate from
Plato and a Platonic world adapted to some preconception of what a
history book ought to be is a combination that is unlikely to prove very
fertile. Even those philosophers and epistemologists who claim to be
interested in history do not, in truth, go much further (with the possible
exception of K. R. Popper[60]). Thus, F. Châtelet's book, *Naissance de
l'histoire*[61] juxtaposes to Plato the history of G. Glotz, history which is
composed without Plato, and consequently fails to make any place in
history for Plato. One feels inclined to comment that the poverty of what
historians write about philosophy is matched only by the insignificance of
what philosophers write about the historical context of the works they
study.

This kind of hiatus between on the one hand historical discourse, which
is also, even first and foremost, discourse on historians, and on the other
discourse on philosophers was, however, gauged over a century ago by
one of the greatest historians of the Greek world, George Grote.[62] Having
written his *Greek History*, which did in fact make abundant use of Plato
but nevertheless remained a political history based upon the political
discourse of historians, Grote felt his task was not yet completed. In 1865
he published three volumes on 'Plato and the other companions of Socrates', which he himself described as a 'sequel and supplement to my
history of Greece', explaining that he had wished to write 'the history
speculative as well as active of the Hellenic race'. Grote then went on to
contrast the subject of this 'speculative' history, namely eminent individuals who enquire, theorize, reason and refute, with the subject of 'active'
history, based on 'those collective political and social manifestations which
constitute the contents of history and which modern writers deduce from
Herodotus, Thucydides and Xenophon'.[63] He could not have put it more
clearly. But therein lies the crux of the problem: is it not really a matter
of a single history and would it not be possible to fuse those two accounts
which Grote did manage to produce, albeit separately?

And if it *is* a matter of fusing them, it cannot be done by ignoring the
differences. For example, can tragedy be of use to the historian if it ceases

to be tragedy? It all depends on what one means by 'be of use'. Obviously, there are some types of data that one can try to extract from the texts, whatever their nature. Thus an account of Salamis could be based on both Herodotus and Aeschylus. A similar limited yet not entirely negligible use could be made of philosophical texts. Information about social life in Athens can be gleaned from the *Protagoras* and even from the *Parmenides*, not to mention specific chronological points. But as New Testament specialists have taught us over the past few decades, there is another history too, the kind that considers the form itself of a text to provide irreducible data. The form of a dialogue by Plato, as Victor Goldschmidt, among others, has helped to define it, provides just such data.

To write history using philosophy, as a historian, means being willing to enter into the difficult but necessary game of being a philosopher when amongst philosophers, cutting up the text 'where the natural joints are', like a good butcher (*mageiros*), as Plato says in the *Phaedrus*.[64] And then, of course, one has to go further, comparing what has not been compared before, setting in serial order what has never been serialized, revealing the ideological fragility of what has hitherto been considered knowledge, demolishing what are claimed to be certainties, trying to turn up the cards to see what they conceal, in short playing the role which has always fallen to the historian, the role of the traitor.[65]

PS   An Italian version of this text, published in *Quaderni di storia*, 18, 1983, pp. 61–77, prompted a response from A. Momigliano in *Rivista storica italiana*, XCV, 2, 1983, pp. 447–450, reprinted in *Ottavo contributo*, Rome, Ed. di storia e letteratura, 1987, pp. 427–430. Without wishing to reply to the polemical aspects of this article, I will simply note that in it Momigliano points out that, as anyone can see from reading Croce, the Italian historical school has suffered from an excess of philosophy rather than a dearth of it, and that he quite deliberately laid the emphasis on Isocrates rather than on Plato. I am happy to publicize this point.

Notes

1 See, in V. Goldschmidt, *Platonisme et pensée contemporaine*, Aubier, Paris, 1970, the essay entitled 'Les querelles sur le platonisme'.
2 Le Monnier, Florence, 1934, reprinted with an expanded bibliography, Milan, Guerini, 1987. I truly did make this experiment without knowing what would transpire. Momigliano's book is naturally focused on Philip, and Plato died in 347, well before the victory of this royal house was assured. That being said, Momigliano

certainly does not limit himself to a strictly chronological view of the conflict that he is studying.

3 On pp. 36, 25, 36, 132, to which I refer the reader in that order.

4 *Epistle V*, 322a. This is probably the source of the famous line that Musset gives Rolla: 'Je suis venu trop tard dans un siècle trop vieux' (I arrived too late in a century too old).

5 Müller, *Fragmenta Historicorum Graecorum*, IV, p. 356.

6 See M. M. Markle, 'Support of Athenian Intellectuals for Philip', *Journal of Hellenic Studies*, 96, 1976, pp. 80–99.

7 The authenticity of this letter had been upheld by E. Bikerman and J. Sykutris, with arguments that had convinced most readers, in their edition with commentary of the text, Leipzig, 1928. Against the generally accepted dating (343–342) and the letter's authenticity, see L. Bertelli, *Atti Accad. di Torino, Cl. sc. mor. stor. e fil.*, 110, 1976, pp. 275–300, and 111, 1977, pp. 76–115.

8 The title of an article printed in *Quaderni di Storia*, 12, July–December 1980, pp. 55–81. I cite from p. 57. V. Goldschmidt refers to this study in the latest article that he has sent me: 'Remarques sur la méthode structurale en histoire de la philosophie', *Festschrift F. Brunner*, Neuchâtel, La Baconnière, 1981, p. 223.

9 See my essay 'Hérodote et l'Atlantide: entre les Grecs et les Juifs. Réflexions sur l'historiographie du siècle des Lumières', *Quaderni di Storia*, 16, July–December 1982, pp. 3–76, and chapter 2 below, pp. 38–65.

10 *Hellenica*, I, 7, 14–15.

11 *Apology*, 32b.

12 Thucydides, VIII, 68, 1; 90, 1–2.

13 *Hellenica*, I, 5, 6. The same number, of 6 *strategoi*, is given by Philochorus, 328F142 Jacoby; I will not comment in detail on this debate, an account of which is to be found in, for example, W. P. Henry: *Greek Historical Writing: A Historiographical Essay based on Xenophon's 'Hellenica'*, Chicago, Argonaut Publ., 1967, pp. 100–7, the conclusions of which, however, I do not accept at all. On the subject of the story and the institutions themselves, the most convincing study is G. Giannantoni's 'La Pritania di Socrate', *Rivista critica di storia della filosofia*, 17, 1962, pp. 3–25, but even this article fails to provide an evaluation of the various separate sources.

14 See L. Marin, *Le récit est un piège*, Ed. de Minuit, Paris 1978.

15 473e–474a.

16 My suggestion here probably goes rather further than is altogether justified by the texts: it is the scholiast to the *Gorgias* (473e), *s.v.* ἐπιψηφίζειν (p. 146, Greene), who is our sole source of clear – if indirect – evidence on the matter, apart from Xenophon's text cited below, n. 28. The whole problem deserves to be tackled by means of an evaluation of the various sources, one by one. An anti-model of the method to be followed is provided by P. J. Rhodes, *The Athenian Boule*, Clarendon Press, Oxford, 1972, pp. 23–4 and 62, n. 1, who blithely confuses evidence of the most disparate nature.

17 *Theaetetus*, 174a.

18 'Socrate contrepoison de l'oraison funèbre' is the title of an article by N. Loraux in *L'Antiquité classique*, 1974, pp. 172–211.
19 *Gorgias*, 474a.
20 Ibid., 503c.
21 Ibid., 470d.
22 I will not attempt to summarize the conclusions that have been drawn from all these data.
23 See N. Loraux, *The Invention of Athens*, tr. Alan Sheridan, Harvard University Press, Cambridge, Mass. and London, 1986, p. 466.
24 *Gorgias*, 515c–516d.
25 Ibid., 517b.
26 Ibid., 516d–e. The author of the *Axiochus* (368d) was to make use of this passage in the *Gorgias* when he, in his turn, alluded to the Arginusae affair, but taking care to mention that one day elapsed between Socrates' refusal and the judgement passed on the *strategoi*.
27 *Memorabilia*, I, 1, 18.
28 Ibid., IV, 4, 2.
29 The transparency shifts from the *demos* to the individual. There is a subject of research here, starting from the concepts elaborated by M. Richir: 'Révolution et transparence sociale', Foreword to J. G. Fichte, *Considérations sur la Révolution française*, Payot, coll. 'Critique de la politique', Paris, 1974, pp. 7–74, and N. Loraux, 'Aux origines de la démocratie: sur la "transparence" démocratique', *Raison présente*, 49, 1979, pp. 3–13.
30 *Antiquities*, XVIII, 63–4; XX, 200.
31 See Epicrates' famous dichotomy of the gourd, in Athenaeus, II, 59d.
32 See most recently L. Canfora, 'Tucidide Erodoteo', *Quaderni di Storia*, 16, July–December 1982, pp. 77–84.
33 *Theopompus and Fifth Century Athens*, Washington (DC), Center for Hellenistic Studies, Harvard University Press, Cambridge, Mass., 1968. See also the study by L. Canfora, in L. Firpo (ed.), *Storia delle idee politiche, economiche e sociali*, I, Turin, UTET, 1982, pp. 399–406, and the bibliography, pp. 418–19.
34 *Letter to Pompey*, 6; this is the test. 20 in Jacoby's *corpus*, where Theopompus is positioned at 115.
35 Athenaeus, XI, 508c–d, fr. 259 Jacoby.
36 Fr. 75 Jacoby.
37 Diogenes Laertius, III, 40.
38 See A. Momigliano, 'Ancient History and the Antiquarian', *Studies in Historiography*, 1950, repr. Harper Torchbooks, New York, 1966, pp. 1–39.
39 Fr. 59 Jacoby (Philochorus is at no. 328 in this collection).
40 Fr. 224.
41 Polybius, VI, 5, 1.
42 C. Mossé, *La Fin de la démocratie athénienne*, PUF, Paris, 1962, pp. 348–9; repr. Arno Press, New York, 1979.
43 Op. cit., pp. 398–9.

44 On this point I venture to refer the reader to the pages devoted to Plato in my book, *The Black Hunter*, and also to my article, 'La Société platonicienne des dialogues', in *Aux Origines de l'hellénisme, la Crète et la Grèce, hommage à Henri Van Effenterre*, Publications de la Sorbonne, Paris 1984 and also in my *La Démocratie vue d'ailleurs*, Flammarion, Paris, 1990, pp. 95–119.

45 See the works cited above, R. Clavaud's *Le Ménexène de Platon et la rhétorique de son temps*, Les Belles-Lettres, Paris, 1980, and above all N. Loraux's *The Invention of Athens*, op. cit.

46 It is true that a more thorough search through C. Mossé's book reveals a few more references to the *Critias*, the *Phaedrus*, the *Phaedo* and the *Theaetetus*, but proportionately they do not make much difference.

47 I know of at least one attempt to relate the decomposition of the One in the *Parmenides* to that of the model city in the *Republic*: See the Norwegian philosopher E. A. Wyller, *Platons 'Parmenides' in seinem Zusammenhang mit 'Symposium' und 'Politeia'*, Aschehoug, Oslo, 1960, and, more briefly, 'Zerfall und Verfall nach Platon: 'Politeia' VIII, 3–IX, 3 und 'Parmenides', 3–9 hypothesis', *Dialogos. Festschrift H. Patzl*, Steiner, Wiesbaden, 1975, pp. 67–78.

48 *The Class Struggle in the Ancient Greek World*, Duckworth, London, 1981.

49 Amongst the exceptions, the *Gorgias*, p. 271, the *Euthyphron*, p. 185, the *Menexenus*, p. 416.

50 It is a pity that Sainte-Croix does not reveal to whom he is alluding. Perhaps Karl Popper? But he is not named.

51 Sainte-Croix, op. cit., p. 70.

52 *Republic*, VIII, 550c–552e. Sainte-Croix refers the reader to two linked studies by A. Fuks: 'Plato and the Social Question: The Problem of Poverty and Riches in the "Republic"', 'Plato and the Social Question: The Problem of Poverty and Riches in the "Laws"', *Social Conflicts in Ancient Greece*, Brill, Leiden, 1984, pp. 80–114, 126–71; on this question it is also worth referring to the old article by L. Robin, 'Platon et la science sociale', *Revue de métaphysique et de morale*, 1913, reprinted in *La Pensée hellénique des origines à Épicure*, PUF, Paris, 1942, pp. 177–230. It is worth noting that Sainte-Croix makes no use of the book by the sociologist A. W. Gouldner, *Enter Plato: Classical Greece and the Origins of Social Theory*, Basic Books, New York and London, 1965.

53 See *A History of Education in Antiquity*, the first French edition of which (Seuil) appeared in 1948. Marrou criticized W. Jaeger for having sacrificed Isocrates to Plato in his *Paideia*; see 'Le siècle de Platon, à propos d'un livre récent', *Revue historique*, 196, 1946, pp. 142–9.

54 Hegel hardly figures at all in Sainte-Croix's book; the only allusions to him are to be found on pp. 26, 55, 56.

55 See, for example, the use of Plato made by Y. Garlan in *Slavery in Ancient Greece*, Cornell University Press, 1988, pp. 122–8, and in his *Guerre et économie*, pp. 24–6.

56 In July 1981 I had what was for me an extremely memorable radio conversation on this subject with Philippe Gauthier, who, like Sainte-Croix, is an Aristotelian scholar.

57 I am here thinking principally of historians of society: of course qualifications could be made and exceptions found.

58 A. W. Gouldner, op. cit., n. 52.

59 Except in the conclusion, pp. 156–8.

60 K. R. Popper, *The Open Society and its Enemies*, Routledge, London, 1966. This is not the place to express my own opinions on this book, which is fiercely debated – seldom, however, by historians – and the French translation of which (*La Cité ouverte et ses ennemis*, tr. J. Bernard and P. Monod, I, *L'Ascendant de Platon*, Seuil, Paris, 1979) was not published until ten years after the appearance of the original English edition.

61 Ed. de Minuit, Paris, 1962.

62 On Grote, see A. Momigliano's classic study, 'George Grote and the Study of Greek History', *Studies in Historiography*, pp. 56–74, and *Problèmes d'historiographie*, pp. 361–82.

63 G. Grote, *Plato and the Other Companions of Socrates*, I, p. xii.

64 *Phaedrus*, 265e–266a.

65 Among the works that seem to develop along the right lines, I should mention, apart from those by N. Loraux cited above, on the 'philosopher' side, the studies by I. Labriola, 'Tucidide e Platone sulla democrazia ateniese', *Quaderni di Storia*, 11, January–June 1980, pp. 207–29; 'Atene fra tradizione e progetto (sul 'Menesseno' di Platone)', *Rivista critica di storia della filosofia*, 3, 1981, pp. 235–52, and, more generally, the book by G. Cambiano, *La filosofia in Grecia e a Roma*, Bari, Laterza, 1983; on the 'historian' side, the many works by S. Dusanič, most recently 'Plato's Atlantis', *Antiquité classique*, 51, 1982, pp. 25–32, go beyond what the sources have to say, but are truly innovative.

2

Atlantis and the Nations

The story is a strange one. It starts in about 355 BC, with Plato's *Timaeus* and *Critias*. I say 'it starts' advisedly, for, despite all efforts, nobody has been able to prove that this myth was ever told before Plato recounted it. The tale itself is so well known that I need hardly summarize the essentials. Plato presents it as a story, a *muthos* that is told to the Athenian lawgiver and poet Solon, 'the wisest of the Seven' wise men,[1] by an old priest of the goddess Neïth at Sais in Egypt. Solon has just been telling what he believes to be the oldest legends of the Greek people, but the priest knows better. 'O Solon, Solon, you Greeks are always children: there is not such a thing as an old Greek' (T, 22B). The Athenians do not know their own history, recorded in the archives of Egypt. These go back eight thousand years, but as much as nine thousand years before Solon's time (T, 23D–E), Athens used to be a model city, that is to say a city constructed according to Plato's own principles. This Athens was a perfect city, a land-based and consequently hoplite power that came up against an antimodel, Atlantis, a huge island power, 'larger than Asia and Libya [Africa] together' (T, 24E). Constantly evolving, this kingdom, founded by Poseidon to shelter the children that he fathered by the nymph Clito, became at once a sea power and an evil power – two associated, or even twin, concepts in Plato's view.[2] Naturally, Atlantis was an imperial power, and, although situated in the West, it puts one in mind of the Persia of the Persian Wars. Atlantis launched its ships and soldiers against the Mediterranean and clashed with the Athenian army. The Athenians

This chapter was published in French as 'L'Atlantide et les nations' in Pierre Vidal-Naquet, *La Démocratie grecque vue d'ailleurs: essais d'historiographie ancienne et moderne*, Paris, 1990, pp. 130–59, and has many points in common with my article 'Hérodote et l'Atlantide: entre les Grecs et les Juifs; réflexions sur l'historiographie du siècle des lumières,' *Quaderni di storia* 16, July–December 1982: pp. 3–76.

won the day, but thereupon vanquished and victors alike were swallowed up by a great flood. Atlantis disappeared into the ocean that now bears its name. It no longer existed except in the archives and memories of the Egyptians. Athens did survive, reduced however to the mere bones of the ancient city. Thanks to the priest in Sais, Solon carried the heroic story back to Athens, where he passed it on to Critias, then a child, to be handed down to his descendants, of whom Plato was one of the best known.

I will not dwell overlong on the meaning of this story. But let me make two essential points. Plato tells us this story as though it were true: it is 'a tale which, though passing strange, is yet wholly true.'[3] Those words were to be translated into every language in the world and used to justify the most realistic fantasies. That is quite understandable, for Plato's story started something new.[4] With a perversity that was to ensure him great success, Plato had laid the foundations for the historical novel, that is to say the novel set in a particular place and a particular time.[5] We are now quite accustomed to historical novels, and we also know that in every detective story there comes a moment when the detective declares that real life is not much like what happens in detective stories; it is far more complicated. But that was not the case in the fourth century BC. Plato's words were taken seriously, not by everyone, but by many, down through the centuries. And it is not too hard to see that some people continue to take them seriously today.

As for the meaning, following others and together with others, I have tried elsewhere to show that essentially it is quite clear: the Athens and Atlantis of ancient lore represent the two faces of Plato's own Athens.[6] The former, the old primordial Athens, is what Plato would have liked the city of which he was a citizen to be; the latter is what Athens was in the age of Pericles and Cleon, an imperialistic power whose very existence constituted a threat to other Greek cities.[7]

That was the starting point. Has there ever been an end to the story? A glance at the newspaper, which Hegel called 'the prayer of a realist's morning', shows that there never has been. As recently as September 1984 a Soviet flotilla of submarines gave up the search for Atlantis, offshore from Gibraltar.[8] As we shall see, similar forays in Sweden might have been equally justified. More recently still, an archaeologist from Ghent situated the capital of Atlantis in the neighborhood of Sens, where he was hoping to find Viking remains. His tactful discovery won him vociferous praise.[9]

However, I shall not explore those avenues, for there are too many of them and they are too overgrown. But when did *scholars*, or at least people considered to be such, cease to look for Atlantis? In 1841 Thomas-Henri Martin, a philosophy professor at Rennes University and a disciple of

Victor Cousin, published in Paris a work that has become a classic: *Études sur le Timée de Platon*. It included a long and passionate 'Dissertation sur l'Atlantide' in which the author patiently noted all or virtually all the identifications that had been proposed for the continent described by Plato. In Martin's view their very number proved that no single one could definitively outbid the rest. He concluded: 'Some people have seen the New World as Atlantis. But no: it belongs to *another world*, one that exists not in the domain of space but in that of thought.'[10] Of course 1841 did not mark the end of the quest,[11] or even arrest it momentarily, but for historians of the 'real world' it certainly represents a turning point.

The year 1841 is interesting at another level, too. It was at some time between 1830 and 1840 that a new form of history, based on archives, came into its own. Archives – that is, the use of archives – became the test of scientificity.[12] Of course, in the quest for origins, the myth did not disappear: this was, after all, the period when, from Finland right across to the Balkans, emerging nations were trying to discover *Iliads* of their own. Where national history was concerned, however, the myth was now beside the point. Until this time, national archives had been an instrument of the government; now they became the historian's 'laboratory'.

Martin spoke of 'the domain of thought'. Today we should speak, rather, of the realm of imaginary representations, a realm that also has a history, fed not by 'facts' alone but also by 'interpretations'.[13] Martin may seem to have established the principles for that kind of history, but he certainly did not begin to practise it. One is bound to be struck by the fact that, in his list, he sees no need to distinguish between identifications of the location of Atlantis, on the one hand, and interpretations of the text on the other. He is content to prove that there never was an Atlantis that could be shown on a map in the way that so many people had tried to show it. He makes no attempt to understand what so many imaginative interpretations had contributed to the idea of Atlantis.[14] Of course, space limitations preclude me from considering the subject exhaustively here, so I shall limit myself to a single theme: what I shall call the 'nationalistic' aspect of the story of Atlantis.

Let us therefore leave to one side the intellectual debate that followed the appearance of the *Timaeus* and the *Critias*, a debate that was devoted to the question of whether Plato's description and story should be taken literally. Aristotle and Eratosthenes, for their part, were sceptical. The debate even split the Academy, as we know from the detailed commentary on the *Timaeus* left us by Proclus.

Our point of departure must be a series of events that were completely unforeseeable, however much theologians, followed by historians, have striven to detect a rationality in them. In the second and third centuries AD, the Mediterranean world began to turn Christian. Particularly for the intellectuals who sought to come to terms with the change, this meant replacing their mythology and history, from the War of the Giants down to the Trojan War, with the mythology and history of the Hebrews and the Jews, from Adam down to the birth of Christ.

Of course, it was not as simple as that. A compromise between Jewish chronology and Greek chronology had already begun to be elaborated as early as the second century BC, as is evident from the ancient parts of the *Sibylline Oracles*. At that point, it was the Jews who were seeking to be included, and it was up to them to assimilate themselves into the Greek systems. When the Christian church began to seek to dominate and, in the time first of Constantine, then of Theodosius, even acquired the instruments of domination, the Greek intellectuals at work in that world – Clement of Alexandria and Eusebius of Caesarea for example – were, in their turn, obliged to elaborate a compromise.[15] They acknowledged the greatness of Plato and the existence of the Trojan War, but it was fundamental that Plato should be a disciple of Moses and that this Jewish lawgiver should antedate the time of Achilles. This 'Eusebian compromise' was to have a long and tenacious life, lasting in its essentials right down to the seventeenth century.

How did Atlantis fare in this colossal reorganization? Occasionally, Plato's story is evoked as an exemplum by Jewish or Christian authors,[16] but the only really significant text is to be found in the *Christian Topography* written by Cosmas Indicopleustès, who was probably a monk from the East and who declares that he had travelled in the Orient in the sixth century AD. The story of Atlantis is presented here as at once Greek fiction and Eastern truth. Moses, followed by the Chaldeans, are said to be its distant authors. The West is said to have been substituted for the East, for instead of Solon receiving instruction from an Egyptian priest, it was Plato to whom an Egyptian, by the strange name of Solomon, addressed the famous exclamation: 'You Greeks are always children.'[17] We should take good note of this date, for it records the first meeting between Atlantis and the Jews.

I could, at a pinch, now leap over more than nine centuries and come to the event that, on its own, radically altered the situation: the discovery of America. But a few markers at least, over the intervening years, may be helpful.

We Europeans have become accustomed to think that our nations began with the collapse of the Roman Empire in the West. For example, the title of Suzanne Teillet's book is *Des Goths à la nation gothique: Les origines de l'idée de nation en Occident du Ve au VIIe siècle*.[18] The nation in question is the 'Gothic nation' of Spain, but at least one other European nation, Sweden, was also to discover its roots in a Gothic tradition or myth (it is not always easy to choose between those two terms). And it would assuredly be possible to write a similar work on the Franks. I cannot summarize Teillet's book here, but let me make a few points, rather more forcefully perhaps than that scholarly author did.

These emerging 'nations', or rather the intellectuals who claimed to speak in their name – their ideologists is really what they should be called – were faced with a choice between two models of sovereignty: the imperial Roman model or the royal Hebrew one. They had to choose between Caesar and David. In what was to become France, as in what was to become Spain, the choice – except in the brief Carolingian interval – fell upon Israelite royalty, a fact that is not without relevance to the elabora-tion of the concept of 'magic kings'.[19] The Visigoth King Wamba was probably the first Western sovereign, in 672, to receive the royal unction, in accordance with an Israelite model reworked and rethought by Isidore of Seville and Julian of Toledo, whose *Vita Wambae* is modelled on the Book of Kings in the Bible.[20] And when Gregory of Tours speaks of the *gentes* fighting against Clovis, he most explicitly assimilates them to the *goyim*, peoples foreign to Israel.[21]

This produced one essential consequence, namely a proliferation of 'chosen peoples': a spin-off from ancient Israel. Traces of that prolifera-tion still survive today, and from the Renaissance on it played a role of capital importance in the ideological landscape first of Europe, then of America; but it goes right back to the times that followed the collapse of the Roman Empire in the West. However, it was not enough to be a chosen people, or rather, that idea could not simply apply to the entire people. The established aristocracies and royal families had to have their own particular genealogies. In Spain, the Goths – a minority if ever there were one – remained the largely mythical ancestors of the nobility, even when, following the Arab invasion, they had disappeared as a community. The 'Gothic Blood', pure blood *par excellence*, was to be transmitted through the ages. In France, a legend borrowed from the pagan tradition, namely the legend of Troy, was used to confer prestige on the three successive royal dynasties.[22] France, like Spain – but unlike, for instance, Sweden – was a country where two 'races' coexisted. The Trojan legend was used to give one of those races a sense of superiority.

All these elements were present centuries before the Renaissance. But, of course, with the Renaissance and the renewal of the Latin culture, they received a definite boost. Nor was biblical mythology forgotten, nor that strange association that had been established between Greek literature and the Jewish tradition between the second and the fourth centuries AD.

During the Renaissance, Noah was a particularly important figure.[23] It was, of course, generally accepted that all men were descended from Noah, but, to adapt George Orwell's expression, some were descended better and more directly than others. Naturally, Ham's descendants were accursed, but various claims to primogeniture could be and indeed were advanced in connection with the descendants of Shem and Japheth.

As an ancestor, Japheth was all the more distinguished in that he enjoyed the immense advantage, made known by the *Sibylline Oracles*, of being both the son of Noah and, at the same time, Iapetus, the Titan of Greek mythology, the father of Prometheus and Atlas, the latter himself a namesake of Atlantis.[24]

True, the masses took little interest in speculations such as these, but in this period from the late sixth century on, which witnessed a large-scale reappearance of imperialistic policies in the shape of the Italian Wars, ideologists were in a position to play an important role. Here is one remarkable example. At the end of the fifteenth century, in 1498, Giovanni Nanni, better known as Annius of Viterbo, published a whole series of false fragments from famous historians of classical and Hellenistic Greece and ancient Rome, figures as widely diverse as Cato, Xenophon and the Chaldean Berosus. Some of these pagans were apparently perfectly familiar with Noah, whom they called Janus, and his sons. Ham remained accursed. An unknown son of Noah, who bore almost the same name as the Tuisto whom Tacitus made the ancestor of the Germans, was Tuyscon, who reigned over the Germanic territories. One of Japheth's sons, Gomer, also known as Gallus, sent his son Samothes from Italy to found the kingdom of France.[25] What language did these distant ancestors speak? The classic answer, which had already incurred Dante's criticism, was that it was Hebrew.[26]

The ideologists of the various nations had a natural tendency to claim that their own language was the primordial one. In the sixteenth century, the Florentine Giovanni Battista Gelli similarly tried to prove that, in the course of his travels, Noah-Janus, later buried beneath the Janiculum in Rome, had founded Florence;[27] meanwhile, Annius of Viterbo claimed that the honour of being founded by Noah-Janus went to his own home town.

As was to be expected, the intellectuals of France soon reacted to these Italian claims. A strange cabalist by the name of Guillaume Postel, one of the fathers of Celtomania, declared that Japheth had been banished from Italy by the ghastly Ham and had come to Gaul to work on his astronomical investigations. As for Noah himself, he had travelled all over the world, including – of course – in Atlantis.[28]

The next step was taken by Postel's disciple Guy Le Fèvre de la Broderie, who, in his *Galliade, ou de la Révolution des arts et sciences* (1578), declared that Gaul was the first piece of land to emerge from the Flood. Finally, a century later, Pierre Audigier hit upon the perfect solution: Noah's true name, quite simply, was Gallus.[29] To which it should be added that the kings of France were said to be the descendants of both Japheth and Shem – which made it possible for them to claim cousinship with Jesus and Mary.[30]

Now that that general framework is sketched in, the question is: what happened to Atlantis? The myth had quietly survived throughout the Middle Ages, mainly transmitted by the prologue to the *Timaeus*, made known by Calcidius' translation.[31] Perhaps it can also be detected in the Irish legend of Saint Brendan.[32] Medieval maps speculated on the whereabouts of plenty of mythical lands, ranging from the earthly paradise to the land of Gog and Magog and the kingdom of Prester John, which was where the Antichrist was going to manifest himself. One example was the 1375 *Catalan Atlas*, another the map commissioned from the Venetian Fra Mauro in 1459, at the time of the discoveries by Alfonso of Portugal. However, Atlantis was not included among those mythical places. *A fortiori*, no nation at that time claimed any kind of monopoly over Atlantis. In 1485 the humanist Marsilio Ficino translated Plato's works into Latin, accompanying his translation of the *Critias* with a commentary. His verdict was that the story was true, but only in the Platonic sense of the word, which did not make it possible to locate Atlantis on a map. He too connected Plato with the biblical tradition.[33]

Seven years after this translation, however, something happened that was to change everything: America was discovered. True, it is not known whether Christopher Columbus himself knew of Plato's story, although it has sometimes been mentioned in this connection.[34] But Atlantis was soon to enter into general circulation. As has been pointed out,

> a continent barely touched by man lay exposed to men whose greed could no longer be satisfied by their own continent. Everything would be called into question by this second sin: God, morality and law. In simultaneous yet contradictory fashion, everything would be verified in practice and revoked in principle: the Garden of Eden, the Golden Age of antiquity, the Fountain of youth, Atlantis, the Hesperides, the Islands of the Blessed, would be found to be true; but revelation, salvation, customs and law would be challenged by the spectacle of a purer, happier race of men (who, of course, were not really purer or happier, although a deep-seated remorse made them appear so).[35]

The discovery of America marked the decisive turning point. It was certainly very quickly recognized that this was a 'new world', that is to say a different world.[36] But, as Lévi-Strauss has explained, this 'brave new world', to which Shakespeare was to refer in *The Tempest*, could at first be apprehended only by means of the concepts and ideas derived from the twofold tradition that informed the works of the period: the classical culture and the Christian – and hence Jewish – culture, a twofold tradition which, it must be said, was regarded as a single one by most educated people.[37]

In the name of logic, we should recognize that, in the theories that were elaborated after 1492, Atlantis occupied every logical position that might *a priori* be conceived. In the name of the human mind and to its glory, we should add that, at least by the end of the sixteenth century, sceptics were making themselves heard, particularly Montaigne in France and, in Spain, José de Acosta, the founder of modern anthropology.[38]

What solutions were conceivable? America could either be biblical or Platonic, that is to say, Atlantis. Atlantis itself could be interpreted either through the Bible or in the light of the great new discoveries; and these were all solutions that could easily be combined as well as opposed. The common preoccupation that united them was the now primary need, except for the sceptics, to locate Atlantis – a need that was characteristic of the sixteenth century,[39] although it had, in contrast, been quite absent from works such as Ficino's.

In his edition of Plato, Jean de Serres (Serranus) provided a commentary on both the *Timaeus* and the *Critias*. In it he suggested that the Greeks were indeed children, as the Egyptian priest had observed to Solon. If we compare Plato 'with the simple truth of history as told by Moses', it becomes evident that the description of Atlantis is quite simply a picture of the world before the Flood, before Noah.[40] That is just one text, but it is one that we should not forget because, in the eighteenth century, many scholars were to refine that solution, 'proving' that Atlantis was, quite simply, Palestine.

And what was America supposed to be? For many scholars and ideologists, it was the country where the ten tribes of Israel had found refuge. This myth of the disappearance and reappearance of the ten tribes was a particularly splendid one. And it was not only in connection with America that it was seized on, for in 1944 I was most seriously assured that the tribe of Dan had become Denmark. The origin of these traditions is to be found in a famous passage from the biblical Apocrypha:

Then you saw him collecting a different company, a peaceful one.
They are the ten tribes which were taken off into exile in the time
of King Hoshea, whom Shalmaneser king of Assyria took prisoner.
He deported them beyond the River, and they were taken away into

a strange country. But then they resolved to leave the country popu-
lated by the Gentiles and go to a distant land never yet inhabited by
man, and there at last to be obedient to their laws, which in their own
country they had failed to keep.[41]

In the sixteenth century, echoes from that text resounded widely through
the Christian world. But some Jews also accepted it – notably Manasseh
ben Israel, a friend of Rembrandt's in Amsterdam, who took it up in his
Esperança de Israel (1648), illustrating it in a novel, in which, however,
he insisted upon the crucial qualification that only a fraction of the Indians – those most remarkable for their beauty – should be identified as
Jews.[42]

It was also possible to interpret America without the Bible, using Plato's text on its own,[43] and this was indeed done early on, earlier than is
generally believed[44] – in fact by 1527 – to take account only of published
works: at this date, the illustrious Bartolomé de las Casas was declaring
that Christopher Columbus could be reasonably sure that at least part of
the continent described by Plato had been unaffected by the disaster.[45] It
was logically predictable that the two models, the Atlantic and the biblical, should eventually be combined, as indeed they were by Francis Bacon
in his Utopia, *New Atlantis*, published posthumously in 1627.[46] Here,
Atlantis is an island situated to the west of Peru, in the 'southern seas',
where Hebrew, Greek and excellent Spanish are all spoken, for this is a
perfect society of scholars. It is a fragment that was detached from the
island that Plato described and is Jewish by origin and Christian by con-
version, but with a respected Jewish minority. In this particular case,
Plato and the Bible complemented one another. In 1655, however, it was
just the other way around: in *Prae-Adamitae*, the work of a pro-Jewish
Protestant by the name of Isaac de la Peyrère, Adam is regarded as, not
the first man, but the first Jew. In this author's view, the traditional biblical chronology was clearly incompatible with the nine thousand years
that preceded Solon, whom Plato had credited with the idea of Atlantis.
Atlantis must accordingly have been inhabited by men who predated
Adam.[47]

But to my mind what is of essential interest is the link that is henceforth established between the lands of fable, of which Atlantis is probably
the most famous, and the nationalistic myths that we have seen sprouting
from the ruins of the Roman Empire and being forcefully resuscitated
during the Renaissance. If a German jurist could discern in the language
of the Indians *'nescio quid Cimbricum, seu priscum Teutonicum'*
['something or other that brings to mind the *Cimbres* and the ancient
Teutons'], for example the word 'papa', which is 'common both to us

Europeans and to Americans', we may be sure that he was not alone in doing so.[48]

For obvious reasons, the place *par excellence* where the fusion between the lands and times of fable and the modernized ideology of the chosen people took place was the Spain of the Conquistadors. It began, as it happened, not with Atlantis but with the ancient garden of the Hesperides. Gonzalo Fernandez de Oviedo, who was appointed official chronicler of the Indies in 1532, produced the first part of his *Historia general y natural de las Indias* in 1535. In it he declared that the Antilles, that is to say the land of the Hesperides, had already long been possessions of the Spanish Crown. Charles V, informed in advance of these investigations and discoveries, on 25 October 1533 expressed his keen satisfaction at learning that 'for three thousand and ninety-one years these lands have been among the royal possessions of Spain, so that it is not surprising that, after so many years, God has restored them to their owner.'[49]

The next step was taken by a Flemish subject of the King of Spain, Jan van Gorop (Goropius Becanus). According to him, ancient Tartessus, the Tartessus of both the Bible and Herodotus, was the ancestor of modern Spain and the capital of Atlantis, which had been founded by two brothers, Atlas-Tartessus and Ulysses-Hesperus, both grandsons of Japheth. Of the two it was the elder, Atlas-Tartessus, who held the power of primogeniture, and his descendants, the kings of Spain, thus possessed obvious rights over Atlantic Africa and America.[50]

The clearest formulation of what we may now call Atlanto-nationalism was produced in 1572, for the sole profit of Philip II of Spain, by Pedro Sarmiento de Gamboa, in his *Historia general llamada Indica*.[51] On the basis of the Platonic text, which places Atlantis beyond the Pillars of Hercules, Sarmiento claimed that this was a continent that, long ago, had adjoined Spain. America, its distant remains, thus belonged by divine right to the Spanish Crown.[52]

Spain had thus made use of both the Gothic myth and the myth of Atlantis. But here, so far as I know, there was not the slightest connection between the two. That was not to be the case in another country that also used the Gothic myth, namely Sweden.

Now we must tackle a question of considerable importance: what became of the myth of Atlantis during the Enlightenment, that is to say from about 1670, the beginning of what Paul Hazard has called *la crise de la conscience européenne*, down to the French Revolution? The early years of those extremely troubled times saw the appearance of the work of the man who, following Sarmiento but with infinitely more brilliance, was the real creator of the nationalistic Atlantis myth: Olof Rudbeck.[53]

A few rules of interpretation need to be sketched in at this point. What I shall refer to as the Enlightenment was faced with a huge problem, just the opposite of that which had faced the Greek Fathers of the second to the fourth centuries and which, by and large, had been retackled by the men of the Renaissance. The task of the Fathers was to reconcile Greek historiography and the biblical tradition as best they could. The men of the Enlightenment had, on the contrary, to put paid to using the Jewish people as a vector of universal history, a role in which they had been most splendidly confirmed by Jacques Bénigne Bossuet's *Discours sur l'histoire universelle* as late as 1681. What now needed to be done was to find a new chosen people, even if – provisionally – this meant resuscitating some form of paganism.[54] And of course, the men of the Enlightenment were not alone. There were rivals to be contended with, who knew how to turn the tables. In the eighteenth century, one was just as likely to discover a Jewish prophet behind Plato or Homer as to find a pagan god behind the sacred figure of Jesus Christ. The Enlightenment was, it need hardly be said, not a conscious movement at all levels or where all its participants were concerned. Many helped in practice to 'crush the beast', quite unaware that they were collaborating in that endeavour.

At the time of the Enlightenment, Atlantis was a kind of substitute for the Jewish people in the economy of universal history. But what I should like to discuss, more specifically, is Atlantis used as a *national* substitute. The people who once constituted Atlantis were a chosen people and, as such, deserved the primacy that every imperial power believes itself to possess.

Admittedly, Atlantis as a national substitute was not the only function of the myth in the Enlightenment. Quite apart from any particular national ancestry, Atlantis could be considered as the origin of all the nations, or as a golden age, which is indeed how the astronomer Jean Sylvain Bailly regarded it. Beyond humanity and above it, Atlantis, for Nicolas Boulanger, was a cosmic episode, one particular moment in the universal floods that, he believed, punctuate history.[55] But Atlantis also always functioned as a substitute.

Olof Rudbeck (1630–1702) was rector of Uppsala University. In his immense work *Atlantica (Atland eller Manheim)*, he set out to show that Atlantis, the cradle of human civilization, was none other than Sweden, with its capital at Uppsala.[56]

I must confess that ever since I first came across Rudbeck's oeuvre, over a quarter of a century ago, the man and his work have always fascinated me. He was a scholar of considerable stature, a great anatomist who discovered the network of lymph ducts, and was also responsible for the construction of an amphitheatre that still stands today in Uppsala. But he was not only a doctor and a biologist. He knew everything there was to be known about language and history, and he used it all in *Atlantica*, the work to which he devoted his maturity and old age. There is no truth in the idea that there were two Rudbecks, one a doctor, the other a historian,[57] any more than in the notion that there were two Descartes, one responsible for the *Cogito*, the other the author of reflections on the circulation of the blood that today seem totally risible.

Throughout his work, Rudbeck remained faithful to an empiricism inherited from Francis Bacon. Yet some of his contemporaries, Pierre Bayle in particular,[58] realized that that empiricism bordered on paranoia. Unquestionably, he was well aware of the dangers of his project – as we all should be when it comes to speculations of our own. In his first volume, Rudbeck presents a discussion on the subject of the Indies, presided over by Apollo, in which the participants are a number of august scholars and one humble gardener, Hortulanus. Apollo and the eminent doctors have much to say on this rich subject, but the little gardener does not agree with them, dismissing all that he has heard as *chimerae atque deliramenta*, 'fantasies and nonsense'. He tells his interlocutors: 'Assuredly, *et nos homines* we too are men';[59] but so, equally, are the great doctors: *et vos homines*. On the frontispiece of his atlas (figure 1), Rudbeck, the great scholar *par excellence,* had that maxim repeated – ET NOS HOMINES – thereby feigning to cast himself in the role of a little gardener, possibly sensing that he had laid himself open to the attacks of any other little gardener who happened along.

As the scholar who devoted the greater part of his life to the mystery of Atlantis, Rudbeck managed to create a national myth comprising two separate elements: the quest for Noah and his heirs, with which we are well familiar, and the Gothic myth, one of whose early manifestations we have noted in Visigoth Spain.[60] I will not embark here on the history of that myth from its distant origins in the sixth century AD down to the point at which it was solemnly revived at the Council of Basel in 1434, when the bishop Nicholas Ragvaldi forcefully claimed that the kingdom of Sweden was older, more powerful, and more noble than any other. Far from having been conquered by the monarchs of Rome, it had forced the Romans themselves to become its allies.

It was mainly in the seventeenth century, in the period of history when Sweden was known as a great power, namely the reign of Gustavus Adolphus (1611–32), that the primacy of the Goths became the national myth of the Swedish people.

To show how the quest for Noah was fused with the Gothic ideology of Sweden, let us limit ourselves to the study of two documents. The first is the frontispiece of volume 1 of the *Atlantica* (figure 1). Originating in

Figure 1 The tree of Shem and that of Atlas: religion and power. Frontispiece of the first volume of Rudbeck's *Atlantica*. Photo: François Demerliac.

Noah, seated somewhere in the vicinity of Mount Ararat, three lines of descent branch out. One, that of Ham, is soon lost in the sands of Africa. The other two, those of Shem and Japheth, are closely intertwined, as in the French monarchical tradition. Shem's family tree is a vine, the top of which is watered by the blood of Jesus (Rudbeck definitely remained Christian). The other tree, which is thicker, belongs to Japheth only up to the point where it is taken over by his son Atlas, a figure from Greek mythology. Atlas's tree grows in Sweden. It is an apple tree and is accordingly assimilated to the tree of the Garden of Eden, whose apples thud to the ground, symbolizing all the different nations. These include the Turks, the Trojans, the Goths of Spain, the Moors and the Gauls. The Greeks are absent from this symbolism. Atlas is directly succeeded by Boreas, who in turn is directly succeeded by kings who bear Swedish names: Eric, Gustavus and so forth. The tree of power thus interweaves its branches with those of the tree of religion, still present at this point. One day, it was to disappear.

The second document shows Rudbeck himself, very much the great scholar, portrayed as a geographer and an anatomist (see figure 2).[61] He is the central figure in this picture, the anatomist and archaeologist who is to discover Atlantis right under the skin of Sweden. He is surrounded by eleven other figures, bringing the number in this group up to that of the apostles (the only biblical reference in the picture). The first of these figures, on Rudbeck's right and recognized by his scythe, is Time (Chronos); then, ringing the globe, come the rest, all but one of them named: Hesiod, Plato, Aristotle, Apollodorus, Tacitus, Ulysses, Ptolemy, Plutarch, the anonymous one and Orpheus. The anonymous figure really does not need to be named for, blind as he is and crowned with a laurel wreath, he is clearly Homer. One great figure is conspicuous by his absence: Herodotus, who was guilty of having failed to mention the peoples with Germanic languages. Those who are present, however, are the most eminent representatives of classical culture and learning, and they are gathered here to proclaim the primacy of Sweden, the land of Origins *par excellence*.

Confronted with this totalitarian proclamation, it was Bayle, exiled in Rotterdam, who assumed the role of the little gardener.[62] He quite simply pointed out that there were many nations in the world and that each one could lay claim to primacy with equally good arguments. In 1676, after all, Pierre Audigier, a Frenchman, had similarly announced the primacy of Gaul.[63]

Giambattista Vico was a citizen in a country that was still no more than 'a geographical expression', but the Lombards provided it with an

Figure 2 Olof Rudbeck, anatomist and geographer: Atlantis-Sweden revealed.
Frontispiece to the atlas of Rudbeck's *Atlantica*. Photo: Bibliothèque Nationale.

equivalent to the Goths and furthermore could draw on the Etruscans, whose claims to be hailed as the princes of Origins were very serious indeed. In his first major work, *De antiquissima Italorum sapientia* (1710), Vico was momentarily tempted by an argument resembling Rudbeck's, which he had read but then rejected, rallying to the view that, in the eyes of God and in the Cycle of History, all nations are equal.[64] Elsewhere, notably in France and Germany, Rudbeck's discourse on Origins was turned around and restored to the Christian faith. Atlantis was indeed the place of Origins, but that place was none other than Palestine.[65]

Rudbeck's nationalistic Atlantism, like the Gothic myth, was a typical product of the period of great powers. In 1779, seven years after King Gustavus III had seized power to set on the ruins of party oppositions a typical enlightened despotism, the political climate was very different. It was then that a Piedmontese scholar, Giuseppe Bartoli, published and commented on the inaugural speech that the king of Sweden had delivered to the Riksdag in 1778. The Gothic-inspired ideology had collapsed, following the failure of the latest venture of Swedish nationalism led by Charles XII (king from 1697 to 1718). When Bartoli successfully argued that Atlantis was an image of imperialistic Athens, he was in truth referring to Sweden, but to a Sweden now disabused of its illusions.[66]

Meanwhile, what Bayle had foreseen and predicted came to pass. The ideologists of other countries also saw themselves as heirs to Atlantis; and they must be mentioned here, if only to note a certain degeneration from the level of myth to that of the novel, to speak in the manner of Georges Dumézil and Lévi-Strauss.[67]

France, however, was not affected by this particular malady; and the explanation is simple enough. What with her confidence in her own great king,[68] her status as a great nation, and her own great emperor, she was sufficient unto herself and, in so far as she indulged in talk of Origins, the Gauls, the Romans and the Franks provided quite enough material to satisfy any ideologist. Atlantis was, it is true, a favourite topic of the intelligentsia, but it was a prenational Atlantis (a golden age), a cosmic or Christian Atlantis (Palestine) or a geographical Atlantis (the Canary Islands or America), not a national Atlantis. There was one exception that proved the rule. In 1808 a native of Avignon by the name of Fortia d'Urban published a thesis designed to show that a primitive people composed of Celts and Iberians had brought the civilization of Atlantis from Spain to France.[69] But this Atlanto-Occitanism had very little impact.

Italy, for its part, did have a problem with Origins, and during the Enlightenment there were numerous candidates for the position of primacy, with the Italici, the Etruscans, the Germans and the Greeks all to the fore. The nationalistic-Atlantic theme did also manage to slip in its own little say, however. Its first spokesman was Count Gianrinaldo Carli (1720–95), an interesting reformist figure.[70] Carli produced what was, *a priori*, an unpredictable merger between the American theme of Atlantis and the thesis of Italian primacy at the origins of civilization. At the time of Atlantis, according to him, Italy was the link between America and the eastern Mediterranean. After Janus, the indigenous king, Saturn came from Atlantis to Italy, and it was Italy that then transmitted to Greece all the arts and virtues of Atlantis.

Much later, in 1840, Angelo Mazzoldi explained that Italy actually *had been* Atlantis and, as such, had civilized the entire eastern Mediterranean.[71] What he was doing – and he was not the first to do so – was turning upside down the tradition of Greece as the ancient origin of civilization. At this late date, his book was received with respect.

England poses a different problem. So far as I know, there was no nationalistic-Atlantism there, neither in the seventeenth century nor in the Enlightenment. James Harrington's *Commonwealth of Oceana* (1656) was dedicated to Oliver Cromwell, who was later to send the author to prison. As John Toland pointed out in his biographical essay, when the work could finally be published at the beginning of the eighteenth century, it was 'written after the manner of a Romance, in imitation of Plato's *Atlantic Story*', but except as a literary genre, this apologia for a Republican and merchant England had nothing at all in common with Plato.[72]

The two nationalistic versions of Atlantis that I have found in England belong to the occultist and preromantic tradition rather than to the tradition of the Enlightenment proper. It is accordingly more rewarding to compare them to works such as that of Fabre d'Olivet than to Rudbeck's.

They are worth mentioning, however. William Blake (1757–1827) produced a strange combination of Celtic, Jewish and Atlantic lore. According to him, Atlas was another name for the Breton patriarch Albion; Abraham and Noah were both druids; and the vanished continent was a link between England and the new America that Blake exalted in so many of his poems. The underlying principle here is that 'the antiquities of every Nation under Heaven, is no less sacred than that of the Jews',[73] but the consequences that Blake drew from that fundamental principle of modern nationalist messianism made for fusion rather than for distinction. England was the land of the twelve tribes of Israel.[74]

One of Blake's contemporaries, Captain F. Wilford, an Indianist, with great originality discovered in the *Puranas* some faraway white islands in the West. Combining these texts with a number of others culled from Greek sources, he concluded that these white isles (the *S'weta-dwípa*) were at once Great Britain and Atlantis, going on to observe forthrightly, 'admitting my position to be right, I am conscious that *Britain* cannot receive any additional lustre from it.'[75] The myth was, in fact, to pass from England to Ireland, where it was extremely popular in the nineteenth century.[76]

At this point, having covered the chronological ground that I set out to, I could well come to a halt. But I cannot refrain from mentioning two other nationalistic versions of Atlantis that belong to times much closer to our own. It was Plato's bitter patriotism that gave birth to the myth of Atlantis, the antithetical model to that of an Athens which was itself imaginary. The most popular modern identification of Plato's continent assimilates the destruction of Atlantis to the explosion that partially destroyed the island of Santorini around the middle of the second millennium BC. This theory, which is as absurd as all the others, owes much to the patriotism of the Greek archaeologist Spyridon Marinatos and his disciples,[77] and it has continued to be exploited for patriotic ends.[78] As an irony of history would have it, however, the name of the Greek ship sent to collect the unfortunate Yasir Arafat from Beirut in 1982 happened to be *Atlantis* too. In a more optimistic vein, it is perhaps worth noting that Atlantis was also the name given to one of the American space shuttles of the late 1980s.

The Atlantis of German National Socialism was an idea that had much more far-reaching consequences, the repercussions of which still have not died out. The last disciples of Rudbeck were to be found among Hitler's National Socialists even before they came to power. Alfred Rosenberg's *Myth of the Twentieth Century* explained that the people of Atlantis, the ancestors of the Germanic peoples, had spread all over the world, including Palestine, a fact that made it very likely, indeed certain, that Jesus, a Galilean and accordingly a foreigner, was not a Jew.[79] After the Nazis came to power, the same thesis was advanced in a book written by a geographer, Albert Herrmann (a professor at the University of Berlin but also the *Führer* of the German press).[80] This was a remarkable example of imperialism in which North Africa, for example, was represented as part of the Atlanto-Germanic heritage and the Roman amphitheatre of El Djem in Tunisia was also claimed as the work of the Atlantic race. Similar ideas were diffused in occupied Europe, particularly in France.[81]

This was no isolated phenomenon. In the notorious Ahnenerbe Institut [National Heritage Institute], the agency set up to foster SS ideology, Atlantis was a frequently mentioned subject and one in which the Reichsführer-SS Heinrich Himmler himself took a personal interest.[82] It was within this institute that the name for the island of Helgoland (*das heilige Land*, sacred or holy land) was first proposed.[83] The purpose here was clearly to find German names for German origins, so that these could display a superiority that owed nothing to Abraham. After the war, similar ideas were repeated by Jürgen Spanuth, a Nazi pastor who pretended

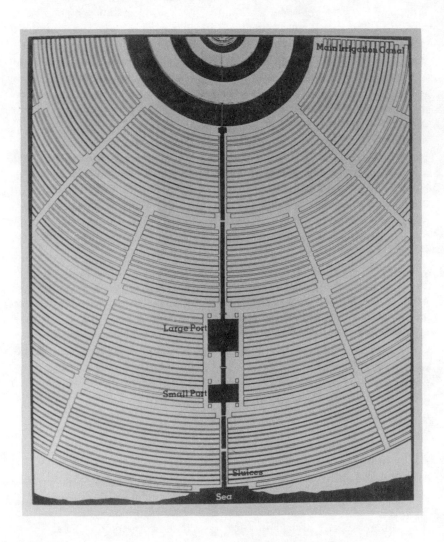

Figure 3 Putting Atlantis to good use: the Platonic city and its system of canals at the centre of the sea, according to H. R. Stahel, *Atlantis Illustrated* (New York, 1982), p. 91.

that it was he who had discovered the identity of Atlantis and Helgoland and for a while enjoyed a certain success in Germany.[84] It seems hardly necessary to point out that such ideas are still not dead.

The time has come to bring this inquiry to a close. The successive nationalistic versions of Atlantis that we have examined represent but one aspect of a widespread ideological phenomenon: the quest for Origins, which is to be found among proud and humiliated peoples alike. It draws on monuments, ancient texts, unknown or little-known peoples, and even, as in the case of Atlantis, imaginary peoples. Seven Greek cities all claimed the honour of being the birthplace of Homer. But where was Troy? One theory, which has recently enjoyed considerable success in Yugoslavia, is that Homer's Troy was situated not at Hissarlik, in Turkey, but between Split and Dubrovnik, at the mouth of the Neretva.[85] This theory has not crossed the Albanian border; but in Albania, which passionately claims descent from the ancient Illyrians,[86] serious consideration has apparently been given to the idea that during the Trojan War the Illyrians played a role of crucial importance.[87] As for the Etruscans, is it not obvious that they were Turks?[88] That is one way of settling a few old scores with the Greeks.

Faced with so many fantasies, what is to be done with Atlantis? In the first place, we should study its history as a history of human imaginary representations, and that, indeed, is what I have briefly attempted to do here. But also – why not? – we can make pictures of it, setting down on paper drawings of the geometric colony precisely imagined by Plato (figure 3).[89] Perhaps that is the best use to which Atlantis can be put in this day and age.

Notes

1 Plato, *Timaeus* 20D; hereafter abbreviated *T*.
2 For more details, see my 'Athènes et l'Atlantide: structure et signification d'un mythe platonicien', *Revue des études grecques*, 77, July–December 1964, pp. 420–44, which also appears in a more complete form in my *Black Hunter: Forms of Thought and Forms of Society in the Greek World*, tr. Andrew Szegedy-Maszak, Baltimore, 1986, pp. 263–84. Parallel and complementary points have also been treated in Luc Brisson, 'De la philosophie politique à l'épopée: le "Critias" de Platon', *Revue de métaphysique et de morale*, 75, October–December 1970, pp. 402–38, and *Platon, les mots et les mythes*, Paris, 1982; Christopher Gill, 'The Origin of the Atlantis Myth', *Trivium*, 11, 1976, pp. 1–11; 'The Genre of the Atlantis Story', *Classical Philology*, 72, July 1977, pp. 287–304; and *Plato, the Atlantis Story*, Bristol, 1980. These works, together with my own article 'Hérodote

et l'Atlantide: entre les Grecs et les Juifs; réflexions sur l'historiographie du siècle des lumières', *Quaderni di storia*, 16, July–December 1982, pp. 3–76, provide a very full bibliography. The whole succession of works on this subject, most of them quite mad, may be followed thanks to the Platonic bibliographies published in *Lustrum*, first under the editorship of Harold F. Cherniss and then under Luc Brisson. For an example of the unbelievable seriousness of some of these works, see Barbara Pischel, *Die Atlantische Lehre: Übersetzung und Interpretation der Platon-Texte aus Timaios und Kritias*, Frankfurt am Main, 1982.

3 The Greek text reads: 'λόγου μάλα μὲν ἀτόπου, παντάπασί γε μὴν ἀληθοῦς' (*T*, 20D).

4 A number of precedents exist: Xenophon's *Cyropaedia*, more or less contemporary with the *Republic* (about 380 BC) and, as Sally Humphreys has pointed out to me, in Herodotus, the Persian leaders' discussion on the subject of the best constitution, which the author presents as authentic. See Herodotus, *The Histories*, 3.80 and 6.43.

5 See in particular the works by Brisson mentioned above in n. 2, which show how carefully Plato planned the setting for his story.

6 See the works by Vidal-Naquet, Brisson and Gill mentioned above in n. 2.

7 It was the Piedmontese scholar Giuseppe Bartoli, I believe, who first hit on this explanation for the myth. See his *Essai sur l'explication historique que Platon a donnée de sa 'République' et de son Atlantide et qu'on n'a pas considérée jusqu'à maintenant*, Stockholm, 1779–80.

8 See 'Russians Say Site Is Not Atlantis', *International Herald Tribune*, 20 September 1984, p. 7. I am grateful to Jesper Svenbro for telling me that more information is to be found in 'Tracked Soviet Mini-submarine', *International Defense Review*, 17, November 1984, p. 1601. There we learn, for instance, that the Soviet 'archeological' explorations were taking place from 1973 to 1984.

9 See the article in *Courrier de Gand*, 22 February 1985: 'The huge work of M. Mestdagh, the exemplary discretion and scientific rigor, shows – if it needed to be shown – that there are still natives of Ghent who bring honor both to their own land and to their neighbor's.' I am indebted to Yvon Garlan for this press clipping.

10 Thomas-Henri Martin, *Études sur le Timée de Platon*, Paris, 1841, p. 332. The 'Dissertation' fills pp. 257–332.

11 This was shown by the identification of Atlantis and Italy just the year before. See n. 71 below.

12 See Pierre Nora, 'Archives et construction d'une histoire nationale: le cas français', in Jacques Berque and Dominique Chevallier (eds), *Les Arabes par leurs archives (XVIᵉ–XXᵉ siècles)*, Paris, 1979, pp. 321–32. See also Marcel Gauchet, 'Les "Lettres sur l'histoire de France" d'Augustin Thierry', in Nora (ed.), *Les Lieux de la mémoire*, 2 vols., Paris, 1986, 2: pp. 247–316.

13 On this point Alexander von Humboldt, a very eminent scholar in the synoptic vein, was less radical in his critique than Martin, but showed more scholarly imagination regarding the 'mythical geography' of the Greeks. See Alexander von Humboldt, *Histoire de la géographie du nouveau continent et des progrès de l'astronomie nautique aux quinzième et seizième siècles*, 5 vols., Paris, 1836–9, especially. 1: pp. 112–15 and 1: pp. 167–80.

14 Fairly recent studies on this may be found in the (not altogether reliable) book by Lyon Sprague de Camp, *Lost Continents: The Atlantis Theme in History, Science, and Literature*, New York, 1954, and in Edwin S. Ramage (ed.), *Atlantis, Fact or Fiction?*, Bloomington, Ind., 1978.

15 See, for example, Jean Sirinelli, *Les Vues historiques d'Eusèbe de Césarée durant la période prénicéenne*, Dakar, 1961.

16 The references may be found in my 'Hérodote et l'Atlantide', p. 50, n. 24.

17 See Cosmas Indicopleustès, *Topographie Chrétienne*, trs. Wanda Wolska-Conus, 3 vols., Paris, 1968–73, bk. 12, §§ 2–3, 7.

18 See Suzanne Teillet, *Des Goths à la nation gothique: les origines de l'idée de nation en Occident du Ve au VIIe siècle*, Paris, 1984.

19 Here I would refer the reader to Marc Bloch, *Les Rois thaumaturges: études sur le caractère surnaturel attribué à la puissance royale, particulièrement en France et en Angleterre*, 1924; Paris, 1983; tr. J. E. Anderson, under the title *The Royal Touch: Sacred Monarchy and Scrofula in England and France*, London, 1973.

20 See Teillet, *Des Goths à la nation gothique*, pp. 602–11. On Isidore of Seville's ideas on royalty, see Marc Reydellet, *La Royauté dans la littérature latine, de Sidoine Apollinaire à Isidore de Séville*, Rome, 1981, pp. 556–68. Reydellet stresses the mediatory role played by the image of Christ. The fundamental work on the medieval concept of kingship is still Ernst Hartwig Kantorowicz, *The King's Two Bodies: A Study in Medieval Political Theology*, Princeton, NJ, 1957.

21 See Teillet, *Des Goths à la nation gothique*, p. 404.

22 On these questions the basic work is Arno Borst, *Der Turmbau von Babel: Geschichte der Meinungen über Ursprung und Vielfalt der Sprachen und Völker*, 4 vols., Stuttgart, 1957–63. See also Léon Poliakov, *Le Mythe aryen: essai sur les sources du racisme et du nationalisme*, Paris, 1971; Brussels, 1987.

23 Apart from Borst's book, the essential work on this question is Don Cameron Allen, *The Legend of Noah: Renaissance Rationalism in Art, Science and Letters*, Urbana, Ill., 1949.

24 See the *Sibylline Oracles*, bk. 3, 1. 110.

25 I know of only one recent general work on Annius of Viterbo: Giovanni Baffioni and Paolo Mattiangeli, *Annio da Viterbo: documenti e ricerche* (Rome, 1981). It is essentially devoted to a critical edition of a new history of Viterbo and iconographical studies, and contains a full bibliography (p. 24). Among the works that I have found useful are: Allen, *The Legend of Noah*; Borst, *Der Turmbau von Babel*, especially 3: pp. 975–7 and *passim*; and Eugène Napoleon Tigerstedt, 'Iohannes Annius and "Graecia Mendax" ', in Charles Henderson, Jr. (ed.), *Classical, Mediaeval and Renaissance Studies in Honor of Berthold Louis Ullman*, 2 vols., Rome, 1964, 2: pp. 293–310.

Annius of Viterbo's Italian patriotism, which was, in truth, an extension of his local patriotism, is marked by the fact that the earliest of his forgeries, attributed to Myrsilus of Lesbos and Cato, are devoted to the 'origins' of the Italians and the Etruscans, but his text potentially offered glorious lineages to most nations. He was particularly enthusiastic about Spain, the Spanish ambassador having helped to finance the publication of his book.

26 See Maurice Olender, *Les Langues du paradis: Ayrens et Sémites, un couple inprovidentiel*, Paris, 1989, especially pp. 26, 124–6.

27 Giovanni Battista Gelli's *Delle origini di Firenze* dates from 1542. See Paolo Simoncelli, *La Lingua di Adamo: Guillaume Postel tra accademici e fuorusciti Fiorentini*, Florence, 1984, p. 18.

28 On Guillaume Postel and Celtomania, see Claude-Gilbert Dubois, *Celtes et Gaulois au XVIᵉ siècle: le développement littéraire d'un mythe nationaliste*, Paris, 1972; on the relationships with Annius of Viterbo, see p. 85. See also the essential work by William James Bouwsma, *Concordi Mundi: The Career and Thought of Guillaume Postel, 1510–1581*, Cambridge, 1957; on the travels of Noah, see pp. 257–8.

29 See Pierre Audigier, *L'Origine des François et de leur empire*, 2 vols., Paris, 1676, especially pp. 214–17.

30 See Joseph R. Strayer, 'France: The Holy Land, the Chosen People and the Most Christian King', in Theodore K. Rabb and Jerrold E. Seigel (eds), *Action and Conviction in Early Modern Europe: Essays in Memory of E. H. Harbison*, Princeton, NJ, 1969, pp. 3–16. On similar themes in Germany, see Frank L. Borchardt, *German Antiquity in Renaissance Myth*, Baltimore, 1971. For a comparative study, the essential work is Orest Ranum (ed.), *National Consciousness, History, and Political Culture in Early-Modern Europe*, Baltimore, 1975.

31 See Raymond Klibansky, *The Continuity of the Platonic Tradition during the Middle Ages*, London, 1939, which also served as the introduction to the *Corpus Platonicum Medii Aevi*, 4 vols., London, 1951–75; vol. 4 is the *Timaeus*, ed. J. H. Waszink, whose commentary shows the extent to which the importance of the Hebrew influence on Plato was considered to go without saying, but makes no mention of Atlantis.

32 See the Introduction by Ian Short and Brian Merrilees to Benedict, *The Anglo-Norman Voyage of St. Brendan*, ed. Short and Merrilees, Manchester, 1979.

33 See Raymond Marcel, *Marsile Ficin, 1433–1499*, Paris, 1958, especially pp. 630–1.

34 In particular by von Humboldt, whose intellectual portrait of Columbus remains unrivalled, despite the errors in the first two volumes of the *Histoire*. Charles Minguet's study on this text does not really do him justice. See Minguet, *Alexandre de Humboldt, historien et géographe de l'Amérique espagnole, 1799–1804*, Paris, 1969, pp. 584–603. Von Humboldt notes the absence of any mention of Atlantis from Columbus's writings but nevertheless maintains that Columbus 'took pleasure in Solon's references to Atlantis' (von Humboldt, *Histoire de la géographie du nouveau continent*, 1:167). Nor is it true that Columbus's son, Fernando, in his biography of his father, made any connections, even in a muddled fashion, between his father's achievements and Plato's myth. Although he does refer to Atlantis in a polemic directed against Gonzalo Fernandez de Oviedo, it is as a story with which his father was, precisely, unfamiliar. See Fernando Colón, *The Life of the Admiral Christopher Columbus by His Son, Ferdinand*, tr. Benjamin Keen, New Brunswick, NJ, 1959, pp. 28–34. The original Spanish text has been lost; all modern editions refer to the Italian translation.

35 Claude Lévi-Strauss, *Tristes Tropiques*, tr. John and Doreen Weightman, New

York, 1973, p. 74. Contrary to what is frequently ascribed to him through quoting him incorrectly, Lévi-Strauss nowhere states that the Spaniards went off 'to verify old legends', including that of Atlantis. Anyone interested in this little polemic is referred to Jacques Lafaye, *Les Conquistadors*, Paris, 1964, p. 111; Marianne Mahn-Lot, *La Découverte de l'Amérique*, Paris, 1970, p. 90; and Numa Broc, *La Géographie de la Renaissance (1420–1620)*, Paris, 1980, p. 166. All refer to and quote each other without having taken the trouble to check the text by Lévi-Strauss, which is incorrectly cited by Lafaye. Lévi-Strauss himself has provided me with the correct reference.

36 The credit for recognizing this must go in the first place to Pietro Martire d'Anghiera's letter from Barcelona to Cardinal Ascanio; Amerigo Vespucci's intervention came a full ten years later. See W. G. L. Randles, 'Le Nouveau Monde, l'autre monde et la pluralité des mondes', *Congresso international de história dos descobrimentos*, vol. 4, Lisbon, 1961.

37 On Atlantis and the great discoveries, the two essential works are Ida Rodriguez Prampolini, *La Atlantida de Platón en los cronistas del siglo XVI*, Mexico City, 1947, and Giuliano Gliozzi, *Adamo e il nuovo mondo: la nascita dell'antropologia come ideologia coloniale, dalle genealogie bibliche alle teorie razziali (1500–1700)*, Florence, 1977, especially pp. 177–246. Antonello Gerbi's *La Natura delle Indie nove: da Cristoforo Colombo a Gonzalo Fernandez de Oviedo*, Milan, 1975, although extremely scholarly, manages to make no reference at all to Atlantis except in an insignificant note on p. 379.

38 See Montaigne's famous 'On Cannibals', *The Essays of Montaigne*, tr. George B. Ives, 4 vols., Cambridge, Mass., 1925, bk. 1, ch. 31. See also José de Acosta, *Historia natural y moral de las Indias*, Seville, 1590, bk. 1, ch. 20.

39 On this point the essential works are Gliozzi, *Adamo e il nuovo mondo*, and Broc, *La Géographie de la Renaissance*.

40 Jean de Serres in the commentary to his translation of Plato, *Opera quae extant omnia*, 3 vols., Geneva, 1578, 3:105.

41 2 Esd. 13:39–42. The astonishing history of this text has been studied in a vast work entitled *Moïse géographe: recherches sur les représentations juives et chrétiennes de l'espace*, ed. Alan Desreumaux and Francis Schmidt, Paris, 1988. A basic commentary and bibliography are also to be found in Manasseh ben Joseph ben Israel, *The Hope of Israel*, tr. Moses Wall, ed. Henry Méchoulan and Gérard Nahon, 1648; New York, 1987.

42 On this subject see also Marcel Bataillon, 'L'Unité du genre humain du P. Acosta au P. Clavigero', *Mélanges à la mémoire de Jean Sarrailh*, 2 vols., Paris, 1966, 1: pp. 75–95; Lee Eldridge Huddleston, *Origins of the American Indians: European Concepts 1492–1729*, Austin, Tex., 1967; and Lynn Glaser, *Indians or Jews: An Introduction to a Reprint*, Gilroy, Calif., 1973. On the Spanish side to the question, see Méchoulan, *Le Sang de l'autre ou l'honneur de Dieu: Juifs, Indiens et Maures au siècle d'or*, Paris, 1979.

43 In de Acosta, the two major solutions to the mystery of America, both of which he refutes, are (1) the ten tribes and (2) Atlantis. See de Acosta, *Historia natural y moral de las Indias*.

44 The text usually mentioned here is Francisco López de Gómara, *Historia General*

de las Indias, Zaragoza, 1553. Gliozzi's *Adamo e il nuovo mondo* goes farther back, citing Girolamo Fracastoros, *Syphilidis, sive morbi Gallici*, Verona, 1530, bk. 3, 11. 165–86.

45 See Bartolomé de las Casas, *Historia de las Indias*, ed. Juan Perez de Tudela Bueso, Madrid, 1957, pp. 36–9. The *Historia* was begun in 1520 and completed in 1561, but was not published until 1875–6. I am indebted to Ida Rodriguez Prampolini for referring me to this work.

46 See the commentary by Michèle Le Doeuff and Margaret Llasera in Francis Bacon, *La Nouvelle Atlantide: voyage dans la pensée baroque*, tr. and ed. Le Doeuff and Llasera, Paris, 1983.

47 See Isaac de la Peyrère, *Prae-adamitae, sive exercitatio super versibus duodecimo, decimotertio et decimoquarto capitis quinti epistolae d. Pauli ad Romanos: quibus inducuntur primi homines ante Adamum conditi*, Amsterdam, 1655, pp. 176–80. This very logical line of argument by la Peyrère has not been noted in the works on him that I have read, not even in the excellent *Thèse de troisième cycle* by J.-P. Oddos, *Recherches sur la vie et l'oeuvre d'Isaac de la Peyrère*, Grenoble, 1977. The same applies to Richard H. Popkin's indispensable *Isaac la Peyrère (1596–1676): His Life, Work, and Influence*, New York, 1987.

48 Christoph Besold, *De novo orbe, conjectanea*, in *Dissertationes singulares*, Tübingen, 1619, p. 24.

49 Gonzalo Fernandez de Oviedo y Valdés, *Historia general y natural de las Indias*, Seville, 1535, pp. 379–80; on the question of the Hesperides, see pp. 365–83; the whole mythico-biblical argument (Tubal-Hercules and so on) is derived from Annius of Viterbo. The essential work on Oviedo is Gerbi, *La natura delle Indie nuove*.

50 See Jan Goropius Becanus, *Hispanica*, in *Opera hactenus in lucem non edita*, Antwerp, 1580, pp. 35, 62, 105–58. See also Gliozzi, *Adamo e il nuovo mondo*, pp. 25–7. Van Gorop having died in 1574, his book was published posthumously. His hispanophilia did not prevent him from also discovering a number of connections between the Indian languages and Flemish. The link between Tartessus and Atlantis was to be 'rediscovered' in the twentieth century by Adolf Schulten; see his *Tartessos: Ein Beitrag zur ältesten Geschichte des Westen*, Hamburg, 1922, especially pp. 53–6.

51 Pedro Sarmiento de Gamboa's *Historia general llamada Indica* was not published until 1902. I am referring to the version that appears in the appendix to Garcilaso de la Vega, *Obras completas del Inca Garcilaso de la Vega*, ed. Carmelo Sáenz de Santa María, 4 vols., Madrid, 1960, especially 4: pp. 201–5.

52 Carles Miralles, my colleague from Barcelona, has pointed out that the nationalistic Atlantis myth appeared in Catalonia in the late nineteenth century in the form of a Catalan epic by Jacinto Verdaguer, *L'Atlantida*, Barcelona, 1877, and was later set to music by Manuel de Falla. Here again we find a fusion of the legends of the Hesperides and Atlantis, for the last queen of Atlantis, saved by Hercules and installed by him in Spain as his wife, is none other than Hesperis. A French translation by Albert Savine of Verdaguer's text is entitled *L'Atlantide*, Paris, 1883. See also the vast bibliography cited in Carles Miralles, 'L'Arbre i la Lira', in *Festschrift Antoni Comas*, Barcelona, 1985, pp. 289–304.

53 For a more detailed account of the Atlantis myth in the Enlightenment, see my 'Hérodote et l'Atlantide'.
54 The literature on this subject is, of course, extensive. Outstanding for their clarity are Peter Gay, *The Enlightenment: An Interpretation*, 2 vols., New York, 1966–9 and Frank E. Manuel, *The Eighteenth Century Confronts the Gods*, New York, 1959; repr., 1967. See also Jean Starobinski, 'Le Mythe au XVIIIe siècle', review of *The Rise of Modern Mythology, 1680–1860*, by Burton Feldman and Robert D. Richardson, *Critique* 33, November 1977, pp. 975–97.
55 These points are developed fully in my 'Hérodote et l'Atlantide'.
56 See Olof Rudbeck, *Atlantica*, 3 vols., Uppsala, 1679–1702; see the more modern edition, *Atland eller Manheim*, ed. Axel Nelson, 4 vols., Uppsala, 1937–50; volume 4 contains a very useful collection of *testimonia* on the reception of the work (pp. 205–65). There is a vast bibliography on Rudbeck and Gothically inclined ideology, most of it in Swedish. I will cite only a handful here: Erika Simon, *Réveil national et culture populaire en Scandinavie: la genèse de la Højskole nordique, 1844–1878*, Paris, 1960; Ernst Ekman, 'Gothic Patriotism and Olof Rudbeck', *Journal of Modern History*, 34, March 1962' pp. 52–63; Josef Gusten Algot Svennung, *Zur Geschichte des Goticismus*, Stockholm, 1967; of capital importance with a large bibliography is Jesper Svenbro, 'L'Idéologie "gothisante" et l'*Atlantica* d'Olof Rudbeck: le mythe platonicien de l'Atlantide au service de l'Empire suédois du XVIIe siècle', *Quaderni di storia*, 11, January–June 1980, pp. 121–56; Gunnar Eriksson, 'Gestalter i Svensk lärdomhistoria I: Olof Rudbeck D. Ä.', *Lychnos*, 1984, pp. 77–119; English summary: 'Swedes in the History of Science and Learning I: Olaus Rudbecksen', pp. 116–18; thanks to Svenbro for this reference. I would like to express my warmest thanks to Nils and Renée Andersson for showing me, in Uppsala, the places and images connected with the Rudbeck saga. I notice, in the articles cited above in note 8, however, that when the Soviet submarines 'visited' the Stockholm archipelago in October 1982, no mention was made of the identification of Atlantis and Sweden, nor of Atlantis's capital with Uppsala.
57 Only Rudbeck the doctor is mentioned in *Petit Larousse*, Paris, 1973. However, Rudbeck's unity as a baroque scholar is strongly underlined in Eriksson, 'Gestalter i Svensk lärdomhistoria I', n. 61.
58 See Pierre Bayle, 'Olavi Rudbeckii *Atlantica* sive *Manheim*', *Nouvelles de la république de lettres*, 3, January and February 1685, pp. 49–69 and 119–36.
59 See Rudbeck, *Atlantica*, 1:890.
60 But we should not forget that as early as the sixth century, Cassiodorus's *History of the Goths*, which survives only in an abridgement by Jordanes, created the myth of the Goths as a Nordic people. See Teillet, *Des Goths à la nation gothique*, pp. 305–34; and, on the specifically mythical aspect, see Gilbert Dagron and Marin, 'Discours utopique et récit des origines', *Annales: Économies, Sociétés, Civilisations*, 26, March–April 1971, pp. 290–327.
61 I owe much to the commentary by Allan Ellenius, 'Olaus Rudbecks Atlantiska Anatomi', *Lychnos*, 1959, pp. 40–54; English summary: 'Olaus Rudbeck's Atlantic Anatomy', pp. 53–4.

62 See Bayle, 'Olavi Rudbeckii *Atlantica* sive *Manheim*'.

63 See Audigier, *L'Origine des François*.

64 See Gustavo Costa, *Le Antichità germaniche nella cultura italiana da Machiavelli a Vico*, Naples, 1977.

65 My 'Hérodote et l'Atlantide', pp. 25–8, provides all the necessary references.

66 On Bartoli and Sweden, see my 'Hérodote et l'Atlantide', pp. 43–6, and, more recently, Franco Venturi, *Il Patriotismo repubblicano e gli imperi dell'Est*, vol. 4, bk. 2 of *Settecento Riformatore*, Turin, 1984, p. 899.

67 See Georges Dumézil, *Du mythe au roman: La Saga de Hadingus et autres essais*, Paris, 1970, and Lévi-Strauss, *Anthropologie Structurale (Deux)*, Paris, 1973, pp. 312–15.

68 On French historiography and Louis XIV, see the fundamental work by Ranum, *Artisans of Glory, Writers and Historical Thought in Seventeenth-Century France*, Chapel Hill, NC, 1980 and, more recently, Blandine Barret-Kriegel, *Les Historiens et la monarchie*, 4 vols., Paris, 1988.

69 See Fortia d'Urban, *Antiquités et monuments du département du Vaucluse*, 2 vols., Paris, 1808, 2:408–79.

70 See the article on Gianrinaldo Carli (also known as Giovanni Rinaldo Carli in some bibliographies) in *Illuministi italiani: Riformatori Lombardi, Piemontesi e Toscani*, ed. Venturi, vol. 46, bk. 3 of Raffaele Mattioli, Pietro Pancrazi, and Alfredo Schiaffini (eds), *La letteratura italiana: storia e testi*, Milan, 1958, pp. 419–79; on the subject with which we are concerned here, the essential work by Carli is *Lettere americane (1770–1781)*, in *Opere*, Milan, 1779; tr. Jean Baptiste Lefebvre de Villebrune, under the title *Lettres américaines*, 2 vols., Paris, 1788. For more information, see my 'Hérodote et l'Atlantide'.

71 See Angelo Mazzoldi, *Delle origini italiche e della diffusione dell'incivilmento italiano alla Fenicia, alla Grecia e a tutte le nazioni asiatiche poste sul Mediterraneo*, Milan, 1840, pp. 44, 172–87. On the respectful reception given to the book, see Benedetto Croce, *Storia della storiografica italiana nel secolo decimonono*, vol. 15 of *Scritti di storia letteraria e politica*, Bari, 1921, p. 56.

72 John Toland, 'The Life of James Harrington', in Toland (ed.), *The Oceana of James Harrington and His Other Works*, London, 1700, p. 2.

73 William Blake, 'A Descriptive Catalogue', *The Complete Writings of William Blake*, ed. Geoffrey Keynes, London, 1966, p. 578.

74 See Blake, 'Jerusalem', *The Complete Writings of William Blake*, pp. 635–6. For more details and a bibliography, see my 'Hérodote et l'Atlantide', p. 24.

75 F. Wilford, 'An Essay on the Sacred Isles in the West', *Asiatic Researches*, 8, 1808, p. 246.

76 The best illustration is provided by Henry O'Brien's novel, *The Round Towers of Ireland; Or, The History of the Tuath-de-Danaans for the First Time Unveiled*, London, 1834, recently reprinted under the title *Atlantis in Ireland*, Blauvelt, NY, 1976.

77 Marinatos published this theory in an article well before his own excavations revealed the splendours of Minoan Santorini. See Spyridon Nikolaos Marinatos, 'On the Atlantis Legend' (in Greek), *Kretika Chronika*, 4, 1950, pp. 195–213; tr. under the title *Some Words about the Legend of Atlantis*, Athens, 1969. For a

general account of the thesis, see John Victor Luce, *Lost Atlantis: New Light on an Old Legend*, New York, 1969.

78 See James W. Mavor, Jr., *Voyage to Atlantis*, New York, 1969.
79 See Alfred Rosenberg, *Der Mythus des 20. Jahrhunderts: Eine Wertung der Seelischgeistigen Gestaltenkämpfe Unserer Zeit*, Munich, 1930, pp. 43–8.
80 See Albert Herrmann, *Unsere Ahnen und Atlantis: Nordische Seeherrschaft von Skandinavien bis nach Nordafrika*, Berlin, 1934.
81 See Pascal Ory, *Le Petit Nazi illustré; une pédagogie hitlérienne en culture française: 'Le Téméraire' (1943–1944)*, ed. Ory, Paris, 1979, pp. 53–7. My colleague Axel Seeberg of the University of Oslo tells me that a similar pedagogical cartoon strip was published at the same time in occupied Norway, presumably on orders from Berlin.
82 See the fundamental work by Michael H. Kater, *Das 'Ahnenerbe' der SS 1935–1945: Ein Beitrag zur Kulturpolitik des Dritten Reiches*, Stuttgart, 1974, especially pp. 51, 71, 372 (Himmler's intervention), 378.
83 Ibid., p. 378, n. 109. Herrmann, who was a correspondent for the Institute, interpreted Atlantis as *Adland*, the *noble* land (p. 51).
84 See Jürgen Spanuth, *Das Enträtselte Atlantis*, Stuttgart, 1953; tr. Henri Daussy, under the title *L'Atlantide retrouvée*, Paris, 1954; and Spanuth, *Atlantis, Heimat, Reich und Schicksal der Germanen*, Tübingen, 1965. The latter was published by Grabert Verlag, an openly Nazi publisher.
85 See Roberto Salinas Price, *Homer's Blind Audience: An Essay on the 'Iliad''s Geographical Prerequisites for the Site of Ilion*, San Antonio, Tex., 1984.
86 See S. Islami (ed.), *Les Illyriens*, Tirana, 1985. Although this book is not free of retrospective nationalism, it is a worthy work of serious scholarship.
87 See Engjëll Sedaj, 'Les Tribus illyriennes dans les chansons homériques', *Studia Albanica*, 23, 1986, pp. 157–72.
88 See Adile Ayda, *Les Etrusques étaient des Turcs,* Ankara, 1985. Other examples from the Middle East may be found in my 'Flavius Josèphe et les prophètes', *Cahiers du Centre d'études du Proche-Orient ancien*, Geneva, 1989, pp. 11–31.
89 See the splendid collection made by the architect H. R. Stahel, *Atlantis Illustrated*, New York, 1982. I am most grateful to Alain Schnapp for bringing this work to my attention, and I have borrowed figure 3 from it. Unfortunately, in his preface to Stahel's book, Isaac Asimov echoes Marinatos's theory on Santorini, as does Kater in his *Das 'Ahnenerbe' der SS 1935–1945*, p. 372, n. 119. Jean-Pierre Adam (in his *Passé recomposé: chroniques d'archéologie fantasque*, Paris, 1988, especially pp. 38–64) certainly puts a number of mad theories in their place but only to replace them with a hypothesis that is neither new nor convincing. But then, clearly, one cannot expect everything.

3

The Enlightenment in the Greek City-state

Every historian of a past world – and every world which is the subject of a historical study is a past world, even if that past goes back no more than a few hours – is caught in an insoluble quandary. His most primary duty is to show wherein and how that world differs from our own, that its values are not the same as ours, its institutions do not function in exactly the same way as ours, and that even when our words derive from its language, as our political vocabulary does from Latin and Greek, for us they do not have the same meaning. The Republic is not the *res publica*, even if it is true that without the *res publica* there never would have been republics in Venice, Geneva and Paris.

As for the word *politeia*, which we translate as 'Republic' when it appears in the title of works by Plato and Aristotle and which Rousseau was still using in his *Social Contract*[1] in the form '*politie*', in French it has also produced more surprising descendants, such as the one used by Montaigne when (*Essais* I, II) he wishes to evoke the '*police* which [Plato] forges as he will'. But, as is well known, the word has since acquired other meanings which carry it even further from the sense of 'Republic'.

We ought to distance ourselves from Antiquity and avoid anachronisms; yet what anachronism could be greater than associating the huge states of today with the modest circumstances of the ancient city? Surely we hardly need to be reminded that Attica, that is to say the city of Athens, town and countryside included, the *astu* and the *chora* together, covered an area no larger than the Grand Duchy of Luxemburg.

However true all this may be and however aware of it we may be, the fact remains that the eyes with which we survey the past, whether or not

This paper was first published in *Citoyenneté et urbanité*, Éditions Esprit, Paris, 1991.

we happen to be historians, are twentieth-century eyes. Historians, to be sure, are – or ought to be – more conscious of the differences which it is their task to catalogue, as Paul Veyne put it.[2] But no rejection of anachronisms, however deliberate, can change a person of the late twentieth century into a contemporary of Pericles. And while we need to destroy the illusion that Pericles thought as we do, we need equally to destroy the illusion that we can think as Pericles did, adapting easily to his way of thinking and reasoning.

'Desperately foreign' is the expression used by Moses Finley in *Aspects of Antiquity*,[3] to describe not the Greek civilization in general even, but tragedy in particular, that is to say the medium through which we form the impression that we are effortlessly communicating with the Greek classical world, if only because the tragedies of Aeschylus, Sophocles and Euripides are performed and adapted for us every year. Yet that same Moses Finley was also the author of a little book entitled *Democracy Ancient and Modern*,[4] a timely second French edition of which has recently appeared. It is a book that it is tempting to associate with 1968, in which Finley argues, in the name of the values of ancient democracy, against modern theorists of 'apathy', such as Seymour Martin Lipset in America and Julien Freund in France, who reckon that democracy is able to function only because, precisely, citizens are so little interested in politics that they do not even bother to vote. In opposition to that passive democracy Finley sets the kind of activist democracy which, admittedly, did condemn Socrates (who had in truth rather asked for it) but which is also capable of taking such momentous decisions as to send a man to the moon or to construct an atomic bomb, the kind of things that, in the contemporary world, are decided behind the closed doors of committees rather than out in the open at a people's assembly.

Even if it is true that we can only be historians of the past to the extent that we belong to the modern world, we should also recognize that our relationship with Antiquity is an integral part of our own world. Admittedly, Antiquity may be less intensely present in our present world than it was when the young Charles Péguy was fighting what he called his 'Battle of Orange', that is to say struggling to prise from his mother enough money to go and see *Antigone* and *Oedipus Rex* performed in the Roman theatre of Orange;[5] admittedly also, models other than those of Antiquity have penetrated our culture: ethnographic or even ethnological ones. But let me recount an anecdote that goes back about twenty years. The scene is the École des Hautes Études, where it was a matter of electing a successor to Fernand Braudel. Jacques Le Goff was the only candidate and, to flatter us, he said: 'I feel as though I was up before an assembly of kings.' It was an allusion to Cineas' account of Pyrrhus being received by the Roman

Senate and exclaiming, 'I felt I was up before an assembly of Kings!'[6]
But as we left the electors' meeting, Serge Moscovici remarked to me:
'What has just taken place was exactly like what happens among baboons,
when an old baboon is replaced by a younger one.' That image is undoubtedly more accessible to us than Cineas' image of Pyrrhus.

Nevertheless, Antiquity *is* still with us; and Euphronios, a painter and
potter of the late sixth century BC never mentioned in any text, whose
name would certainly have been unknown to a contemporary of Plato,
was quite recently exhibited at the Louvre – a fact that would have aston-
ished Isocrates, who was indignant at the very idea that he himself should
be compared to a sophist or that Phidias should be compared to a painter
of little pictures such as those produced by Euphronios. Likewise, the
Paris Métro has even housed an exhibition entitled 'Cité des images',[7] an
expression which certainly would not have been understood by Euphronios,
Aeschylus or Pericles (not that this is meant as a criticism). Furthermore,
a double bill of the *Oresteia* and *Iphigenia at Aulis* has recently been put
on at the Cartoucherie Theatre and another production of the *Oresteia* has
even been shown late at night on television, Solzhenitsyn has recommended
that an ailing Russia consider the lessons and virtues of the Greek city,[8]
and if Castoriadis refers to the Greek city in his vision of a socialist
Utopia entitled *Sur le contenu du socialisme*,[9] it is certainly not solely
because he himself is Greek. With the aid of a few examples, it will
perhaps be possible to throw some light upon the relationship that links
us with the Greek city. I will take a small selection of words, or syntagms
if you prefer, and one by one see with whom they are associated in
Antiquity, who took them over in modern Europe, and how. So I shall be
operating on two levels: that of what is known as classical Greece, the
Greece of the fifth and fourth centuries, to which many of Plutarch's
Lives hark back, and that of the France of the Age of Enlightenment,
Revolutionary France and the France of the nineteenth and twentieth centuries. It would, of course, be perfectly possible to pick a different
chronological framework – for the Italian cities of the Middle Ages and
the Renaissance, the fourteenth and fifteenth centuries, also thought much
about Antiquity (and in Padua it is still possible to see a tomb, erected in
the twelfth century, which purports to be that of a Trojan hero, Antenor);
However, our relations with the Age of Enlightenment are more direct
and closer.

The first syntagm is that of democratic transparency. What does that
mean? It means that 'politics is identified with what is rational',[10] but
equally it implies that there was a time when a democratic society functioned under the sign of transparency between the leaders and the led,
when not the slightest obstacle was interposed between the peasant seated

on the steps of the Pnyx and the *strategos* who went off to implement the decisions taken by the people's assembly, when both peasant and *strategos* concerned themselves not only with their own affairs but also with those of the community: that is how Plato defines justice. There can be no doubt that this image of Athenian democracy is a Greek image. It is the image that Aeschylus created of the democratic vote in *The Suppliant Maidens* (about 464 BC), in which, for the first time ever in Athens, the noun *demos* was associated with the verb *krateîn*, to command. The people's decision to grant residents' rights to the Danaids fleeing marriage with their first cousins is passed unanimously by a show of hands after arguments of persuasion have been heard and Zeus, the supreme authority, has ratified it: a single decision, a single vote from everyone involved, from Zeus down, through the king, to the humblest citizen. A perfect model of transparency. The remarkable point, one forcefully made by Nicole Loraux both in her monograph[11] and in her 1979 article on democratic 'transparency', is that this unanimity is also to be found in the funeral orations – in the one known as Pericles' speech in Thucydides and in others too – which constitute *par excellence* the city's ideal discourse on the subject of itself.

All the things that constituted the democratic originality of the City were excised, erased from the City's discourse on itself: for example, the drawing of lots for magistracies (something that always astonishes the moderns: just imagine suggesting that the President of the French Republic be selected by lot . . .) and the remuneration provided for those serving as magistrates, the *misthophoria*. Pericles' funeral oration praised democracy in only the most aristocratic of terms. It exalted democracy not as a *mode of power*, simply as the regime which could best accommodate *arete*, a word we translate somewhat inadequately as 'virtue', as Montesquieu – among others – did.

This leads me to make three remarks. First, if the Greeks were responsible for the invention of politics, which we regularly ascribe to them, it must be said that they certainly did not exalt that invention. What do I mean by that? The human world is by nature conflictual, and political activity involves considering conflicts objectively, setting them out openly even without hope of resolving them. A political decision is taken by a leader speaking not, as so often happened, in the name of a deity; nor even, as was usual, in the name of a more or less unanimous consensus; but in the name of the majority. Aeschylus himself, in *The Suppliant Maidens*, before having it announced that the vote was unanimous, confronts the speaker with the following question: 'Tell us where it has alighted, the decision taken according to the law of the popular ballot in which the majority prevails' (literally: 'where the sovereign hand of the people decides, through the majority, [to fall]'). But though conflict may be expected, for practically all those who refer to it – Thucydides being a prime exception – it is not something to be accommodated, rather a sickness. And this sickness from which the City suffers is known as *stasis*, or sedition. To the Greek way of thinking, the link between political conflict and civil war cannot be resolved by any continuous process. The ambiguity between the *demos* as a popular faction and the *démos* which represents the entire city was never dispelled. In Athens, no political party was ever formed with a programme that envisaged functioning alongside other political parties. The nearest to what we call political parties were oligarchic associations whose very nature was conspiratorial, since *oligoi* were bound by definition to be minorities with no hope of acquiring power through the free interplay of the city's institutions. In consequence, strange though it may seem, we do not know whether any electoral campaigns ever took place there, as they did in Rome. In 346, when it was a matter of selecting the members of an embassy to obtain the oath of Philip of Macedon, nobody asked Aeschines or Demosthenes, both of whom were included, whether they belonged to the same political tendency.

My second remark is this: this democracy on which the moderns are so keen inspired not a single philosophical or political treatise that set out the principles of democracy or was composed in its praise. It is true that we have the funeral orations, but they exalt democracy by non-democratic means. The only democratic philosopher known to us to have written a theoretical text on democracy that has survived is Protagoras of Abdera, who explained to Socrates[12] how it was that in Athens anybody could express his opinion on political matters and who went so far in his justification of democracy as to involve not only the citizens but everybody, including even women. And we owe even this brief treatise on justifications for the existence of democracy to the magnanimity of Plato, who appears to have respected Protagoras enough not to distort his ideas as he so blithely did all those of his predecessors. In Greek literature, it is the historical works that show us how democracy functioned. It is Herodotus who tells us (V, 78) that the Athenians owed their greatness and their primacy to *iségorìe*, equality in freedom of speech; while Thucydides declares that, in truth, democracy means government by the 'first' citizen (II, 65, 9). And in the Greece of the fifth century it was tragedy (which is democratic in its very essence since what it shows in a sense is princes summoned before courts composed of their contemporary peoples) that was the democratic institution *par excellence*. But, as I have already pointed out, even tragedy does not elude the fictitious rule of unanimity. Aeschylus' tragedies contain only one vote that is not unanimous, the one in *The Eumenides* which absolves Orestes and which is obtained only thanks to Athena's intervention. When an Athenian tragic poet wished to show a city in a state of conflict he never chose Athens, but used Argos or even more often Thebes, which, in Greek classical tragedy, is the city of *stasis par excellence*.

My third remark is that this democracy, which is so rarely praised by political theorists and so seldom represented pictorially (there was just one fourth-century relief which showed 'Democracy' crowning 'Demos') was, in contrast, violently criticized throughout the classical period and thereafter, in the Hellenistic and Roman periods: by intellectuals who were entranced by the mirage of Sparta, by philosophers such as Plato who dreamed of a hierarchical society and would accept a touch of democracy only provided it was controlled and gagged, and by orators who, from Isocrates down to Plutarch, were constantly praising a so-called ancestral constitution generally placed under the patronage of Theseus or Solon which, thanks to a judicious interplay of checks and balances under the control of the Areopagus, should have been able to avoid the excesses of radical democracy. At this price, Athens could be forgiven for being a democracy and Isocrates could afford the luxury of preferring his native city to Sparta. Within the heritage that we have received from Greece, how strong is the tradition that inspired the men of the Age of Enlightenment?

As is well known, if ever there was a moment in the history of France when the ideology of power was that of the Ancient City it was the revolutionary period or, to be more exact, the period of Montagnard power, when Robespierre's and Saint-Just's speeches were expounding how a republic should be when based on virtue, as Montesquieu had wished.[13] And for Robespierre, as for Montesquieu, virtue was the principle upon which democracy was founded. However, the model democracy was not Athens at all, even though Montesquieu did occasionally refer to Demosthenes, Socrates and Aristides. It was Sparta, known as the city of the Peers (*homoioi*), that 'shone out like a flash of lightning amid an immense darkness' (Robespierre), Sparta that embodied the model of social transparency.

Robespierre and Saint-Just used Sparta to create a vision of their own society as transparent and ideally united. They rejected any idea of class conflicts, interests and parties. They recognized only on the one hand men who were pure, on the other traitors and rogues whom it was legitimate to eliminate. On the face of it, how strange it seems that men who were democrats out of principle should turn to Sparta which, faced with Athens in the fifth century, placed itself at the head of a coalition of oligarchies and connived at the establishment of the regime of the Thirty Tyrants in Athens – a regime which, not without reason, has been compared to Vichy during the Second World War both by Jules Isaac, who took refuge in the

Cévennes, and by Pierre Jouguet, a Gaullist and director of the IFAO (Institut français d'archéologie orientale).[14] Under the Montagnard dictatorship, only Camille Desmoulins dared to side with Athens in the name of democracy, freedom of the press (Aristophanes!) and the right to make mistakes. What is the explanation for that strange identification, later to be rejected by Volney and Benjamin Constant as early as the Thermidor period, by Marx in *The Holy Family*, by Fustel de Coulanges, in his preface to *The Ancient City* in 1864, and by many others too?

The eighteenth century was divided over whether to support Sparta or Athens, virtuous austerity or slightly degenerate luxury. Athens' partisans, Voltaire amongst them, were those who exalted not democracy itself but commerce and the freedom to think and to write. And Sparta? Let us consider the question which is still being asked by some scholars today:[15] was it all the fault of Rousseau (following Mably)? Was Rousseau the generator of the image of the totalitarianism which functioned in Year II?

It is true that Rousseau, nurtured on Plutarch and a citizen of Geneva, sided with Sparta in the argument between Sparta and Athens. In 1752, in his *Dernière réponse aux adversaires du Discours sur les Sciences et les Arts*, he wrote: 'The embarrassment of our opponents is patent every time the subject of Sparta arises. What would they not give for that fatal Sparta never to have existed?'[16] In what it is fair to describe as 'Rousseau's system', to borrow Victor Goldschmidt's expression,[17] two models come into confrontation: man and citizen. Man as nature made him, a theoretical construction and an object of melancholic nostalgia, if he ever existed, which Rousseau very much doubts: 'The happy life of the Golden Age was always a state unknown to the human race, either because it did not recognize it when it might have enjoyed it, or because it lost it when it might have known it.'[18] In other words, part of the very essence of the golden age is that it never existed except (if I may so put it) as a possible impossibility. Faced with man as nature made him, Rousseau constructs an antithesis, the function of which has been excellently analysed by Yves Touchefeu in a recent article:[19] the very best product of history (not nature), the product the most resistant to degeneration, namely the citizen. It was a theme that provided him with scope to speak of Sparta, Rome and Geneva all in the same breath: 'I love to fasten upon those venerable images of Antiquity in which I see men raised by sublime institutions to the highest degree of greatness and virtue attainable to human wisdom.'[20] Sparta is a kind of rock that, in Rousseau's vision, resists the law of historical degeneration which he himself assumes to function.

But even if Sparta did once exist, can it exist today? For a long time Rousseau thought that Geneva could be Sparta, but having been condemned within his own city and forced to renounce forever his rights as a citizen of Geneva, in 1764 he sternly warned the people of Geneva that they were 'not Romans, not even Athenians': 'You are merchants, artisans, bourgeois, always concerned with your own private interests, people for whom liberty itself is simply a means of acquiring possessions without let or hindrance and possessing them in security.'[21] In other words, Sparta, Rome and even Athens are as inaccessible as the Golden Age. When Rousseau speaks of democracy in *The Social Contract*, it is to rally to the principle that Montesquieu, following Pericles, considered the basis of democracy, but also to add, as a final remark: 'If there were a people of gods, they would govern themselves democratically.'[22] True, Rousseau does sometimes borrow from that part of history which he knows to be inaccessible. For instance, his plan for Corsica is crammed with ancient references, prefiguring Saint-Just's *Institutions républicaines*. Rousseau's plan was one of exclusion. It excluded from the right of citizenship all those who were not married by the age of forty and all foreigners: every fifty years just one foreigner could be granted citizenship.[23] Nobody, I think, could deny that a kind of totalitarian temptation is detectable in Rousseau, a temptation which finds expression in the notion of the 'general will'. The fact that he countered this temptation from within and that 'the obstacle' (to borrow the title of Starobinski's splendid book) always rose up to block transparency is what, to my way of thinking, makes Rousseau a truly tragic character, in the Greek sense of the expression. But that was something that his readers of 1793 were not necessarily in a position to understand.

Of all the words that we translate from Greek and Latin, none perhaps is more resonant for us than the word 'liberty', nor is any more equivocal or embedded in a more complex history. The slogan of the Revolution, 'liberty or death', obviously related not to the individual but to the nation. The Greeks clearly experienced that liberty; and what has been called the 'Marseillaise' of Salamis (Brasillach's expression), in Aeschylus' *Persians*, translates easily into the diction of 1793: 'Come, children of the Greeks, liberate the motherland, liberate your children and your wives, the sanctuaries of the gods of your fathers and the tombs of your ancestors: this is the supreme struggle (literally: the battle to decide everything)' (except that in the French translation with which the men of the Revolution were familiar, produced by Du Theil in 1785, the word 'save' was used instead of 'liberate'). In his *Essai sur les révolutions* of 1797, Chateaubriand is clearly aware of this. There can be no doubt that modern patriotism reflects ancient patriotism, even if *Greek* patriotism is, it is true, something exceptional (as indeed was the war against the Persians), the most common form of patriotism being that of the city, but here again the words translate easily.

The real problem posed by the liberty of the Ancients in relation to the liberty of the moderns was raised following the Montagnard experience, in the last years of the eighteenth century and the first of the nineteenth, by Benjamin Constant for one, but also by many others.

The liberty of the Ancients stands in contrast to that of the moderns as impulse stands in contrast to calculation, war to (basic) commerce, participation to enjoyment, what is immediate to what is deferred and, finally, as the slavery of the majority stands in contrast to the individual liberty of all. It was the men of Thermidor who rediscovered the fundamental role played by slavery in Greek society, with Athenian society no exception. This raises a number of points and I will tackle them in a way different from my procedure so far. That is to say, instead of moving from the Ancients to the moderns, I will first consider the fortunes of Greece in the nineteenth century, and only later return to what we understand by Greece itself. For the discovery of Constant and his contemporaries turned out to entail decisive consequences.

The first was the progressive elimination of Sparta, which was thereafter shifted to the right, even the extreme right, of the political spectrum. The shift began with Joseph de Maistre, but it was not completed in a day. Under the Empire, the Restoration and even the July Monarchy, general public instruction was more Spartan than Athenian. For Constant, Athens was, to be sure, a society based on slave-ownership, and liberty there was certainly not the individual liberty guaranteed by the principles of 1789 and the very existence of the civic society; nevertheless, it offered more liberties than Sparta, 'that vast monastery'. Sparta thus moved to its place on the right, having previously been positioned on the extreme left. It also established itself on a solid footing on the other side of the Rhine.[24] The Dorian myth (K. O. Müller) was a specifically Germanic myth which naturally gave rise to a counter-myth in France. In the second half of the nineteenth century and the first half of the twentieth, France and Germany clashed on the Athens/Sparta issue. The 'Republic of lawyers' destroyed by Philip of Macedon bore a strange resemblance to the Third Republic. As a result, from Victor Duruy, the historian and minister of the Second Empire, down to Glotz, this model of a liberal Athens or, as Nicole Loraux and I have ventured to call it, a bourgeois Athens, which needed only a little more in the way of a representative system and a little more sense of national unity, gradually became a dominant model in France. It was, it is true, always in competition with Rome: for the purposes of colonizing Algeria, it was better to be Roman than Greek; and in France the spiritual identification with Antiquity never became so strongly rooted as in the Germany of Hölderlin and Heidegger. Nevertheless, even though France did not rediscover the presocratics and the philosophy of being until relatively recently, it unquestionably did find in Athenian liberty, Athenian *parrhésia* (Euripides, *Hippolytus*, 422 etc.) a model which, though interpreted in a census-based form at the beginning of the century, was then taken over by the democratic movement and converted into universal suffrage. And that model was traced to a very specific period: the fifth century BC and it alone.

Decadence set in with the Peloponnesian War. This point was arrived at by way of some strange procedures. Reading the *Histoire grecque* by Glotz, who died in 1936 and whose word was still law when I was a student, reading this work closely one noticed that his sources for the most part came from the fourth century, for the simple reason that it was in the fourth century that Athens became a city of writing, whereas in the fifth century writing had still been exceptional. And a historian such as Glotz arranged his sources in two categories: anything that suggested the harmonious functioning of the city institutions was classified as fifth-century; anything that suggested discord and crisis was allocated to the fourth century. As for the Hellenistic period, that could be left to the Americans or the English.

That was the predominant image conveyed both by the textbooks used in public education and by the university tradition. But needless to say, a number of contrasting images were also purveyed. In response to the *Prière sur l'Acropole* by Renan, who was concerned that the *cella* of Athena might be a little constricting for the modern world ('if your *cella* turned out to be large enough to accommodate a crowd, it would collapse'), Barrès in his *Voyage de Sparte* wrote as follows: 'An oriental song poisons a passing soul. But the clear vision of a number of cruel facts revives us and acts as a tonic. Man is made not to dream but to bite and rend.' In Sparta, as in Mistra, Barrès was filled with enthusiasm; in Athens he 'analysed his disarray'. As for Maurras, his reply to Renan was to retort that there was no need whatsoever to lodge a crowd in Athena's quarters.[25] A hierarchical Greece, engendered by Plato, has always co-existed alongside democratic Greece and, were it necessary, one could, as in truth everyone recognizes, demonstrate that democracy was itself exclusive. Mme Stirbois, the sole deputy representing the National Front, recently[26] found it easy enough to call upon the support of a whole constellation of authorities, including Glotz by the way, as she reminded the National Assembly that it was not easy for a metic to become an Athenian and that in Greece citizenship was not granted simply on the strength of a person's place of birth. In truth, Switzerland, which does not recognize the *jus soli*, is closer to the Greek tradition than France. The only thing that Mme Stirbois forgot to mention in the course of the scholarly address to which she treated the National Assembly was that in Athens, not only foreigners and slaves but also women were excluded from the political domain.

This leads me to raise the last question that I shall tackle in this study: was the Greek city a closed society, in the Bergsonian or Popperian sense of the expression, or even a totalitarian society? The question is not a new one. Paradoxically enough, it was deliberately raised by one of the men who was to be most categorically accused of perversely imitating the ancient city, namely Saint-Just. Admittedly, that was in 1791, not 1793 or 1794: 'The ancient legislators did everything for the Republic, France has done everything for man. Human rights would have been the undoing of Athens or Sparta. There, one recognized only one's own dear motherland, it was for its sake that one forgot oneself.'[27] In the declaration of 26 August 1789 there is, in truth, only one word that refers us to Antiquity and that is 'citizen', which, precisely, is not a word that Saint-Just used in the text I have just cited. Since then, this theme has recurred repeatedly. Volney introduced it, in blunt terms, in the aftermath of Thermidor, in his famous *Leçons de l'an III*, showing that the greatness and beauty of Athens rested upon 'a system of extortion and plunder' and that 'these so-called democrats' lived in a world in which 'the despotic regime of our colonies of America' had been established.[28] It was taken up again by Fustel de Coulanges, in his own particular way, in 1864. Modern theorists of totalitarianism, Hannah Arendt in particular, were on the whole more prudent, although Sparta continued to be a candidate for this kind of definition. Marrou, writing his *History of Education in Antiquity* during the Occupation, could not avoid comparing Sparta to Hitler's Germany, particularly as the Nazis themselves subscribed to that identification, to which they gave a positive interpretation.

But let us now set aside Sparta, which in the fourth century did, after all, become an exception in the Greek world; and let us turn to Athens. It was, it is true, a relatively closed world and a hard one. The professors of the Third Republic who idealized Athens would not have found it easy to live there, any more than we would. It is also true that it was a world capable of imposing its domination upon others, a domination which could go so far as massacre, as in the famous case of Melos, where the Athenians told the Melians: 'We are in the right since we are the strongest',[29] yet a world not capable of integrating the countries which it had dominated. The *hyperhoria*, the world beyond the frontiers, as they called it in Athens, began as close to home as Mount Cithaeron and included the cities Athens had subjugated just as it did enemy cities and neutral cities. The contrast with Rome was striking and was perceived to be so as early as the Hellenistic period.[30] In the period of imperial Rome, Lucian amused himself in connection with Athens, reintroducing the word *hyperhoria* but situating the frontier of Athens, which had become a university town, somewhere on the Euphrates. Saint Paul was a Roman citizen; but he could certainly not have been a citizen of Athens in the classical period. It is also a fact that in Athens liberty was strictly connected with participation. Every Athenian had a reasonable chance of taking part in the decision-taking deliberations of the city, of belonging, for example, to the Council (*Boulè*), for membership of which lots were drawn and which our grandfathers mistakenly translated as 'Senate'. It is also quite true that not everyone did participate. But a normal attendance of six thousand Athenians at the meetings of the *ekklesia*, even if that did represent only 20 per cent of the citizen population, was certainly a large attendance for the ancient world. A perverse and intelligent opponent of Athenian democracy, such as the writer known as pseudo-Xenophon or the Old Oligarch, and who accused the Athenians, among others, of being exaggeratedly tolerant towards slaves and metics who, he claimed, enjoyed as much freedom of speech as citizens, which was assuredly excessive, made the following telling observation:

> For oligarchic cities it is necessary to keep to alliances and oaths. If they do not abide by agreements or if injustice is done, there are the names of the few who made the agreement. But whatever agreements the populace makes can be repudiated by referring the blame to the one who spoke or took the vote, while the others declare that they were absent or did not approve of the agreement made in the full assembly.[31]

This criticism has a somewhat caricatural air, for the treaties Athens concluded were the subject of oaths by which all the Athenians were bound. But it is true that every decree and every law did have one responsible author in particular: once an individual had spoken, *eipen*, this – possibly since the decisive democratic reform of 462–461 – might lead to a *graphé para nomôn*, an accusation of illegality made against, not the people as a whole, but the individual who had led the people into error. Since the people could not condemn itself, it turned against an individual whom it made responsible. But this was not a totalitarian institution; it was one which, in the last analysis, was devised in order to counter thoughtless and precipitate action, such as that which, in 406, led to the execution of the *strategoi* who had been victorious in the battle of Arginusae, when the people declared that it was a crime to prevent it doing as it wished.[32] The question of individual liberty, freedom of speech and thought, is quite a different matter. Clearly, values in Athens were not the same as those of today in New York, London and Paris. The crime of impiety, established by the law of Diopeithès, led to the exile of Anaxagoras, and a charge of corruption of the young led, in 399, to the death of Socrates, who had attracted dangerous disciples in the shape of men such as Alcibiades and Critias.

But is that all there is to be said about liberty in Athens? Along with Finley and many others, my answer would be no. Let us return to the Old Oligarch (*circa* 430). He writes as follows:

> They do not permit the people to be ill-spoken of in comedy, so that they may not have a bad reputation; but if anyone wants to attack private persons, they bid him do so, knowing perfectly well that the person so treated in comedy does not, for the most part, come from the populace and mass of people but is a person of either wealth, high birth or influence. Some few poor and plebeian types are indeed abused in comedy, but only if they have been meddling in others' affairs and trying to rise above their class so that the people feel no vexation at seeing such persons abused in comedy.[33]

Yet the whole of Aristophanes' *opus* gives the lie to this declaration. In 424 (that is about six years later), in *The Knights*, he set *Demos* on stage and the effect of the very structure of his plays is that Athens puts itself in the dock. Camille Desmoulins was not altogether mistaken when, in 1794, he invoked this example against Robespierre and claimed that, under the Terror, Aristophanes would have been sent straight to the guillotine; and Renan *was* mistaken when, in *L'Avenir de la Science* (1848), he claimed that the normal state of Athens was one of terror and that this had in no way hindered the construction of the Parthenon. Athens certainly did have its moments of collective hysteria (in 415, at the time of the 'mutilation of the Herms'; and in 406, after the Arginusae affair); but permanent terror of either the hot or the icy variety, no.

Three remarks in conclusion:

The Greek city, a place of collective decision, of decisions which emanated neither from the Gods – at the head of decrees, the most ever written was 'the Gods' or 'to good luck' – nor from a divine king, nor from a king subject to the Gods, represented a mutation of huge importance in the Mediterranean of the first millennium.

In Athens and under the influence of Athens, democracy, in the strict sense of the word, however limited, constituted another mutation of huge importance. It is not just a matter of possibilities for bold and exciting ventures being created by a city capable of mobilizing 30,000 citizens in 480 BC (Salamis), in contrast to the 9,000 it had barely managed to muster in 490 (Marathon). What is also so important is that the three great processes of reform introduced by Solon, Cleisthenes and Ephialtes were followed by that incredible miracle the peasant-citizen. His appearance constituted a radical innovation not only in the Mediterranean world but also in Greece itself where, for the most part, peasants were rural dependants (the Helots of Sparta provide the clearest example). A price had to be paid for this, as it does for every step forward, and in this case it was a very high one for, to borrow Finley's expression, slavery and liberty went 'hand in hand'.[34]

Those who are determined to seek in Greek Antiquity for a model of the totalitarian societies of the modern world will not find it in Athenian democracy nor even in the oligarchy of Sparta. They are more likely to find it in the blueprint that democracy's most determined enemy devised to remedy the evils of Greek society: Plato. Everything is to be found here, from history rewritten to serve ideology to the establishment of concentration camps known as 'places of reflection' (*sophronistèria*, *Laws*, 908a), where the wrong-headed and the ill-behaved have all the time in the world to meditate upon the best of all constitutions.

Notes

1 J. J. Rousseau, *Oeuvres complètes*, Gallimard, Pléiade, III, Paris 1964, p. 410 and *Political Writings*, tr. and ed. F. Watkins, Nelson, London, 1953, p. 78.

2 Paul Veyne, *L'Inventaire des différences*, Seuil, Paris, 1976.

3 M. I. Finley, 'Desperately Foreign', in *Aspects of Antiquity*, Chatto & Windus, London, 1968, 2nd edn 1977, pp. 1–6.

4 *Democracy Ancient and Modern*, Chatto & Windus, London, 1973. The French translation, *Démocratie antique et démocratie moderne*, Payot, Paris, 1990 is prefaced by P. Vidal-Naquet's 'Tradition de la démocratie grecque'.

5 See Simone Fraisse, *Péguy et le monde antique*, Armand Colin, Paris, 1973, pp. 64–6 and 195.

6 Plutarch, *Life of Pyrrhus*, 6.

7 See Cl. Bérard et al. *A city of Images: Religion and Society in Ancient Greece*, Princeton University Press, Princeton, 1989.

8 A. Solzhenitsyn, *Comment réaménager notre Russie*, French transl. G. and J. Johannet, Fayard, Paris, 1990, p. 90.

9 See as well as *Sur le contenu du socialisme*, Christian Bourgeois, coll. 10–18, Paris, 1979, 'La *polis* grecque et la création de la démocratie', in *Domaines de l'homme, les carrefours du labyrinthe*, II, Seuil, Paris, 1968, pp. 261–306.

10 Cf. N. Loraux, 'Aux origines de la démocratie: sur la *transparence* démocratique', *Raison présente*, 49, 1979, pp. 3–13.

11 *The Invention of Athens: The Funeral Oration in the Classical City*, tr. Alan Sheridan, Harvard University Press, Cambridge, Mass. and London, 1986.

12 In Plato's *Protagoras*, 320c–323c. There are good reasons to believe that this text was inspired by the real Protagoras; to this reference one could add a few tiny fragments of Democritus.

13 I also tackle this point in chapter 5, pp. 141–169.

14 See P. Jouguet, *Révolution dans la défaite*, Éditions de la *Revue du Caire*, Cairo, 1942 and J. Isaac, *Les Oligarques, essai d'histoire partiale*, Éditions de Minuit, Paris, 1946.

15 For example, J. Julliard, *C'est la faute à Rousseau*, Seuil, Paris, 1985.

16 J. J. Rousseau, *Oeuvres complètes*, op. cit., p. 83.

17 Cf. V. Goldschmidt, *Anthropologie et politique: les principes du système de Rousseau*, Vrin, Paris, 1974.

18 The first version of the *Social Contract*, in *Oeuvres complètes*, op. cit., p. 283.

19 'Le sauvage et le citoyen, le mythe des origines dans le système de Rousseau', in Chantal Grell and Christian Michel (eds), *Primitivisme et mythe des origines dans la France des Lumières (1686–1820)*, Presses de l'Université de Paris-Sorbonne, Paris, 1989, pp. 177–92.

20 *Parallèle entre Sparte et Rome*, in *Oeuvres complètes*, op. cit., p. 538.

21 *Lettres écrites de la Montagne*, ix, in *Oeuvres complètes*, op. cit., p. 881.

22 *The Social Contract*, in *Political Writings*, op. cit., p. 73.

23 J. J. Rousseau, *Oeuvres complètes*, op. cit., p. 941.

24 See the essential book by E. Will, *Doriens et Ioniens: essai sur la valeur du critère ethnique appliqué à l'étude de l'histoire et de la civilisation grecque*, Belles Lettres, Strasbourg and Paris, 1950.

25 See C. Maurras, *Anthinéa*, Juven, Paris, 1901, p. 92 and M. Barrès, *Le Voyage de Sparte*, Plon et Nourrit, Paris, 1922, p. 186; a work that I have found very useful is F. Le Bot's 'mémoire de maîtrise', *La Représentation de la Grèce dans les doctrines d'extrême droite en France, à travers les écrits de C. Maurras et M. Barrès*, Paris-VIII, 1990.

26 In her speech in the Assemblée nationale of 2 May 1990, which is the subject of a detailed commentary by N. Loraux, in R. P. Droit (ed.), *Les grecs, les romains et nous: l'antiquité est-elle moderne?*, Le Monde Éditions, Paris, 1991; see also, in this volume, N. Loraux, 'La démocratie à l'épreuve de l'étranger', (*Athènes, Paris*), pp. 161–89, in particular pp. 177–87.

27 *L'Esprit de la Révolution et de la Constitution (1791)*, in *Oeuvres complètes*, Champ libre, Paris 1984, p. 287.

28 For the references, cf. chapter 5 below, pp. 141–169.

29 I am paraphrasing Thucydides, V, 84–112.

30 For example, King Philip V of Macedon, addressing the Greek city of Larissa in 219, reproached it for its selfishness in the granting of citizenship and drew a contrast with the Roman example; G. Dittenberger, *Sylloge inscriptionum graecarum*, 3rd ed., n° 543.

31 Pseudo-Xenophon, *The Constitution of the Athenians*, I, 17.
32 Xenophon, *Hellenica*, I, 7, 12.
33 Pseudo-Xenophon, op. cit., 18.
34 M. I. Finley, *Economy and Society in Ancient Greece*, Penguin, Harmondsworth, 1983, p. 115.

4

The Formation of Bourgeois Athens: An Essay on Historiography between 1750 and 1850

In a recent article, Zvi Yavetz asked 'Why Rome?',[1] by which he meant, why did ancient history become established as a scholarly discipline in Germany on the basis of B. G. Niebuhr's *Römische Geschichte*, the first two volumes of which appeared in 1811–12? Yavetz found this surprising since it was Greece that, to borrow a well-used expression, was then exerting its 'tyranny' over German minds.[2] According to this Israeli historian, the answer was to be found in the fact that the model for the interpretation of Roman history was the conflict between Prussian lords and peasants at the beginning of the nineteenth century, a conflict that was resolved after the battle of Jena (1806) by reformist arbitration on the part of the State (Stein, Hardenberg, Scharnhorst, Gneisenau . . .). Niebuhr, after starting his career as a civil servant in the service of the king of Denmark, had, after all, become a close collaborator of Stein's.

The problem is certainly a real one, but we believe that it is necessary to look further afield.[3] It is true that the absorption of the peasant revolt by the reformed Prussian State provided a model for the interpretation of the clash between the patricians and the plebs and also for an understanding of the crises of the second and first centuries BC, but it is not only Rome and Prussia that are involved here. Niebuhr's intellectual development was, in large measure, a reaction to the huge 'event' which had ushered in contemporary history, namely the French Revolution. The revival of the 'agrarian question' in Germany was partly a result of the fact that in 1789 the French peasants had already raised that question and

This extract is from R. R. Bolgar, *Classical Influences on Western Thought, AD 1650–1870*, Cambridge University Press, 1979, dedicated to Geoffrey Lloyd. Co-author: Nicole Loraux.

partially resolved it, with a degree of energy that is all too well known. Niebuhr had been an attentive observer of that upheaval. Having at first been violently hostile to the Montagnards of Year II, he had rallied from afar to the Thermidor republic, which he believed would disseminate a 'generalized *Aufklärung*'. He even considered going to study at the École normale in Year II, when Volney was to be teaching there.[4]

A few years before Niebuhr's great work, another German scholar, A. H. L. Heeren, had put the matter very clearly in a textbook published in 1799, which was to enjoy an enduring success in several languages. He had written as follows:

The events of our time have shed upon ancient history a light and an interest which it had lacked and was bound to have lacked up until now ... and if, by chance, several parts of my work, in particular those on the history of the Roman republic, are found to contain similarities with the events that occurred during the ten years preceding the publication of the present work, I feel that no apologies are due on that account.[5]

That the political conflicts of Antiquity might confirm and shed light upon the modern world and themselves be illuminated by the latter was an idea that had occurred to some thinkers even before the Revolution. In 1772, Diderot had written as follows: 'It was in the midst of the continuous storms in Greece that that land was filled with painters, sculptors and poets. And it was at the time when the wild beast known as the Roman people was either devouring itself or busy devouring other nations that historians wrote and poets sang.' And even if, in modern times, 'the spirit of commerce [was] incontestably the dominant spirit of the age', what was certainly continuing, through it, was a political struggle and 'the passion for conquest'.[6]

In Germany, as in France, the connection with the Roman world led to reflection on the State, whether in the form of a republic or in that of an empire. In contrast, the problem that the Greek city raised was, rather, that of political action and its place in society. So the question that we shall be addressing in this study of France and Athens is how and (if possible) why, for French teachers and their students, Athens became the model of a liberal and bourgeois society and even, in the last analysis, of a 'civil society' detached from political society but nevertheless possessing a history with a beginning, a climax and a decline.

The culmination of that line of thought is not in serious doubt. In 1851, Victor Duruy, then teaching at the Lycée Saint-Louis, published the first edition of his *Histoire grecque*. It presents every aspect of the view of

Athens which later, with the necessary transitions, was to become the vision of Glotz and so many others. Duruy wrote as follows: 'The link between civil institutions and political institutions is less evident in Athens than in Sparta . . . In Athens, property is not absorbed by the State . . . Here, the family preserves all its mystery.'[7] Liberty, trade, property, the family: all the elements of a bourgeois Athens are put together for the delectation of the humble and the great alike. But what was the starting point? A whole century before Duruy, in the famous 'Tableau philosophique des progrès successifs de l'esprit humain' which Turgot, then twenty-three years old, delivered in the Sorbonne as his inaugural address as a prior, we are told that while 'barbarity levels all men', progress, for its part, rests upon the inequality of nations. Athens, as opposed to Sparta, is nevertheless 'the model of all nations' and it was 'commerce and the arts' which were later to make Alexandria Athens' rival. 'The known world is, if I may so put it, the trading world.'[8] But, as we shall see, Turgot was here reworking themes used by others before him, although they were themes that by no means encapsulated the entire eighteenth-century attitude to the Greek world.

How best to mark the transitions that took place between Turgot and his predecessors on the one hand and Duruy and his successors on the other? How, that is according to what criteria, should we select our witnesses? By the mid-nineteenth century in France, ancient history had become the preserve of professors. The same thing happened earlier in Germany, later in England where, though George Grote was not himself a professor by training or vocation, he was nevertheless one of the founders of the University of London, set up as a rival to Oxford and Cambridge. But what of the transition from Turgot to Duruy? Professional scholars of the Greek world already existed by the end of the eighteenth century. Men such as D'Ansse de Villoison and Jean Schweighaeuser, publishers and hard-working textual critics, reigned over their domain as surely as Louis Robert reigned over his. A. J. Letronne was born in 1787 and, from the moment that he began to hold forth, in 1814, it was as a professional, even as a contemporary of ourselves. Nevertheless, in 1820 the triumph of the professors was still far from assured. It was considered a toss-up as to who would make the deepest mark in Greek studies, Paul Louis Courier (1772–1825), a colonel in the artillery, or his father-in-law Clavier (1762–1817), a translator of Pausanias and a professor at the Collège de France.

At the outbreak of the Revolution, D'Ansse de Villoison (1750–1805) decided 'not to become involved in the affairs of the Republic' and said so, in Greek of course: $τ\tilde{ω}$ $σοφ\tilde{ω}$ $ο\dot{υ}$ $πολιτ$ $ευτέον$. In a letter dated 17 June 1792, he claimed that the 'long and vast programme of research' demanded to compose his great work, 'a comparative history of Greece in ancient and modern times', justified his retirement from public affairs, but his words brought him no luck for, so immersed was he in his documentation, he never got round to writing the history of which he dreamed.[9]

In contrast, J. Schweighaeuser (1742–1830), who, from Strasbourg, greeted the Revolution with enthusiasm and remained an ardent patriot (despite a few difficulties in Year II), did succeed in publishing his great edition of Polybius between 1789 and 1795, adding the following remark in a letter addressed to a Representative: 'I am sorry and almost ashamed to offer the French Republicans a work first published in a land of slaves.'[10] However, it seemed quite legitimate for Polybius to remain neutral in the opposition between the Revolution and the Counter-Revolution.

But we have picked our principal witnesses from outside this strictly classical academic domain. In a world of specialists, we have decided to offer the floor to men who were not solely specialists of the ancient world. For instance, Pierre-Charles Lévesque (1736–1812), before devoting his life to Thucydides and the Graeco-Roman world, was interested in China and imaginary journeys and also produced an *Histoire de Russie*, in which he wrote as follows: 'The history of one or two small Republics whose domination barely extended to an imperceptible point on the globe [he is, of course, referring to Athens and Sparta] has long been one of the principal subjects of our studies: the very name of the largest empire in the world was unknown to our fathers.'[11] The witnesses whom we have chosen represent the whole gamut which extends from writers and politicians engaged in an essentially ideological struggle – Benjamin Constant, Chateaubriand, Joseph de Maistre – to a *philosophe* who was both an actor and a victim in the Revolution, such as Condorcet, a peculiarly audacious gentleman-enthusiast such as Cornelius de Pauw, and Volney, a famous orientalist who was also an 'ideologue' in the late eighteenth-century sense of the word, a member of the Constituent Assembly and a history professor at the École normale of Year III. Rather than turn to great scholars such as Nicolas Fréret (1688–1749)[12] or Sainte-Croix (1746–1809), it is these men, who were at once citizens of Athens and men of the Revolution, the Empire and Europe, whom we shall ask how it was that Athens came to be considered the supreme achievement of bourgeois history. And although the composition of our group initially seemed rather artificial even to us, gradually, as our enquiry proceeded, it acquired a certain consistency. We had decided to treat these authors as a coherent group and that is indeed what they turned out to be, all complementing one another and all sharing the same basic culture. It was with some surprise, for example, that we came to realize what a central role had been played by a figure such as Cornelius de Pauw (1739–1799), who is more or less unknown to historians of Greek history,[13] but was read and meditated upon by Lévesque, Joseph de Maistre and many others.

Dominating the centre of the historical period that we shall mark out there is, of course, that huge social and intellectual upheaval, the French Revolution. In an earlier work, one of us has tried to define the role played by Greece in the political consciousness of the Revolution and, more precisely, at the centre of its centre, namely Year II.[14] But our present aim is quite different. Our concern here is not to analyse a phenomenon of social identification, in a word the Montagnards' self-identification with a mythical Sparta, a phenomenon which, in the last analysis, could be said to stem from millenarianism. Instead, it is to understand the function of a selection of *oeuvres* which appeared immediately before or immediately after the major crisis, that is to say between 1786 and 1788 or 1795 and 1800. Year II, for example, was a great year for publications and republications.[15] It was at the time of the Thermidor Convention and the Directory that the ideologues, those creators of contemporary secularism, and their opponents were to assess how close to Athens they were or how far distant. At that point the die was cast for many a year.

But before tackling the years immediately before and after the Revolution, let us venture to formulate a few general observations on the age of the Enlightenment as a whole and its relations with Greek Antiquity. It is advisedly that we say 'as a whole', for it would be simplistic to limit ourselves to the rediscovery of 'Antiquity', which triumphed at the end of the century in rhetoric, as well as in architecture and the plastic arts generally. Even more out of the question is any idea of reducing the eighteenth century to whatever prefigured the historicism of the nineteenth century, namely the handful of disciples or emulators of Vico and Herder. To do so would be to judge one age according to the categories of the following one, adopting an attitude that has specifically and with reason been denounced by Cassirer: 'This all too prevalent idea that the eighteenth century is a typically a-historical age is itself a notion with no historical basis, nothing more than a rallying cry emitted by Romanticism, a slogan to launch a campaign against the philosophy of the Enlightenment.[16]

Let us take as our starting point a number of remarks borrowed from an address delivered to the Académie des inscriptions et belles-lettres in 1760 by Jean-Pierre de Bougainville (1722–63), a brother of the explorer and a member of that body:

There can be no doubt that the history of Greece, which has gradually attracted more and more scholars and become increasingly disciplined, offers not so much the spectacle of the destiny of one

nation but rather a perspective in which the entire human race is
depicted in a shortened version of the various stages through which
it has passed. It represents an abridged but complete course of History,
Morality and Politics, for its merit is to incorporate within a short
space all the divers characteristics recorded in the annals of the various
centuries: it shows man from every possible angle, savage, nomadic,
civilized, religious, warlike, mercantile; it provides models of all the
laws, in a word a complete theory, supported by facts, of the formation
of societies, of the birth, propagation and progress of the arts, of
every variety of revolution which the human race can undergo, in all
the forms by which it can be modified. For an attentive observer . . .
Greece is a universe in miniature, and the history of Greece is an
excellent précis of universal history.[17]

Nothing particularly surprising there, you may say. But let us straight
away note the spatial metaphor. The 'short space' here does not allude
solely to the small area that Greece fills on the map. In the eighteenth
century, it was taken for granted that a 'space' could sum up a time,[18]
Space and time, the present and the distant past, the world of the savage
and the world of ancient civilizations, Utopian projects and Utopias realized – on the basis of the debris of the *Discours sur l'histoire universelle*,
every kind of combination was possible in a space-time that was un-
believably expanded.

To understand what Greece meant to the *philosophes*,[19] we must, of
course, see that the distant past served as a weapon that could be deployed
against Christian society, both that of the past and that of the present, and
against the Judaeo-Christian myth which supported it. But above all we
must understand that every association seemed possible, however contradictory. Any time and any space could be used to create fantasies, to seek
for liberty and security. Primitive times and immobile spaces, the newly
conquered and socialized lands of Anglo-Saxon America, the Russian
world, the Chinese world, the world of India, the continent of Africa.
Every combination was possible: immobility and movement, liberty and
enlightened despotism. Where Greece was concerned, Voltaire might
choose Athens rather than Sparta, but that did not prevent him also propa-
gating the mirage of China.[20] Ideally, a detailed study ought to associate
Greece and America, Greece and the world of savages, Greece and Holland,
Greece and Switzerland. Because the end of the century produced the
'bourgeois revolution', it is tempting to think that all that the movement
of ideas retained of Greece was whatever fitted in with the movement of
the age, once it was over. But nothing could be further from the truth. As
much as it embodied victorious reason, Greece served to uphold the dream

of a history that was static[21] or one in which perfection was achieved. That is what Athens itself was for Winckelmann, and Sparta too, where the lawgiver at a stroke instituted a good society – a myth which the Revolution had the effect of multiplying. Just as in modern controversies over the Greek economy,[22] in the eighteenth century Greece was fought over by 'primitivists' and 'modernists', not to mention those for whom it was precisely the place of transition, a group represented well enough by J.-P. de Bougainville. The first of those themes, that of 'primitivism', sketched in as early as 1724 by Father Lafitau,[23] took on a new aspect in the last quarter of the century. Compared with the modern world, the primitive world seemed a place of symbols, allegory, secrets to be deciphered. Court de Gébelin, for instance, in the nine volumes of his *Monde primitif*, published between 1773 and 1782 and one of the rare works in French to have been influenced by Vico, was in quest of the universal language, the immediate expression of natural symbolism, which holds the secret to that world.[24] His quest came to an end in the Greek world ('At last we have reached you, beloved Greece'[25]), the Greek world whose language was in some respects a dialect of Celtic. The Greeks, our ancestors . . . And his disciple, the astronomer Bailly, who was to become the first mayor of Paris, was searching, beyond the Brahmins so dear to Voltaire, for the primitive people from which Plato's inhabitants of Atlantis were an off-shoot and whose greatness accounts for the very existence of the ancient world.[26] Long after the revolutionary period, the descendants of this primitivist symbolism, from Dupuis to Creuzer, continued to be legion.

But we should also note the opposite theme, that of modernity. And what modernity means is 'commerce', for trade made it possible to distinguish Athens from Sparta and compare it to Amsterdam, London or Paris. Initially, this theme made no more than a very discreet appearance in a book, inspired by a Dutch model, which the bishop of Avranches, the famous Huet, published in 1711. Here Athens was seen, with the aid of Xenophon's *Anabasis*, as 'a very commercial town, provided with all kinds of commodities for trading'.[27] But at this level, the opposition between Athens and Sparta led to no serious consequences either in representations of the ancient world or in the preferences of the modern world.

However, 1735 saw the anonymous publication of the *Essai politique sur le commerce* by J.-F. Melon, who was Law's Secretary. This book has a pre-history, mainly English, linking it to Mandeville's *Fable of the Bees*, which developed the idea that morality and economic efficiency are two very distinct things.[28] It also has a post-history, for it gave rise to the controversy, essentially French, over the advantages of luxury for economic development.[29] Athens had a role to play here:

The austere Sparta was neither more victorious nor better governed, nor did it produce more great men than luxury-loving Athens. Plutarch's famous men include four Spartans and seven Athenians, not to mention the forgotten Socrates and Plato. Lycurgus' laws against luxury deserve no more attention than other laws of his that are so offensive to modesty.[30]

The theme of Athens and its luxury now became a commonplace, and Rousseau used it as an argument in his critique.[31]

But it was not just a matter of luxury, for in connection with Rome and Carthage, if not with Athens and Sparta, Melon introduced an opposition which was to acquire a lasting popularity. It was between the spirit of conquest and the spirit of commerce: 'The spirit of conquest and the spirit of commerce are mutually exclusive in a nation.' The reason why Rome, which, up until the Empire, 'was more of a camp than a town', and the Romans, 'whose trading involved only necessities', conquered the Carthaginians was that 'the spirit of commerce and preservation was still, so to speak, in its infancy'.[32] The eighteenth century, the age of commerce and industry, needed to develop its spirit of commerce and enterprise to the limit by, for example, making surgical experiments on those condemned to death or by inflicting upon criminals 'the kind of painful labours which shorten life'. By adopting such means, it could hope for perpetual peace: 'The spirit of peace has at last enlightened our Europe.'[33]

The opposition between the spirit of conquest and the spirit of commerce was also familiar to Montesquieu,[34] but in the *Esprit des Lois* (1748) he was reluctant to attribute a spirit of commerce to Athens, for democracy operated against commerce:

The Athenians ... who were more attentive to extend their maritime empire than to enjoy it; whose political government was such that the common people distributed the public revenues amongst themselves, while the rich were in a state of oppression; the Athenians, I say, did not carry on so extensive a commerce as might be expected from the produce of their mines, from the multitude of their slaves, from the number of their seamen, from their influence over the cities of Greece; and, above all, from the excellent institutions of Solon.

But on the very same page he also remarks, apropos the evidence of the 'Old Oligarch', whom he takes to be the author of the *Anabasis*: 'One would imagine that Xenophon was speaking of England.'[35] Others too were disinclined to identify Athens with a spirit of commerce, in particular

David Hume, who was initially sympathetic to the idea but eventually concluded: 'Great interest of money and great profits of trade are an infallible indication that industry and commerce are but in their infancy', which was a deliberate generalization from the arguments of Thucydides' *Archaeology*.[36]

However, these were isolated voices, and it was the idea of Athens, the city of commerce, that was to prevail. In 1777, in London, Sir William Young published a history of Athens which was to run to two more editions, dated 1786 and 1804.[37] The title of the second edition described the city as 'a free and commercial state', and all that Young, who held an important post in the British Colonial Administration, retained from Montesquieu's views was the comparison with England. According to Young, Athens, thanks to its commerce, represented the state best designed to promote general happiness: 'The free state of Athens, in the high perfection of its establishment, was the state the best calculated for general happiness.'[38] Clearly, the theme here was already that of utilitarian philosophy. But how is it possible to reconcile a 'spirit of commerce' with patriotism, another sentiment that was growing at the end of the century and for which ancient Greece, particularly Athens, almost to the same degree as Sparta, provided a model? When the Marquis de Chastellux, who was one of the theorists of representative government,[39] was travelling in America in the early 1780s, he produced the following portrait of a merchant of Philadelphia:

He is a very wealthy merchant; he is, in consequence, a man of every country, for commerce is the same the world over. In a monarchy he is free, in a Republic an egoist; a foreigner or – you could say – a citizen throughout the world, he excludes both the virtues and the preconceptions which run counter to his interest.[40]

Now let us pause to consider the years immediately prior to the Revolution. The year 1787–1788 saw the publication of two sharply contrasting books whose fortunes were likewise to differ greatly. One is well known, even famous: the six volumes of Abbé Barthélemy's *Voyage du jeune Anacharsis en Grèce*, a monument of erudition that was to run to a string of editions in the course of the nineteenth century. It presented a picture of Athens on the model of Paris or Chanteloup – the Duc de Choiseul's estate in the neighbourhood of Tours, where Barthélemy composed his great work (today a Chinese folly is all that remains standing). 'How very Parisian these Athenians are!' was the comment of all the critics, although they were not sure whether to be amazed or indignant about it.[41] Not much attention was paid to the fact that the traveller was a Scythian or that, like

Rollin, Rousseau and Mably, he preferred Sparta to Athens and Scythia
to Greece. In the end, despite his studies under Plato and Aristotle, this
'noble savage' decided to return home.

The other work was Cornelius de Pauw's *Recherches philosophiques
sur les Grecs*, which appeared in Berlin in 1787 and in Paris in 1788 and
was republished in Year III together with the rest of the author's *oeuvre*
and translated into English. Yet, so far as we know, it has never been the
subject of any scholarly research.[42]

Cornelius de Pauw (1739–99) was a great-nephew of the De Witt
brothers, whose assassination in 1672 harrowed Spinoza, the uncle of
Anacharsis Cloots, the 'orator of the human race', by whose execution
during the Montagnard Terror de Pauw was himself deeply upset. He was
a German born in Amsterdam, and served as ambassador to the town of
Liège. His *Recherches* on Greece were but a part of a much vaster corpus.
'This Protestant polygraph argues against the Jesuits at every opportunity.'[43] In 1768, in Berlin, he published his *Recherches philosophiques sur
les Américains ou Mémoires intéressants pour servir à l'histoire de l'espèce
humaine*, which is by far the best-known of his works.[44] Reacting against
the myth of the noble savage and the Utopia often claimed to be represented by pre-Columbian America,[45] de Pauw set about presenting Indian
America as a vast morass where nothing, neither man nor plant, could
flourish as it should. A few years later, in 1773, he published another
volume of his *Recherches philosophiques*, on the Egyptians and the
Chinese. His purpose was twofold: first, to separate the destiny of Egypt,
which had – erroneously, according to de Pauw – fascinated intellectuals
ever since the Greek period, from that of China. For it had been claimed
– and as late as 1758, by the linguist J. de Guignes – that China, a mirage
of the intellectuals of the eighteenth century, was an Egyptian colony.[46]
Secondly, once that separation was established, it was necessary to show
that the China of which those intellectuals dreamed was, on the evidence
of travellers who had been to Canton, in truth also a mirage.

Shortly before his death, de Pauw destroyed the manuscript of a fourth
work, on Germania. Almost certainly it was devoted to demolishing the
idealized representations which the French nobility cultivated concerning
their ancestors, the 'Franks'.

But amid all this destruction, he did devote himself to the construction
of Greece, or rather of Athens. For Greece meant neither the Spartans
'who never contributed any knowledge to progress or any skills to new
developments', nor the Aetolians, who were compared to wild beasts, nor
the Thessalians, 'amongst whom agriculture was a demeaning activity',
nor the Arcadians, those noble savages of Antiquity who had no political
existence at all until the arrival of Epaminondas.[47] What Greece meant,

first and foremost, was Athens. A democratic Athens, of course, the city
of political speech: 'Here, politics was not obscured beneath veils and
clouds.'[48] All the same, it was a strange Athens, where commerce, which
constituted the entire life of the city, was seen with a pastoral bias, for de
Pauw stressed the Athenians' predeliction for the pastoral life. According
to him, on the evidence of the pseudo-Dichearchos' description, even the
town of Athens boasted no sumptuous edifices.[49] 'The road was agree-
able, running through a countryside well cultivated and with a welcoming
air. But the town was arid and lacked water; it was poorly laid out, in
the archaic manner.'[50] To demonstrate the typically democratic low-key
aspect of Athens, de Pauw writes: 'They feared, with reason, to affront
the essential principles of popular government and the equality that was
its law.'[51] Everything, even the philosophers' 'gardens', was woven into
this pastoral idyll.

However, this countrified Athens had also, since Solon, been a land
of mechanical skills, with a 'huge industrial trade', sustained by 'a prodigious number of factories', in other words it was a kind of London
or Amsterdam.[52] All this was made possible by slavery, the importance
of which de Pauw quite openly recognizes. He even accepts the figure of
400,000 slaves given by the 'census' of Demetrios of Phaleron and recorded
by Athenaeus in a text that is as famous as it is controversial.[53] However,
it should not be thought that de Pauw accepted all the traditional data
unreservedly. His Athens was a historical democracy which certainly did
not begin with Theseus, as classical, Hellenistic and modern rhetoric
claimed. The most ancient period of the 'history' of Athens and the earliest dates, for example on the 'Paros marble', which mentions 'the arrival
of Ceres in Eleusis', were rejected as being totally legendary – in which
de Pauw revealed himself to be in advance of his own time. He describes
Solon's constitution as a mixture, not as purely democratic. According to
him, democracy was not really founded until Aristides, at which point
'the humblest of the Athenians became a king'. De Pauw rejects Rousseau's
notion that 'only gods can live in a democracy'.[54] Commenting on the
pseudo-Aristotelian *Economica*, he writes: 'the author of this remarkable
book entitled the *Economica* says not a word about the economy, but
describes various operations carried out by the satraps of Persia and the
kings of Caria'.[55] These are remarks upon which many commentators of
this treatise on fiscal and family strategy might do well to meditate.[56]

On the eve of the uprising of 1789, the main framework for a bourgeois
Athens had thus been set in place: the whole picture is one that may
appear coherent but that today seems to us flawed by the lack of critical
distance between the eighteenth-century present and the past. A critique
and a distance were to be created by the Revolution.

As is well known, during the 'troubles' Athens lost ground to Sparta, which anyway had never ceased to dominate in college teaching, as also in a major sector of political comment. 'Sparta shines like a flash of lightning in a great darkness' was what Robespierre declared on 18 Floréal in Year II (7 May 1794). Ideologically, it was thanks to Sparta that the Montagnard leaders conceived French society as transparent, that is to say ideally united. The 'revolutionary festival', one of the most deliberate imitations from Antiquity, aimed to be an event that denied an event, wiped out time in the interests of a commemoration, there and then embodying the lawgiver's dream.[57]

At this point we must introduce a parenthesis. Let us, for the moment, turn away from the network of signs that are the true subject of our study and confront what – through an abuse of language – has come to be known as social reality; and let us ask the following question: did this identification with Antiquity, which characterizes the most radical aspect of the Revolution,[58] produce consequences for the educational system, particularly in relation to the teaching of ancient languages, the obvious means of access to this Antiquity that was so much revered?

It is a problem worth considering, for it concerns an important phenomenon upon which the imaginary representations of a whole group of people were concentrated. According to the Prince de Ligne, on one occasion when he was with Frederick the Great, the king 'made a little trip to Rome and Sparta; he liked to visit there'.[59] The English Puritans of the seventeenth century never 'made a little trip' to ancient Israel, for they *were* to a large extent figures from the Bible, not that this meant – far from it – that most of them ever felt any need to learn Hebrew. The most 'Spartan' of them probably did not even feel that their children should learn Greek. They themselves could provide them with living examples to emulate.

Similarly, a rapid glance at the sources and works devoted to this question[60] shows quite clearly that the French Revolutionaries evinced no enthusiasm at all for the study of classical languages or classical history. Thus Mirabeau, who, it is true, was neither Spartan nor Roman, perhaps for that very reason justified himself as follows: 'Far be it from me to proscribe the study of dead languages. What I would like, above all, would be to have the fine Greek language reborn from its embers . . . All the same, I believe it necessary to order that all public teaching should henceforth be in French.'[61] The teaching of Latin was, after all, associated with the most decrepit of teaching institutions. The most that the Montagnard mathematician Gilbert Romme could envisage was associating the study of Latin with 'the Romans' forceful love of liberty in the heroic days of the Republic'. And Condorcet had already declared himself to have many reservations *vis-à-vis* the subject of Latin, 'since today all prejudices must be swept aside'.[62] Le Peletier's famous educational plan for children aged between five and twelve years had good reasons for not mentioning ancient languages,[63] despite the fact that Foucroy, recalling Le Peletier's example, was to declare on 30 July 1793: 'His only guides were the ancient lawgivers. He, like the sages of Greece, considered the sons of citizens to be children of the Republic.' But all Foucroy himself had to suggest was: 'You can imitate Athens, where schools opened at sunrise and closed at sunset.'[64]

At the height of the heated days of Year II, on 15 Brumaire (5 November, 1793), Marie-Joseph Chénier was even heard pronouncing the following critical (but, it must be said, atypical) remarks:

> What we must do is study men and *mores*, times and places and nature, immutable in its principles but ever varied in its results; and then perhaps people will be in less of a hurry to present us with political tales easily constructed on the basis of Plato's *Republic* or the historical stories composed about Sparta.[65]

All the same, the 'ideologue' Chénier, author of a *Caius Gracchus* very much to the taste of his day and performed in 1792, was, it must be said, directly acquainted with the Greek culture.

It was, in truth, in the Thermidorean days that the problem was seriously raised, although the École normale of Year III did not have a chair of ancient languages. The 'central schools' set up at this time in every department did, for their part, make room for those languages.[66] A teacher of general grammar at the central school of the Lot region even wrote to his minister to tell him that 'the Greek language must at last occupy the distinguished place in public teaching that its superiority over all known languages ought to have assured it'.[67] Notwithstanding, the emphasis in teaching was, in extremely innovative fashion, placed on the sciences and political economy. On 16 December 1794 (26 Frimaire, Year III), Lakanal's advice was: 'Read *The Wealth of Nations*, the most useful work for the peoples of Europe.'[68] In principle, the ruling was that the teaching of Latin and Greek should be completed in two years: a ruling which, as can be imagined, provoked an outcry.[69] It was Bonaparte, after Brumaire, and later as Emperor, who progressively re-established the absolute priority of Latin, at the expense of mathematics in particular, restoring to it the socially selective role that it had enjoyed for so long in the past.[70] Rome had, to be sure, 'taken the place of Sparta', but an almost total cleavage now separated the cult of the Revolution from practice in the *lycées* of imperial France.

The proscribed Condorcet, a Girondin and the last great representative of the *Encyclopédistes*, raised what was a minority voice in opposition to the values generally honoured in Year II but one which, little by little, was to become that of most liberal bourgeois (many of whom were at the time quite prepared to lay down their lives for liberty). On 13 Germinal, Year III, on the recommendation of the report of the ideologue Daunou, the Convention decided to acquire 3,000 copies of Condorcet's posthumous work, *Esquisse d'un tableau historique des progrès de l'esprit humain* (the very title conveys the extent of the author's debt to Turgot) and to have it distributed generally, starting with the entire body of its own surviving members.[71] This was the fundamental text through which the ideology of progress elaborated in the eighteenth century was transmitted by the Thermidoreans to the nineteenth century.[72] Bonald, Joseph de Maistre and Chateaubriand were in no doubt of that.[73]

What was Greece's place in this *Tableau*?[74] If it was true that 'the perfectibility of man is truly limitless', it followed that the march of progress 'would never be reversed'.[75] After clans and the emergence of agriculture and writing, the fourth period of the history of humanity was symbolized by 'the progress of the human mind in Greece up to the division of the sciences, about the time of Alexander'.[76] The ninth period, by the way, extended 'from Descartes up until the formation of the French Republic'. The tenth was yet to come.

Condorcet's attitude towards Greece was by no means simplistic. He wrote as follows, and his words had far-reaching implications:

Nearly all the institutions of the Greeks assume the existence of slavery and also the feasibility of bringing together the whole body of citizens in one public place. If we are to judge of the practical value of these institutions and, above all, to assess their relevance to the great nations of the modern age, we must not for a moment lose sight of these two important differences.[77]

To be sure, as Condorcet himself was to point out elsewhere,[78] the printing press rendered direct democracy and Demosthenes' kind of eloquence unnecessary and made representation a viable possibility. But in the last analysis, what is important is that it was Condorcet who in a sense created Athens as a distant historical model: 'There is hardly to be found in any modern republic or in any of those schemes devised by philosophers an institution of which the Greek republics did not provide the model or supply an example.'[79] Here Condorcet refers to the Greek republics in the plural, but he clearly has Athens in mind: 'Apart from Athens, there was for some time possibly no city where the entire citizen body enjoyed full rights.'[80] The fall of kings, at the dawn of Greek history, marked the start of revolutions.

> It is to that same revolution that the human race owes its enlightenment and *will owe* its liberty. It has had a far greater influence upon the destiny of the present nations of Europe than events which are much closer to us, in which our own ancestors were actors and for which their country was the theatre: in a sense it constitutes the first page of *our* history.[81]

Condorcet may have admired Leonidas, without however believing that his death was caused by his obedience to the laws of Sparta, but he nevertheless wrote as follows: 'The battle of Salamis was one of those events, so rare in history, in which the luck of a single day decides the destiny of the human race for centuries to come.'[82] History is progress, but Greece anticipates later developments. In their way, Democritus and Pythagoras prefigure Descartes and Newton.[83] In his double position of both distance from and closeness to Greece, Condorcet is not far from Hegel, and that very comparison suggests that he marks an essential turning point. For his line of discourse was continued by Chateaubriand, criticized by Benjamin Constant and reversed by Joseph de Maistre, who gave it a tragic element.

Athens was both close and distant. Yet one typical Thermidorean man, Volney, had the courage to suggest, with unprecedented vigour, that the closeness was largely illusory and only the distance was real. The compromise from which bourgeois Athens initially emerged was thus denounced from the start.

The particular advantage of Volney (1757–1820) was without doubt that he not only knew Greek and Latin and had read, even had an intimate knowledge of, Herodotus, but was also an orientalist, even an orientalist who knew the Orient.[84] In 1787 Volney, the Man of the Enlightenment (his pseudonym was said to be an amalgamation of *Vol*taire + Fer*ney*) published his *Voyage en Syrie et en Égypte* with the following epigraph, which brilliantly conveys the spirit in which it is written: 'I thought that the genre of travel literature belonged more to history than to the novel.'[85] The date of his journey represents a milestone, for what Volney discovered was not the Orient of *Origins*, not even the land of abstract despotism that had been a source of ambiguous inspiration to so many contemporaries of Louis XIV and Louis XV. Rather, it was what we today call the 'underdeveloped world' or the 'third world'.[86] Volney's book describes a sick world, and, to the surprise of commentators, the first chapter, which classifies its inhabitants, introduces, 'apparently for no reason, a passage on sickness'. This Orient is neither exotic nor picturesque; it is degenerate,[87] and the reason for this is that it took a wrong historical turning. When we read his famous description of Alexandria, there is no mistaking the third world, with its teeming crowds and its crushing poverty:

> Their markets ill supplied with dates and round, flat little loaves; a filthy drove of half-starved dogs roaming through the streets, and a kind of wandering phantoms, which, under a long drapery of a single piece, discover nothing human but two eyes, which shew that they are women . . . the narrow, ill-paved streets, the low houses which, though not calculated to admit much light, are still more obscured by lattice work, the meagre and swarthy inhabitants, who walk barefooted, without other clothing than a blue shirt fastened with a leathern girdle or a red handkerchief.[88]

No doubt Volney's explanation for this degradation seems simplistic, for virtually the only cause that he adduces is Turkish despotism. Volney in fact sets himself up as the inspired spokesman of the Western world, which, for its part, did choose the right direction to take, a path in which the early days of the Revolution fully confirm it. In 1791, he published his *Ruines*, a 'Discourse on secular universal history'.[89] The said 'ruins' are the remains of 'the revolutions of the past', and the work is an appeal for a Lawgiver equal to legislating for the Universe, a legislative people. The 'genius' of the ruins exclaims:

> Let but a virtuous chief arise, a just and powerful people appear and the earth will raise them to supreme power: the world is waiting for a legislative people; it wishes and demands it, and my heart attends the cry . . . Then, turning towards the West: Yes, continued he, a hollow sound already strikes my ear: a cry of *liberty*, proceeding from far-distant shores, resounds on the ancient continent.[90]

This people is, of course, the French people, the people who, with Buonaparte, were soon to invade Egypt, using the work written by Volney – who had not intended this at all – as its guide. Volney the orientalist, for his part, now set about writing Arabic and Hebrew in Roman characters.[91] A disciple of Abbé Raynal though he was, and against the colonial venture on principle, he thus nevertheless played a part in Western aggression by virtue of the very fact that he was a Western philosopher of history.[92]

The French Revolution did not set out along the highway of bourgeois rationality immediately. In Year II, after a taste of prison and having given his famous *leçons* at the École normale, Volney set sail for America. His *Tableau du climat et du sol des États-Unis*, which he published several years after his return, in 1803, and which was anything but enthusiastic about this other branch of the Western adventure, foretold the disappearance of the last of the Indians: 'In a hundred or two hundred years, possibly not one of these peoples will exist.'[93] It was high time their customs and languages were studied and classified. And how should this be done if not with the aid of Greece's past? It was Thucydides' *Archaeology*, cited in the new translation by Pierre-Charles Lévesque,[94] that would make it possible to understand not only Greece but the Iroquois too: 'This fragment seems to me so well suited to my subject that I believe I do my reader a favour in submitting it to him, so that he can make the comparison for himself.'[95] But Volney went much further than Thucydides, at the risk of making the very phenomenon of the Athenian historian's existence incomprehensible, for what was true of Homer was also true of the contemporaries of Pericles – not merely the Aetolians, whose barbarity had struck both Thucydides and Cornelius de Pauw so forcibly, but even the Athenians themselves:

> I am always struck by the analogy that I notice each day between the savages of North America and the much extolled ancient peoples of Greece and Italy. In the Greeks of Homer, especially *those* of the *Iliad*, I find the customs, discourse and behaviour of the *Iroquois*, the *Delaware* and the *Mîami*. The tragedies of Sophocles and Euripides faithfully depict for me, almost literally, the opinions of the *red men* on necessity, fatality, the wretchedness of the human condition and the harshness of blind destiny.[96]

Paradoxically, however, Volney does fleetingly admit, since Thucydides spoke of the special destiny of Attica in his *Archaeology*, that this particular part of Greece did experience occasional causes of civilization.[97]

In Year III, in his lectures at the École normale,[98] Volney had ventured to deliver a radical critique directed against the imitation of Antiquity, which he considered to be a major phenomenon of the Revolution, and against the historicism from which the movement of the ideologues had certainly not been free. It is a famous passage but worth citing again. Volney points out

> that in Athens, that sanctuary of every liberty, there were four slaves for every free individual; that there was not a single house where the despotic regime of our colonies of America was not exercised by these so-called democrats; that of the four million odd souls who

must have made up the population of ancient Greece, over three million were slaves; that the political and civil inequality of men was the dogma accepted by peoples and lawgivers alike; that this was consecrated by Lycurgus and Solon, professed by Aristotle and the divine Plato and also by the generals and ambassadors of Athens, Sparta and Rome who, in Polybius, Livy and Thucydides, all speak as did the ambassadors of Attila and Tchinguizkan [Genghis Khan].[99]

And Volney goes on to say:

Yes, the more I have studied Antiquity and its widely acclaimed governments, the more I have thought that the government of the Mameluks of Egypt and the Dey of Algeria were essentially no different from those of Sparta and Rome; and that all that is lacking in the resemblance in every respect between these highly extolled Greeks and Romans and the Huns and the Vandals are the names that the latter bear.

The 'only just and honourable war was the one against Xerxes'. No sooner was it over than Athens embarked upon its 'insolent vexations'. The masterpieces of Attic art were the 'primary cause' of Athens' downfall, 'because, being the fruit of a system of extortion and plunder, they provoked both the resentment and defection of its allies and the jealousy and cupidity of its enemies, and because those masses of stone, although well cut, everywhere represented a sterile use of labour and a ruinous drain on wealth'.[100] A bourgeois ideology of production is at work here, in harmony with the reading of Thucydides that Lévesque's translation had just produced.

It has sometimes been wondered, in connection with Edward Gibbon, whether the historian of the decadence of the Roman Empire engaged upon his intellectual adventure in harmony with classical historiography or breaking away from it.[101] But in the case of Volney, there can be no doubt at all on that score; in no sense was he a contemporary of Thucydides.

So the break was made. But it was a break that had to be demonstrated repeatedly, a gulf that needed to be dug deeper before the new position could become established. After Thermidor, everything had to be reconsidered, everything had to be understood in a new way. In this attempt to reconstruct the discourse, Greece still had a place. It still had a place, or already had a place: it was still the Greece of the Revolution and already the Greece of the liberals. The time would come, with Pierre-Charles Lévesque and with Benjamin Constant, when the Greek city would be set up as a subject for study. But in the meantime, the first thing to do was make use of Antiquity in order to understand the present that was already in the past: namely the French Revolution. This was Chateaubriand's purpose in writing his *Essai historique sur les révolutions*, published in London in 1797.[102]

It is, in truth, a curious work: written by an *émigré* yet 'dedicated to all parties'; a work of history yet haunted by the timeless law which 'will propel us from one revolution into another until the end of time' (I, ch. LXX, p. 263) and which seeks to tie to Antiquity a present that has strayed from the course of time – France's present and Chateaubriand's, pulled this way and that by the 'imaginary perfections' of over-audacious innovators and the out-of-date obscurantism of those who sought 'to remain men of the fourteenth century in the year 1796';[103] a political essay but one which ends in the dark, amongst the savages of America: 'No more towns, . . . no more Presidents, Republics, kings'; but at the same time a very internal revolution (II, ch. LVII, p. 442). However, we should not be too hasty to condemn the incoherence of this 'strange and disorganized book',[104] for that would be to fall into the trap laid by Chateaubriand himself for the reader when, in 1826, seizing the opportunity afforded by the second edition of the *Essai*, he pretended to distance himself from this text of his youth.[105]

What is a revolution?: 'an entire change in the government of a nation, whether from monarchical to republican or vice versa' (Introduction, p. 48 [p. 6]). On the strength of this definition, Chateaubriand can count twelve revolutions, five of them in Antiquity, including 'the establishment of the republics of Greece' (the first) and 'their subjection by Philip and Alexander' (the second). In other words, while 'the dethronement of Hippias may be considered as the epoch at which happiness returned to Greece and the end of the republican revolution' (I, ch. XII, p. 78 [p. 38]), in the case of Greece it all began with revolution. Chateaubriand takes good care not to carry his analysis any further than that original revolution, as if between 510 BC and 1789 AD time had stood still. His 'space of two moments' in that history[106] may perhaps be regarded to indicate how much Chateaubriand owed to the intellectual climate of the Revolution,[107] but above all it shows the great importance that he attached to the comparative plan that is the inspiration for his *Essai*.

For the only question that really matters is put as follows: 'Among these revolutions, are there any which, from the spirit, manners and enlightened state of the times, can be compared with the French one?' (Introduction, p. 45 [p. 3]; II, ch. LVI, p. 432). Once it is admitted that 'there is nothing new under the sun' and also that history repeats itself, sometimes to the letter (Preface, p. XXIIII, ch. LIX; II, ch. LVI, pp. 220–1), what we have is a book in which the French Revolution serves as a 'common focus' (Introduction, p. 47 [p. 6]) and Greek history as its mirror. But Greek history is never studied on its own account – facts that are 'totally distinct in their causes and effects from those of the French Revolution' are set aside (Introduction, p. 49 [p. 8]) – nor does Chateaubriand make much effort to reconstruct it for himself, for he takes much of his information ready-made from Abbé Barthélemy.[108] However, he feels few scruples on that score and, while his erudition may not be as fantastical as Renan was to claim,[109] it is true that 'there are very few passages that stem from a true historical method'.[110]

As is not hard to guess, thereupon follow a series of bold assimilations, some of them clear enough (the 'Montagnards' of Pisistratus' day and the Montagnards of the Convention;[111] the elegies of Tyrtaeus and the *Marseillaise* – I, ch. XXIII; Draco's laws and the decrees of Robespierre – I, ch. V), many of them disconcerting (Megacles and Tallien – I, ch. VIII; Pythagoras and Bernardin de Saint-Pierre – I, ch. XLI);[112] and above all and providing the *Essai* with its structural framework, the Persian Wars are identified with the revolutionary wars: 'The republicans advanced to death, singing the hymns of Castor and that of the Marseillais. Miracles were achieved amid shouts of *Liberty*. Greece and France boasted the days of Marathon, Salamis, Plataea, Fleurus, Weissemberg and Lodi.'[113] Which is Greece? Which is France? Each of their histories is written in the same timeless present and a single phrase is enough to wipe out the polyphonic time of history: 490 BC = 1793 AD (I, ch. LXV, p. 238).

This levelling of time may be seen as 'the height of nonsense', as the *Essai*'s author himself suggested when, having become Chateaubriand, he looked back over thirty years at his youthful work;[114] and ever since Montlosier, that is exactly how many critics have represented it.[115] Chateaubriand was accused of having failed to recognize 'that great and primary truth which should have provided the basis for his book: . . . namely, that the French Revolution has nothing in common with other revolutions on this earth; . . . [that] in stature, spirit and results, everything was different'.[116] But in truth Chateaubriand was not as naive as all that, for he devoted an entire chapter (I, ch. LXVIII [ch. XLII]) to 'the great general difference between our Age and that in which the Republican Revolution of Greece took place', a chapter in which we are told that 'the dissimilarity of the ages appears . . . in all its force (p. 256 [p. 242]) and that 'it is natural to expect that the revolutionary movements of France would, in their effects, infinitely surpass those produced by the disturbances in Greece' (p. 254 [p. 240]). The author of the *Essai* thus indulged in that most aristocratic luxury of risking 'reducing [his] own system to ruination' (note written in 1826, p. 254). Nevertheless, he did not give up his comparative project, and for us that is the main point.

We may thus regard his project as more than pure nonsense and even detect in it something that Chateaubriand, the former minister and a figure still eligible for ministerial responsibilities in the future, was none too keen, in 1826, to find that he had expressed in 1797, as if, by drawing a comparison between Tyrtaeus and the *Marseillaise*, he had in effect made his peace with the revolutionary process: namely, an understanding of the French Revolution according to his own categories – in short, recognition that imitation had been a theoretical principle of the Revolution. In one of the four chapters devoted to the Jacobins, Chateaubriand put that point forcefully:

> A distinguishing feature of the French revolution is that it is necessary to admit speculative views and abstract doctrines as infinite in their causes. It was in part effected by the men of letters who were rather inhabitants of Rome and Athens than of their own country, and who endeavoured to bring back the manners of antiquity into modern Europe (I, ch. XVII, p. 90 [p. 54]).

To make imitation the central theme of the *Essai* was to try to reflect upon the identification of modernity with Antiquity, the better to denounce the dangers of doing so. With its three protagonists – Sparta, Athens and the French – and universal history as the stage, this was a drama well worth putting on again. Given that 'one race of men, suddenly rising up, had, in its exhilaration, set about sounding the knell for Sparta and Athens (I, ch. LXX, p. 266), the director of proceedings would pass over the 'annals of the other small places' that were 'too little known to be interesting' (I, ch. IV, p. 64 [p. 22]).

This was the starting point in Chateaubriand's strategy to waylay the Revolution in the trap set by its own desires, that is to say its imaginary representations, or its own reality, for exile had taught this *émigré* that 'we never perceive the reality of things', only 'images of them falsely reflected by our own desires' (II, ch. LVI, p. 439). If France had wanted to be Sparta (I, ch. XIII–XVI, pp. 79–91 [pp. 39–55]) it was imperative, at whatever cost, to point out that the copy did not match the original. Certainly, the revolution had been pure in Sparta, 'which had the good fortune to possess in the same man a revolutionist and a legislator' (I, ch. V, p. 64 [p. 22]). But, given that the French and the Athenians were as alike as two peas in a pod,[117] the French had never really imitated anything but Athens, in an imitation that was at once involuntary and inadequate: 'As the age of Solon [always Solon!] surpassed ours in morality, so were the factious of Attica superior in talents to those of France' (I, ch. VIII, p. 71 [p. 30]).

Chateaubriand thus made use of Athens as if it were another France, an ancient France with which he could set the modern France at a distance: an ancient France which 'really possessed . . . the most democratic constitution that ever existed among any people' (I, ch. VI, p. 67 [p. 26]). Better still, Athens proves that a republic is impossible in France, since no true democracy can exist without slavery (I, ch. LXVIII). It is true that in 1826 Chateaubriand confessed that he had not appreciated how wide a gap separated ancient democracy from the representative republic, but the essential point for us is that in 1797, for the purposes of identification, the *Essai sur les révolutions* made slavery the basis of the Athenian system.[118]

France was not Athens, then; but Athens was France, a France better able to accept the consequences of its own behaviour. Thanks to this switch in the identification, Athens acquires a predominant position in the *Essai* ('Fixed at Athens, as a centre, we will follow the revolutionary rays which emanated from it'),[119] just as it does in discourse devoted purely to ancient Greece. As soon as its image pales, in the fourth century, or as soon as the comparison falters, the *Essai* turns into a disparate collection of increasingly strange comparisons, and it is revealed to be a sadly disjointed rhapsody. On the other hand, the *Essai* probably did help to turn Athens into a kind of *analogon* for the whole of Greece, as is borne out by the chapters in which the Persian Wars are so closely confused with the revolutionary wars.[120]

There are many ambiguities in all this. It is true that Chateaubriand, who in his examination of 'the influence of the Republican Revolution upon Greece' (I, ch. XXV–XXVI [ch. XXI]) recognizes 'good things as well as bad', pretends to be speaking solely of Greece. But in every line France shows through, behind Greece, so much so that the reader is prompted to think: have not the French too just lived through 'the age of marvels'? (p. 130 [p. 98]). For them, to be sure, it was a case of bad things being mixed with good, and the liberty of the revolutionary wars being mixed with the exactions of the wars of conquest,[121] but, mediated by Greece, it certainly was revolutionary France that Chateaubriand was admiring,[122] its victories, its 'indomitable valour', its 'constancy in adversity'. In a significantly inconsequential passage, he even goes so far as to credit the Jacobins with the coherence which he was at the same time seeking to deny them.[123] Without wishing to, perhaps, or even realizing it, he was thus adopting the tactics of another *émigré*, the Old Oligarch, who, in the fifth century BC, had credited Athenian democracy with a rational and systematic policy. So it is really not surprising if other émigrés, Chateaubriand's 'companions in misfortune', gave a somewhat cold reception to his *Essai*.[124]

However, the *Essai* held one last surprise for them, and for us. So deeply gripped by ambiguity as to contradict his own contradictions, Chateaubriand, having identified the Athenian democrats with the French republicans, does not hesitate to compare the Thirty to the Convention, the Three Thousand to the Jacobins and Thrasybulos' democrats to the *émigré* royalists (II, ch. IV–VIII). It is worth noting, finally, that, as these very inconsequentialities indicate, Athens had by now become the accepted *topos* for reflecting upon France, one that provided an (inexhaustible) fund of commonplaces.

In that same year, 1797, Joseph de Maistre's *Considérations sur la France*, the *chef d'oeuvre* of reactionary literature on the French Revolution, was published, purportedly in London, but in reality in Basle.[125]

The first classic of this type had been Burke's *Reflections on the Revolution in France*, published in 1790.[126] In it, the theme of Greece is not entirely absent, but Burke, as a loyal heir to the scholastic tradition, does no more than deplore the decline of the Areopagus and the dangers inherent in government by decree (*pséphismata*). In the cases of Louis de Bonald, whose *Théorie du pouvoir politique* appeared in 1796 in Constance, to be seized forthwith on French territory by order of the Directory, and de Maistre, it was a quite different matter.

In his recent study on this 'mystic materialist', Robert Triomphe devoted more than a hundred pages to de Maistre and Hellenism, showing how 'Greece, lying Greece, which dared all in history', obsessed this theorist of the Counter-Revolution who, like so many after him, used Plato to support his attack on what had happened in Athens.[127]

Our present purpose is not to explore this theme anew, but simply to note whatever new perspectives are brought to the traditional discourse by the text of the *Considérations*, that of *L'Étude sur la souveraineté*, dated 1794–6, so written earlier but never published by de Maistre himself,[128] and by the *Fragments sur la France*, produced in the same year as the *Considérations*.[129] Three points seem to be essential. The first is the critique, partially updated from Plato, of all written legislation unless, of course, notwithstanding the difficulties involved, it was dictated by God himself – which was, after all, the case with all good legislation: that of Moses, that of Charlemagne and also that of Numa and that of Lycurgus, to which Joseph de Maistre repeatedly and obsessively returns.[130] Neither his attitude towards the figure of the lawgiver nor his attitude towards Greece altogether resembles that of Bonald, for in the last analysis Bonald recognizes only one constitution, the one dictated by the God of the Jews and the Christians, and categorically sets Lycurgus in opposition to Moses and the divine apocalypse in opposition to the 'prophetic trumpet' sounded by Condorcet.[131] Society preceded man and 'in Greece [we see] the general power of society becoming the particular power of each member of that association, that is to say society becoming man':[132] which is quite the opposite of the liberal vision of Greece. For Bonald, Greece as a whole is the enemy: 'the Greek [may be compared] to a theatre king who, once the play is over, sets down his sceptre and crown and, returning to his original state, intersperses his manners of a valet with the high-flown language of his role'.[133] Sparta is the most hateful of all: 'Sparta, to which some who claim to be the friends of humanity seek constantly to return us, Sparta was simply a school for uncouth warriors.'[134]

Joseph de Maistre was, in truth, in his own way, much closer to the tradition of the Enlightenment. When visiting Lausanne, he insisted, symbolically enough, upon making a pilgrimage to Gibbon's house.[135] For him, the lawgiver is inspired by God, but the lawgiver does exist; and the best legislation is, of course, oral: 'The more that is written down, the weaker the institution; that is why the most vigorous institution of secular Antiquity was in Sparta, where nothing was written down.'[136]

Accordingly – and this is our second point – de Maistre, like Rousseau, Mably and Robespierre, chose Sparta rather than Athens. His hostility towards that great city was fuelled by the works of Mitford, the Tory historian of Greece, and Sir William Young, who painted a picture of a trading democracy.[137] Going beyond the classic critiques of the fickleness of the democratic crowds who acclaimed Miltiades on one day only to condemn him the next,[138] de Maistre claimed that what Athens represented was the idea of deliberation; however, 'what is certain is that a civil constitution of the people is never the result of deliberation'.[139] The institution created by Solon, that exception to the rule according to which 'the greatest Lawgivers were always sovereigns', was 'the most fragile in Antiquity'.[140]

Joseph de Maistre was thus the inaugurator of the modern reactionary use of the Spartan mirage, a use which has persisted down through Nazi Germany and beyond. Within the space of a few years, Sparta, in a remarkable shift, slithered from the side of the Montagnards to that of the most violent of the 'reactors'. De Maistre was writing not against the Montagnards, who were in the past, but against the Thermidoreans, men such as Benjamin Constant; and the *Considérations* were a riposte to the latter's pamphlet 'On the strength of the present government and the need to rally to it'.[141]

Thirdly, de Maistre's relationship to the philosophy of the Enlightenment is in some ways reminiscent of the Marquis de Sade's. For de Sade, the state of nature is pure desire. For de Maistre, in the last analysis, there is no state of nature, since man is always a sociable being and savages are 'degenerate' or 'never acceded' to sociability. As for the 'savage child', a theme then fashionable, it was simply a 'story'.[142] But violence lies within us. 'We are all born despots.' 'Good savages' no more exist than 'peoples of gods' do. To refute the American dream, he draws support from Cornelius de Paux: 'I am not aware that anyone has answered the ingenious author of the *Recherches philosophiques sur les Américains*.'[143]

But this pessimism leads to a truly tragic view of history. Most innovatively, de Maistre uses Greek tragedy, along with Shakespeare, to fuel his philosophy of history. It was through blood sacrifice that humanity bought the right to existence and de Maistre cites Euripides' *Orestes*, in Greek (1. 1639–42): 'Apollo said that the beauty of Helen was simply an instrument which the gods used to set the Greeks against the Trojans and to make blood flow in order to *staunch*, on earth, the iniquity of men, who had become too numerous.'[144] Never mind if that 'iniquity' is a very inadequate translation of the Greek ὕβρισμα (outrage). What followed from this was something nobody in France had dared to say before him and nobody dared to repeat after him, namely that 'the radiant point for the Greeks was the terrible period of the Peloponnesian War'.[145]

Such was the war-machine de Maistre marshalled against Condorcet, 'that philosopher so dear to the Revolution, who spent his whole life preparing the misfortune of the present generation, benignly bequeathing perfection to our descendants'.[146]

However, this was certainly not the ideology of the majority of the liberal bourgeoisie, the ideology that a professional historian will now help us to seize upon.

Leaving London, Basle and emigration, we now return to France. It was in post-Thermidorean, then Napoleonic France, where scholarship, taken in hand by prestigious institutions, had already been reorganized following the 'troubles', that Greece really became established as a historical subject and that Pierre-Charles Lévesque produced his articulate discourse on that subject.

This was certainly the discourse of a specialist, produced in the Institute of which he, together with Volney, had been a founder member in Year IV.[147] But the class of moral and political sciences in which he elaborated that discourse between 1795 and 1803[148] was no ivory tower. Thanks to the presence in force there of the ideologues, it was a hub of intense activity: scholars held forth on the institutions of Sparta and Athens, but also grappled with the process of the formation of language, and the meaning and value of history. In response to the attacks against ancient history launched by the ardent Louis-Sebastien Mercier[149] ('What we are making is also history; let us make that history without models: it will have a better chance of being good'[150]), Lévesque spoke as a professional historian but without underestimating the impact of the event: 'Witnesses of our Revolution are surely well positioned to write the history of past ages. They have seen so many reversals of fortune, so many calamities.'[151] Long live ancient history, then . . . providing it is rooted in everyone's present. That was an obvious necessity, as the Napoleonic authorities were well aware. Thus, the *Report* that Bon-Joseph Dacier, the permanent secretary of the Académie des inscriptions[152] gave, in the presence of the Emperor, on *The progress of ancient history and literature since 1789*, concluded that the ancient texts and historico-philological scholarship 'ought to be made available to all'. Nobody strove harder than Lévesque, who was present at Dacier's side on that occasion, to carry out that programme, for in 1795 he published a translation of Thucydides, aimed at a wide public, in 1807 his *Histoire critique de la République romaine* appeared, and in 1811 his *Études d'histoire ancienne* followed, also in-tended for 'a numerous class of readers'.[153]

The focus of our attention here will be those *Études*, which – signifi-cantly in our view – are (albeit with some of the erudition pruned away) essentially based on the 'Mémoires' which Lévesque had presented in the Institute to his class of moral and political sciences, between 1766 and 1801.[154] Equally significant, in this connection, is the fact that Lévesque's life had not altogether followed the usual pattern for a professor of Greek history: that is indeed what he was recognized as in the Collège de France as early as 1791,[155] but in 1789, when Lévesque became a member of the Académie des inscriptions et belles-lettres, he was honoured there as a historian of Russia and the Middle Ages no less than as the translator of Thucydides. The life of Lévesque, born in 1736, included an early Russian period, for he taught at the Saint Petersburg school for cadets[156] from 1773 to 1780. He made the most of that experience and by 1781 had published an *Histoire de Russie*, followed in 1783 by an *Histoire des différents peuples soumis à la domination des Russes*: first 'a civil and political history', then 'a natural history of man', as he himself put it.[157] However, while still in Saint Petersburg, he had already published, in Amsterdam, *L'Homme moral* and *L'Homme pensant*, essays in which his thinking on the progress of humanity helped him to formulate the main lines of his general, measuredly liberal thought.[158] In 1788, he tackled the history of France, in a work on *La France sous les cinq premiers Valois* and, after beating a prudent retreat during the Terror, in 1795 he produced his translation of Thucydides. Then followed numerous 'Mémoires', presented in the Institute, and, finally, two works devoted to the history of Antiquity: *L'Histoire critique de la République romaine* in 1817 and, in 1811, one year before his death, the *Études*.

No hiatus interrupted the sequence of all these lines of research. When the author of the *Études d'histoire ancienne* claims the right to speak 'as a Frenchman proud of his country and as a European glorying in the progress of modern Europe', and not to limit himself 'to a humble adoration of ancient Greece',[159] we recognize the preoccupations which, thirty years earlier, had prompted Lévesque to explain to his compatriots that Russia was a part of Europe. Opposing the myth of a Moscow that was 'a desert inhabited by a few wild animals that [Peter the Great] managed to turn into men',[160] Lévesque opened up a new era in the historiography of Russia;[161] in fact, he strikingly demonstrated the determination to destroy all mirages by which his entire *oeuvre* is characterized: the mirage of Peter the Great, the mirage of 'Frankish democracy', that of the 'Roman republic', the Spartan mirage: they all came under attack from Lévesque.[162]

He used 'moral history' to explode the Roman republic and its 'fanaticism for liberty',[163] and history 'as science and as art' to examine Russia, ancient Greece and medieval France. For those are the three subjects that dominate Lévesque's work. In his view, there were many affinities between sixteenth-century Russia and ancient Greece,[164] and this does not surprise him; then, concluding from the links between their respective languages that the Slav and the Greek peoples were related, he goes on to declare that the Greeks originated in the North.[165] On the other hand, France's links with Greece came from the South, and it is through the South that the French language reveals its Greek origins; and this leads on to Lévesque reminding us of 'the ancient colony founded at Marseilles by the Phocaeans'.[166]

Russia, Greece and France: it is hard to distinguish between the parts played by the historian's itinerary of scholarly research on the one hand and his theoretico-emotional commitments on the other.

The Greece of Pierre-Charles Lévesque is a composite construction in which the heritage of Isocrates and Plutarch, that is to say Abbé Barthélemy,[167] coexists, not without a number of glaring contradictions, alongside his reading of Thucydides. Thus, on the very same page in the *Études*, Lévesque describes Pericles both as the demagogue who changed the democracy of Theseus and Solon into a 'violently conflict-ridden regime' and also as an irreplaceable statesman, whose death delivered up the Athenians to 'upstart wretches such as Cleon'.[168] But in general, Lévesque does make a choice; and his choice is for Thucydides, 'of all the ancient historians, the one who deserves the most trust'[169] and, better still, the one who, in the context of an emerging liberal State, 'should be studied more than all others in countries where all the citizens may one day take part in government'; at which point he goes on to remark: 'A most enlightened member of the English Parliament has said that there could be no controversial question that arose in the two chambers upon which Thucydides could not shed some light.'[170] What Lévesque thus prescribes is a Thucydides who can be of use to a good bourgeoisie, a Thucydides whose return, in the middle of the Thermidorean period, marked a definitive break with the imaginary representation of the Greece of the lawgivers so dear to the Revolutionaries.[171] However, the French Revolution sheds new light upon this Thucydides from whom each and everyone can henceforth learn about 'the political action of peoples in relation to other peoples'.[172] If the historian of *The Peloponnesian War* mentions the presence of slaves or the active involvement of women alongside the *demos* of Corcyra, in their struggle against the *oligoi*, Lévesque intervenes to stress how natural that alliance between the people and the slaves was or to explain the conduct of the women, 'always more extreme than men in movements of sedition'.[173] In actual fact, Thucydides had said the exact opposite, explaining that 'the women overcame their natural inclinations, to join in the tumult' (III, 74). But for Lévesque, clearly, fidelity to the text was less important than being effective; and his readers understood, as they recalled how the society of 'Revolutionary women' had constituted the most pugnacious of all the *Enragés*' supporters.[174]

The Revolution had thus interposed itself between Greece and its historian and when, this time using Herodotus as his source, Lévesque recounted how the exiled Pisistratus had made use of the services of a false Athena to effect his return to Athens, it was hardly surprising that the modern historian turned this flower-girl disguised as 'Wisdom' into a figure, allegorical even for the Athenians, who was a Greek prefiguration of all the 'Goddesses of Reason' of the Revolutionary festivals.[175] The recent history of France thus illuminated that of Greece or – to be more precise – of Athens. For to illuminate the history of Sparta, Lévesque goes further back in the history of France, to a time he knew well since he had studied it, the time of 'the odious aristocracy which afflicted France under the first and second races, when a small and privileged caste commandeered the name of the French people for itself alone'.[176]

Hostile to work, commerce and industry, totally devoted to the profession of arms, 'ignorant, ferocious and uncouth': such were the Spartans, 'those men whom one may justly call nobles' (and at this point there was no need to go right back to the Merovingians to understand the allusion).[177] It is accordingly hardly surprising that Lévesque should choose Athens rather than Sparta, Athens and the 'truth of facts' rather than Sparta and 'consecrated ideas about the excellence of the Lacedaemonian constitution'.[178] 'One admires warrior Sparta . . . but one loves its rival',[179] he declares forthrightly. And even that admiration is somewhat grudgingly given: as the author of an *Essai sur l'histoire de l'esprit humain*, who as early as 1779 was criticizing 'the exclusive esteem reserved for warriors',[180] Lévesque could hardly wholeheartedly admire a 'warrior monastery' which the reforms of Lycurgus arrested at a stage of 'ignorance and barbarity'.[181] And how could he admire the Spartan education which he had condemned in 1775 in his *L'Homme moral* and which the Jacobins wished to use as a model? If the law of civil society is the preservation of property – and, for Lévesque, children were property – how could he accept the 'tyranny' of a republican State which took the education of children out of the hands of the family?[182] Even the organization of his *Études* reflects the Athenian sympathies of its author: it is surely not by chance that the dark ages of Greece are evoked in the chapter devoted to Sparta, or that the history of Sparta is explicitly introduced simply to fill in gaps in the history of Athens,[183] whereas the history of Athens, in contrast, illuminates the whole history of Greece down to Alexander; in fact, it affects the whole of humanity, as Lévesque intimates before embarking upon his account of the Peloponnesian War, which was to be so damaging to Athens.[184]

Respect for property and for private life and the promotion of commerce, work and industry:[185] these are the principal characteristics of Lévesque's Athens. Had he in fact created the very paradigm of bourgeois Athens, a construction of liberal imaginary representations to cater for every development in history? Bearing in mind the fact that, in this model of civil liberty, democracy is something as it were tacked on, at the most an inevitable evil, that would perhaps be an over-hasty conclusion. There is no doubt about it: what Lévesque loves in Athens is the industrious city far more than the democratic *polis* ... Not that he had any liking for the opponents of the Athenian regime: 'the ferocious oligarchy' of the Thirty was much too reminiscent of the Terror for him to feel any sympathy with it.[186] However, of all the leaders of the democrats in the classical period, Thrasybulos did deserve to be known as the 'friend of liberty', because he was 'no less a friend of humanity, justice and order'; Lévesque had read Xenophon and appreciated the fact that the victorious Thrasybulos had pleaded for there to be no revolutionary agitation within the restored democracy.[187] It is true that the great period for democracy remained that of Solon, and it was with reference to Solon that Lévesque exalted civil liberty and respect for property. One ought really to cite the entire page in which Lévesque comments upon the arguments with which the lawgiver countered any idea of a division of the land, but let us at any rate note his declaration that 'to strike against property would be to strike against the very principle of association' and that nothing good can come from 'enforced equality', short of employing 'to maintain it, the most violent of means of action; action which would, besides, run counter to the social goal, since one of the objectives that gave rise to societies was the associates' legitimate desire to enjoy the greatest peace, with the support of one another'.[188]

And what of Athenian democracy? Or rather, what of what we twentieth-century historians call 'Athenian democracy', which, ever since Grote and a number of others, has been considered to have begun with Cleisthenes? Lévesque's answer is clear: it was simply a corruption of Solon's democracy, characterized by excess and destined to suffer the misfortunes that inevitably assail 'regimes that are too popular'.[189] Pericles symbolized that democracy, and posterity is invited always to blame him 'for having destroyed strong government'.[190] To recapitulate: between Solon and Thrasybulos, a violently conflictual regime; between 1789 and Thermidor, the Revolution. The juxtaposition speaks for itself, and Athenian democracy certainly seems to have suffered from being judged by the yardstick of 'France's latest troubles'. Admittedly, Lévesque never states that identification openly; but even when he limits himself to the quite contrary comparison between the Thirty and the Montagnards, we should make no mistake about it: for him, the oligarchy of the Thirty is simply the violent and inevitable corollary of democracy. Once again, the history of France makes it possible to interpret that of Athens.

However, the last word goes to distance. In conclusion to the long study devoted to the 'constitution of the Republic of Athens', Lévesque points out that Athens is far away, very distant in time:

> Because Athens shone with the greatest splendour in literature and the arts, we like to believe that everything was fine in that republic – its constitution, its legislation, the form of its tribunals. I admit that in those areas it did leave us some fine models to follow; but I also think that in all these things we are superior to it and to all the republics of Greece. . . . We have not only their experience and that of the Romans, but also that of all the long centuries that we ourselves have lived through.[191]

'We have lived through. . . .' The Revolution is over, Athens is far distant. The time of history is in place.

What Benjamin Constant (1767–1830), a contemporary of both Saint-Just and Napoleon, set out to do was not to produce a historical discourse that established the Greeks as the ancestors of the French liberals, but to find an ideological niche for modern liberalism and, to that end, mark out the necessary distance between, on the one hand, the model capable of inspiring both Saint-Just and Joseph de Maistre and, on the other, the regime he believed to be at once possible and desirable. For him, it was a matter neither of describing a vision of the future, as Condorcet had done, nor of aggressively announcing a break, as Volney did. Rather, it was a matter of establishing a correct distance. And to that end, it would not be enough simply to make use of the Athens-versus-Sparta theme, although Constant certainly did also frequently resort to that already old ploy.[192]

Constant stands out amongst the ideologues of the liberal bourgeoisie in that he possessed not only a college training in Greek and Latin, but also a university education acquired in Erlangen and Edinburgh. He was a personal acquaintance of Gibbon and in 1787 had translated part of the Scot John Gillies's history of Greece. Perhaps that is a detail with symbolic significance for, while Gillies was by no means a democrat, he certainly was not a passionate reactionary as was Mitford, the source of de Maistre's inspiration.[193] Constant was to renew his familiarity with the subject in 1803 and frequently thereafter, in Göttingen, and would become one of the few Frenchmen with a direct knowledge of the emerging German scholarship, acquired not only through his reading of Wolf and Creuzer but also through his conversations with A. W. Schlegel, whom he met in Mme de Stael's entourage. On 14 September 1804, he noted in his diary: 'I shall never be as erudite on the subject of the ancient world as the professional scholars. In order to become so I would have to sacrifice time that I need for thinking.'[194] It was perhaps lucky for Constant that, despite his vastly wide reading, he never did become an erudite scholar, for it is quite true that, where others went in for repetition, he for his part preferred to think.[195]

Constant, like Volney, was a typical Thermidorean, but, unlike Volney, he never became a senator, a count of the Empire or a Restoration peer. In a letter dated 25 May 1795, he wrote as follows: 'Property and talent, those two reasonable reasons for inequality among men, are about to resume their rights.'[196] And *inequality*, along with liberty, was certainly a subject to which he repeatedly returned throughout his *oeuvre*. However, in contrast to Volney, in the early days he subscribed totally to the traditional view of Antiquity, as is demonstrated by the pamphlets and speeches that he published between January 1796 and the summer of 1797.[197] To those dreaming of a Restoration, he predicted the coming of a republican Vendée and heroic rebels: 'Truth would be their religion, history their legend, the great men of Antiquity their saints, liberty their life to come. They would not hope to rise from the dead in three days but they would fight and die as free men.'[198] Refuting those who identified monarchy with virtue, he declared: 'The Roman *monarchy* was founded by brigands and the Roman monarchy never subjugated even a quarter of

Italy. The Roman *republic* was founded by the most austere and virtuous of men.'[199] And, already, there appeared a theme which, in modulated forms, was to continue to resurface throughout his life: 'The ancient republics produced men who were illustrious in every field. Miltiades, Aristides and Xenophon cultivated learning, were army commanders and attracted crowds to the tribune; already such glorious examples are reappearing amongst us.'[200] Not until his famous pamphlet, *De l'esprit de conquête et de l'usurpation*, which was published in Germany in January 1814, did a new and original set of questions appear in Constant's published works. In the mean time, in 1802, Benjamin Constant had been ejected from the *Tribunat*.

The Bibliothèque nationale's recent acquisition of seven manuscripts of works by Constant, completed in 1810[201] but for the most part written between 1806 and 1810, has shown that, as from his ejection, Constant's view of the relations between Hellenism and the modern world crystallized definitively. The two principal texts included in these manuscripts, the *Principes de politique applicables à tous les gouvernements* and the *Fragments d'un ouvrage abandonné sur la possibilité d'une constitution républicaine dans un grand pays* – something that de Maistre had declared to be an impossibility[202] – constituted, word for word, or almost, the source of all that Constant later published on the subject, including the *Esprit de conquête*, whole chapters of which come from the manuscripts now in the Bibliothèque nationale, and the famous lecture of 1819, *De la liberté des Anciens comparée à celle des modernes*.[203]

Like his contemporary, Hegel, Constant speaks of the Greek city as of a harmonious totality.[204] Even in 1827, at the end of his life, he republished, in *Mélanges de littérature et de politique*, a text in which he had written as follows: 'There are some harmonious periods in which man seems to have enjoyed his faculties to the full' and evoked Socrates as a soldier at Potidaea, Aeschylus at Salamis and even Sophocles, the *archon* (which Sophocles never was). And in all this he found arguments to justify the social mobility produced and promoted by the French Revolution. Stable lads became generals. 'Despite all the foreboding predictions, it was precisely because no individual was limited to a single profession that every profession was practised.'[205]

In the last analysis, Benjamin Constant accepts that the liberty of an Athenian citizen was greater than that of a modern individual, even an English or a Swiss one. In an unpublished text, he writes as follows:

Accordingly, we should not say: the Athenians were freer than we are, so the human race is less free than formerly. The Athenians were a small proportion of the inhabitants of Greece; Greece was a small part of Europe, the rest of the world was barbarian, and the vast majority of the inhabitants of Greece itself was composed of slaves.[206]

We are separated from Greece by three revolutions which have constituted undeniable progress, the one that put an end to slavery, the one that destroyed feudalism and the one that put a stop to the privileges of the nobility.[207] All this obviously stems from Condorcet, including the recognition of the importance of slavery, upon which Constant was to pronounce in trenchant fashion in 1819: 'Without the slave population of Athens, twenty thousand Athenians would not have been able to deliberate every day in the public square.'[208] From a modern point of view, then, wherein lies Constant's originality? It finds expression in the triple opposition that he establishes between war and commerce, participation and representation, and the pleasure of action and the pleasure of reflection. That is the set of ideas that we must now consider.

Let us make no mistake: there is a double or even more complicated meaning to this συστοιχία. The war-participation-pleasure in action combination certainly characterizes the ancient world as a whole, and the commerce-representation-pleasure in reflection combination characterizes the modern world. But the first combination also characterizes the period of history which began in 1789 and ended with the fall of Napoleon, a period that was marked by the modern imitation of ancient republics.[209]

Within the ancient world, there was to some extent a similar opposition in respect of the Athens–Sparta pair. And that is the source of all Constant's ambiguity, for he borrows, in particular from Cornelius de Pauw, the description of a modern, trading Athens: 'In Athens, one enjoyed greater individual liberty than in Sparta, because Athens was both a warrior and a trading society.'[210] The Athenians knew how to use a bill of exchange – in short, to a certain degree, this was a modern city: 'It is quite remarkable that it is precisely Athens that our modern reformers avoid adopting as model: the reason for this is that Athens was too much like us;' whereupon Constant proceeds to appeal in the same breath to the examples of Xenophon and Isocrates, to convince the reader 'of the altogether modern character of the Athenians'.[211] That modernity stood in opposition to the warrior and egalitarian monastery of Sparta, so dear to philosophers both ancient and modern (Plato, Mably). But even in Athens, the reign of commerce was not unchallenged for, having read Hume, Constant recognized that 'in Athens, ... the greatest trading republic of Antiquity, the interest in maritime business was about 60 per cent whereas ordinary interest was only 12 per cent, so great was the danger implied by long sea voyages'.[212] Trading peoples did exist in Antiquity, as did an embryonic struggle between the spirit of conquest and the spirit of commerce (for Constant picked up the opposition that we have earlier seen introduced by Jean-François Melon[213]); however, the normal mode of acquiring wealth was warfare: 'We have now arrived at the age of commerce, which must necessarily take the place of the age of war, just as the age of war had necessarily to precede it.' The transition from the one to the other signified progress: 'The one is a savage impulse, the other civilized calculation.' The one can influence the other: 'Commerce has even changed the nature of war.'[214] Carthage was defeated, but the modern Carthage, that is England, was successful: 'If a struggle took place now between Rome and Carthage, the hopes of the entire world would lie with Carthage. It would have modern *mores* and the world spirit as its allies.'[215] It was a case of what Auguste Comte was to call 'a positivist spirit'.

Commerce implies a world of differences, which is why it is associated with representation, not participation. However obvious the oppositions between direct democracies and representative regimes may seem to us – in a sense, since Rousseau – and between Antiquity and the modern world, and however numerous Constant's predecessors, quite apart from those whom he himself cites,[216] the debate was, at the time, far from being considered closed (a point on which, as we shall see, a professional such as Victor Duruy was to be quite mistaken).[217] Constant's own thinking stemmed from as far back as Rousseau, but his immediate masters were, in particular, Condorcet and Sismondi. In his *Histoire des républiques italiennes du Moyen Age*, Sismondi had written:

> In the Republics of Antiquity, there was no such thing as civil liberty: a citizen recognized himself to be a slave of the nation to which he belonged; he abandoned himself entirely to the decisions of the sovereign, never challenging the legislator's right to control all his actions and constrain his will in every respect; but, on the other hand, he was himself, in his turn, that sovereign and that legislator.[218]

The non-existence of a civil society had, as its corollary, a high degree of political participation. But what was liberty, in modern times, if not, first and foremost, 'the peaceful enjoyment of individual independence'?[219] The aim of the modern representative system is to promote that peaceful enjoyment, it being understood that the political pleasure, or pleasure of action that the Ancients enjoyed will no longer be anything but a vicarious pleasure: 'The vast majority, always excluded from power, inevitably takes no more than a fleeting interest in its public existence.'[220] Benjamin Constant makes no attempt to sweeten that pill:

Given that political liberty offers less pleasure than in the past, and that the disorders that it can bring in its train are less easy to bear, we must preserve only what is absolutely necessary from it. In this day and age, to try to use political liberty to console men for the loss of civil liberty is to go against the present spirit of the human race.[221]

And elsewhere he declares that moderns 'are at the very most called to the exercise of sovereignty only through representation, that is to say in a fictitious manner',[222] and so true is it that Constant, like Hegel, is susceptible to nostalgia for the 'fine totality',[223] that he also writes as follows: 'The Ancients possessed total conviction on all matters; we have no more than a flaccid and floating conviction about virtually nothing, and seek in vain to distract ourselves from that incompleteness. The word illusion does not exist in any ancient language, because the word is only created when the thing no longer exists.'[224]

Enjoyment does exist in the modern world, but it is no longer the immediate pleasure of participation. Amongst us, 'immediate pleasure is less acute: it comprises none of the delights of power; it is a pleasure of reflection: for the Ancients, pleasure lay in action. Clearly, our kind of pleasure was less attractive; you could not expect men to make so many sacrifices in order to obtain and preserve it.'[225] Let us by all means give up the idea of all upheavals, since the Revolution is over. Let us abandon all legislative ambitions: 'No more Lycurguses, no more Numas'.[226] However, Constant does not commit himself to the path of bourgeois France without casting a discreet glance over his shoulder – in the direction of the Greek city and its 'modern imitators' of Year II. To be sure, the 'security of private pleasures'[227] is one thing, but a dream is another:

I shall not join the ranks of the detractors of republics. Those of Antiquity, in which men's faculties developed in so wide a field, with such strength from their own resources and with such a sense of energy and dignity, fill any soul of the slightest value with a deep and special kind of emotion. The erstwhile elements of a nature of a, so to speak, earlier kind than ours seem to stir within us with these memories.[228]

Being bourgeois does not stop one from being nostalgic.

As we now near the end of our study, we must consider Victor Duruy and the *Histoire grecque* that he published in 1851,[229] a work that was to run into countless editions.

Clearly, our survey of Thermidorean ideology over half a century of French history and ancient Greek historiography has carried us far beyond Thermidor itself. In this final stage, everything is carefully deliberated. That is because history thrives on decentring shifts and, above all, because the construction of an imaginary representation is never completed in a day: in the event, it was not until the mid-nineteenth century that the bourgeois Athens of the men of Thermidor acquired its effective form as a model, in the historical *oeuvre* of Duruy. At that point its own history was over and its University career began:[230] nothing could more resemble a page by Duruy than a page by Glotz.[231] In the mean time, it is true, the 'real' Greece, the Greece of the 1821 uprising, had to some extent taken over in men's minds from the imaginary Greece we have been considering; and men such as Chateaubriand and Constant had not been unaware of this transformation of philhellenism. However, our own concern, here, is the University.

Others have already remarked upon the determining influence that Duruy exerted upon the teaching of history in France,[232] an influence so immediate and spectacular that the Hachette publishing house was prompted to entrust him with the direction of an *Histoire universelle* series. A crucial fact to note is that well before Victor Duruy the Minister '[mobilized] scholarship to bring it within the grasp of as many people as possible',[233] Duruy the teacher had already decided to place his trust in popularization.[234] The University world in general was to follow him, but not until considerably later (which was really not surprising, as should be apparent by the end of this study).

Duruy, who was a successful textbook author, was teaching at the Lycée Saint-Louis in 1851. He belonged to the generation, nurtured on Michelet, that was inspired by a 'gust of liberalism' and 'researched the destinies of different peoples with sympathy . . . , but with no frantic waving of the flag of democracy'.[235] But given that this specialist of the ancient world (in particular Rome, his lifelong passion) believed that ancient history had something to say on the score of the most contemporary of political issues,[236] it is worth noting that, in mid-nineteenth century France, the pro-Athenian slant of his *Histoire* was still capable of provoking indignation.

It was Charles Nisard who, in the name of university orthodoxy,[237] led the attack in the extremely official *Journal de l'Instruction publique*.[238] Nisard, a confirmed partisan of Sparta, 'that strong, coherent government which ensured the moral superiority of the Dorian aristocracy' and which alone knew how to 'create lasting things',[239] first reproached Duruy for manifesting a 'juvenile admiration' for Athens, then, in condescending vein, proceeded to enumerate the many flaws that reactionary scholarship, in 1851 (and still today), complacently detected in Athenian democracy.[240]

The tone of this quarrel was set from the start: Duruy was a mere school-teacher with views that lacked 'height' and a schoolteacher's language and ideas. We are led to believe that the University remained obdurately Spartan: there were no defectors. But did this mean that, as Nisard implied, secondary teaching had now gone over to Athens? Having consulted the official textbooks in which praise for Cimon and Phocion is accompanied by criticism of the Athenians' 'insatiable ambition',[241] we are not altogether convinced of that. But it is quite true that, under the July Monarchy, there was a tendency to condemn Sparta and its 'terrible policies'.[242] All the same, the battle between Athens and Sparta was not yet won, as Duruy pointed out in his reply to Nisard, a reply that is interesting for a number of reasons: because Duruy, proudly accepting 'the humble condition of schoolteacher', claims the right to 'write a book for those who have to read it'; and above all because the distinction that he draws between Athens on the one hand and its political regime on the other ('it is not democracy that attracts me but the great things that it did') should not be put down solely to prudence. In Duruy's own words, 'My preferences in the past are not political but philosophical . . . In Greece, I am *on the side of Athens, which was productive*, and against Sparta, which was sterile'. This polemic thus clearly set out the antagonistic positions for the future: Sparta and reaction,[243] versus Athens and productivity.

Duruy's type of history set out to be edifying, to draw lessons from facts,[244] but, in its concern to distribute good and bad marks, it was liable to misunderstand a number of essential phenomena: it was thus *de rigueur* to lament 'the insurmountable instinct of municipal isolationism produced by the minute subdivision of the land, which militated against the formation of a great Greek state',[245] but in this schema, the city-State figured as no more than a regrettable incident. In other words, Antiquity was seen more than ever in the light of the present. As a historian of Rome, Duruy interpreted Roman law through the Declaration of Human Rights,[246] and behind the historian of Greece who described Pericles' 'social policies' with such enthusiasm could be glimpsed the minister who, when he introduced contemporary history into the curriculum for *lycées*, made the central point of these studies the defeat of socialism, 'overcome, thanks to the Government's constant efforts . . . to satisfy . . . popular interests'.[247]

To be sure, each form of society has its day, its hour,[248] and the time of Greece had gone forever. But the fact that it was so long gone did not make it impossible for a liberal bourgeois to feel at home in ancient Greece. For Greece was on the right side, the side of commerce, colonization; in a word, civilization, for its geographical destiny had been to be given 'the sea as its domain'.[249] Greece was on the side of the West, as opposed to the 'static East': did it not invent private morality and

civil liberty and, for the first time, lift aloft 'the torch which still illuminates Europe and which Europe in its turn carried on to the New World
discovered a bare three centuries ago and also to the old Orient that it has
just rediscovered'?[250] Greece, finally, was on the side of political liberty,
for an inevitable evolution led the Greeks from royalty to 'the self-
governing city'.[251] Duruy's picture of Greece is a cumbersome schema
which historians of Greece are still finding it difficult to get out of the
way. According to Duruy, Greece was but a short step from inventing the
representative regime. Page xvii of his Preface is worth perusing: 'Greece
saw everything, tried everything. It ended up with the only system that
might have saved it: a moderate democracy, which satisfied its inveterate
instinct for liberty, and a *virtually representative government*, which made
unity possible.' We are led to believe that 'the formation of a great Hellenic
State would have saved Greece' through unity and 'the equal conditions
offered to one and all'.[252] Perhaps fiction provides history's most forward-
looking visions. For, once Duruy stopped dreaming about Greece, he took
instead to regretting bitterly Greece's subordination of the individual to
the State, the dangers that weighed upon property, the civil wars, and
slavery, which prevented the formation of 'a middle class strong enough
to impose peace upon all parties'.[253]

But if, despite everything, ancient Greece is 'the school of the world',
it owes that position to Athens, and, caught between praise and blame,
Duruy's *Histoire grecque* is organized around the opposition between
Sparta and Athens. Sparta, the definitely negative pole, symbolizing
alienation of oneself to the State, is nothing but a war-machine 'incapable
of producing anything' or of participating in 'the common labour of all
humanity'.[254] Athens, the almost wholly positive pole, is gentle with its
slaves, open to foreigners, maternal to its war-orphans.[255] With its 'institutions that were the most humane, the most truly liberal that Antiquity
ever had', this is an Athens that deserves Duruy's 'sympathetic affection'.[256] In Athens, the State – that is, of course, Duruy's own anachron-
istic description – uses its wealth to help its citizens, in a kind of welfare
system for all; property, the family and work are protected by Athena,
'the working goddess who created the olive tree, invented the useful arts
and taught wives all the domestic virtues'.[257] Trade and imperialism are
mutually supportive, to the great benefit of civilization, prosperity and
social equilibrium,[258] and Duruy has nothing but praise for the Athenian
arché, which 'gave these pacified seas over to the spirit of commerce and
the arts'.[259] Better still, commerce and political liberty henceforth went
hand in hand[260] and when Themistocles moved the tribune from which
speeches were delivered to the Pnyx, he did so 'so that orators could,
from this spot, constantly show the people that the sea spread out at their

feet was their domain'.[261] It was by now out of the question for Duruy to criticize democracy and he takes the part of not only Pericles (naturally) but also – perhaps for the first time in the French historiography of Greece – Ephialtes, 'the virtuous Ephialtes' whose only crime was to have 'allowed the Athenians to drink deeply from the cup of liberty',[262] and also the navy at Samos openly defying the oligarchs of the *polis*, 'for Athens was no longer in Athens, but on its ships'.[263]

At this point we will bring our tour through imaginary bourgeois representations to an end, for the paradigm of Athens has been firmly established. But that does not mean that we ourselves have regarded the establishment of this Athens as a victory, as if real progress had been made or an irresistible evolution had finally been accomplished: the silences and contradictions in Duruy's kind of history will continue to weigh heavily on the questions that historians should now be asking about Antiquity. For instance, land, the Greek model of wealth and the Greek criterion of citizenship, is systematically ignored by Duruy in favour of 'commerce, industry and banking';[264] the agrarian crisis of the seventh century goes unrecognized or is avoided, certainly not regarded as worth considering as a possible cause of colonization.[265] Solon is credited only with a monetary reform, and the fortune of the Pentacosiomedimnoi is first calculated in drachmas, then converted into francs.[266] As for democracy, Duruy can accommodate it only by forcing a comparison with census-based or even representative regimes and, even then, not without serious contradictions. Within the space of a few pages, he praises Athens for having turned its citizens into an aristocracy, in relation to which slaves, metics and foreigners constitute the people,[267] and regrets that Pericles limited citizenship to an 'imperceptible minority of fourteen thousand' who were quite incapable of 'keeping in subjection' the multitudes who made up the empire.[268] He even writes as follows: 'The general assembly . . . , placed at the head of the empire, was simply a *chamber of representatives* more numerous than our own.'[269] The empire to which he refers is supposed to be Athens'; the general assembly is the *ekklesia*: the enormity of these inaccuracies hardly needs pointing out. Then, just a few pages later, he writes: 'Even the most obscure citizen feels he is important, for he has a vote in a popular assembly which seldom comprises more than five thousand people.'[270]

Athens or the history of the bourgeoisie? Athens or the bourgeoisie facing its own hesitations: a republic or an empire? An authoritarian empire or a liberal empire? Athens assumes all these faces at once.

In this study we have tried to show how the image of bourgeois Athens became established in France. But in other countries in Europe and elsewhere in the world, other images are to be found and this attempt of ours will only assume its full interest if and when it becomes possible to compare all the different images of all these different concepts of Athens'.

Notes

1 Z. Yavetz, 'Why Rome? "Zeitgeist" and Ancient Historians in Early Nineteenth-Century Germany', *American Journal of Philology*, 97, 1976, pp. 276–96.
2 See E. M. Butler, *The Tyranny of Greece over Germany*, Cambridge University Press, Cambridge, 1935.
3 With the aid, in particular, of the monograph by S. Rytkönen, *Barthold Georg Niebuhr als Politiker und Historiker*, Suomalainen Tiedeakatemia, Helsinki, 1968; this book appears to have escaped the attention of Z. Yavetz. See also, more recently, the book by Alfred Heuss, *Barthold Georg Niebuhrs wissenschaftliche Anfänge*, Vandenhoek & Ruprecht, Göttingen, 1981, in particular pp. 153–88, ch. VI, entitled ' "Lex agraria" und Französische Revolution'.
4 Rytkönen, *Niebuhr*, p. 34.
5 A. H. L. Heeren, *Handbuch der Geschichte der Staate des Alterthums mit besonderer Rücksicht auf ihre Verfassungen, ihren Handel und ire Colonien*, Göttingen, 1799, pp. VII–VIII; we have slightly corrected the translation by A. L. Thurot, Paris, 1827, pp. X–XI, upon which this quotation is based.
6 Diderot, 'Pensées détachées ou fragments politiques échappés au portefeuille d'un philosophe', here cited from *Oeuvres complètes*, vol. X, Club français du livre, Paris, 1971, pp. 81–3; it is worth noting that, in 1743, Diderot had published a translation of the *History of Greece*, in three volumes, by Temple Stanyan.
7 V. Duruy, *Histoire grecque*, Hachette, Paris, 1851, p. 103.
8 Turgot, *Oeuvres*, vol. I, G. Schelle (ed.), Alcan, Paris, 1913, pp. 214–34; we are citing pp. 217, 225–6; the importance of this speech and the one Turgot delivered on the role of Christianity in history is stressed, following others, by F. E. Manuel, *The Prophets of Paris*, Harvard University Press, Cambridge, Mass., 1962, p. 13.
9 See C. Joret, *D'Ansse de Villoison et l'Hellénisme en France pendant le dernier tiers du XVIIIᵉ siècle*, Champion, Paris, 1910, pp. 331–2.
10 See C. Rabany, *Les Schweighaeuser, biographie d'une famille de savants alsaciens d'après leur correspondance inédite*, Berger-Levrault, Paris, 1884, p. 18.
11 P.-C. Lévesque, *Histoire de Russie*, vol. I, Paris, 1782, p. 71. This phrase disappeared when Lévesque re-edited his work for the second time in 1800, then again in 1812; instead, the passage read as follows: 'Our fathers knew very little about Russia; quite a few of them were even in ignorance of the name of this empire, the largest in the world' (vol. I, p. 91 in the 1812 edition). See chapter 5 below, pp. 141–169.
12 See Renée Simon, 'Nicolas Fréret, académicien', *Studies on Voltaire*, vol. XVII, Geneva, 1961. Nicolas Fréret is a central figure in the thesis by Chantal Grell, *Histoire ancienne et érudition: la Grèce et Rome dans les travaux des érudits en*

France au XVIIIe siècle, Paris IV, 1984. See also Mouza Raskolnikoff, *Histoire romaine et critique historique dans l'Europe des Lumières: la naissance de l'hypercritique dans l'historiographie de la Rome antique*, 'thèse d'État', Université de Strasbourg II, 1986.

13 See, however, E. Egger, *L'Hellénisme en France*, Didier, Paris, 1869, vol. II, p. 275; Elizabeth Rawson, *The Spartan Tradition in European Thought*, Clarendon Press, Oxford, 1969, p. 260.

14 P. Vidal-Naquet, 'Tradition de la démocratie grecque', published as the Preface to the French translation (by Monique Alexandre) of M. I. Finley, *Démocratie antique et démocratie moderne*, Payot, Paris, 1976. See also chapter 5 below, pp. 141–169.

15 Also published at this time, as well as Volney's *Leçons d'histoire*, Dupuis's *L'Origine de tous les cultes* and Condorcet's *Tableau historique*. This was also the period when texts such as Adam Smith's *The Wealth of Nations* and the works of C. De Pauw, Condillac and Mably were reprinted or collected together.

16 E. Cassirer, *La Philosophie des Lumières*, tr. P. Quillet, Éd. de Minuit, 1966, p. 207.

17 J.-P. De Bougainville, 'Vues générales sur les antiquités grecques du premier âge, et sur les premières histoires de la nation grecque . . .', *Mémoires de littérature tirés des registres de l'Académie royale des inscriptions et belles-lettres*, vol. XXIX, Paris, 1764, pp. 27–86; we cite from pp. 32–3. A parallel progress was expressed in the following two sets of three: wild, nomad, civilized; priest, warrior, merchant.

18 On the *philosophes'* ideas on space, see the thesis by N. Broc, *La Géographie des philosophes*, Champion, Lille, 1972, and, for the end of the century, S. Moravia, 'Philosophie et géographie à la fin du XVIIIe siècle', *Studies on Voltaire*, vol. LVII, Geneva, 1967, pp. 937–1011.

19 We by no means possess all the studies necessary for such an undertaking. The only work of synthesis in which the problem is seriously tackled is Peter Gay's *The Enlightenment: An Interpretation*, vol. I, *The Rise of Modern Paganism*, Weidenfeld and Nicolson, London, 1967; on the Spartan mirage, see the two chapters devoted to the eighteenth century by E. Rawson, *The Spartan Tradition*, pp. 220–67; on Voltaire, D. H. Jory, 'Voltaire and the Greeks', *Studies on Voltaire*, vol. CLIII, Geneva, 1976, pp. 1169–87; on Rousseau, D. Leduc-Rayette, *Jean-Jacques Rousseau et le mythe de l'Antiquité*, Vrin, Paris, 1974, and above all R. Leigh, 'Jean-Jacques Rousseau and the myth of Antiquity in the Eighteenth Century', in R. R. Bolgar (ed.), *Classical Influences*, pp. 155–68; on Diderot, J. Seznec, *Essais sur Diderot et l'Antiquité*, Oxford University Press, Oxford, 1957; on Montesquieu, an admirable article, possibly the only one that addresses precisely the questions that we have been posing: G. Cambiano, 'Montesquieu e le antiche repubbliche greche', *Rivista di filosofia*, LXV, 2–3, April–September 1974, pp. 93–144. We have, naturally, learnt a great deal from A. Momigliano's *Contributi*, especially his latest article on our subject, 'Eighteenth Century Prelude to Mr Gibbon', *Gibbon et Rome à la lumière de l'historiographie moderne*, P. Ducrey (ed.), Droz, Geneva, 1977, pp. 57–70.

20 See E. Rawson, *The Spartan Tradition*, pp. 255–7, and, on Voltaire and China,

the fundamental synthesis by B. Guy, 'The French Image of China before and after Voltaire', *Studies on Voltaire*, vol. XXI, Geneva, 1963: on Voltaire, pp. 214–84; more recently, S. Pitou, 'Voltaire, Linguet and China', *Studies on Voltaire*, vol. XCVIII, Geneva, 1972, pp. 61–8.

21 On this theme, see J. Ehrard, *L'Idée de la nature en France dans la première moitiè du XVIIIe siècle*, Impr. réunies, Paris, Chambéry, 1963, vol. II, pp. 768–86.

22 See E. Will, 'Trois quarts de siècle de recherches sur l'économie grecque antique', *Annales ESC*, 9, Paris, 1954, pp. 7–22.

23 See P. Vidal-Naquet, 'Recipes for Greek adolescence', *The Black Hunter*, Johns Hopkins Press, Baltimore, 1986; Edna Lemay, 'Histoire de l'Antiquité et découverte du Nouveau Monde chez deux auteurs du XVIIIe siècle', *Studies on Voltaire*, vol. CLI, Geneva, 1967, pp. 1313–28. See also S. Pembroke, 'The Early Human Family: Some Views, 1770–1870', *Classical Influences*, pp. 275–291.

24 See, on Court de Gébelin, apart from the works by his immediate disciple, Rabaut Saint-Étienne, *Oeuvres*, 2 vols., Paris, 1826, vol. I, pp. 355–90; F. Baldensperger, *Mélanges E. Huguet*, Boivin, Paris, 1940, pp. 315–30; F. E. Manuel, *The Eighteenth Century Confronts the Gods*, pp. 250–8; G. Genette, *Mimélogiques*, Seuil, Paris, 1976, pp. 119–48.

25 Court de Gébelin, *Monde primitif*, vol. IX, p. I.

26 J. S. Bailly, *Histoire de l'astronomie ancienne*, Paris, 1776; *Lettres sur l'origine des sciences et sur celle des peuples de l'Asie*, London, Paris, 1779. See chapter 2 above, pp. 38–65.

27 P. D. Huet, *Histoire du commerce et de la navigation des Anciens*, Paris, 1711, p. 75; the following year, Huet published the *Grand trésor historique et politique du florissant commerce des Hollandais*. See, on Huet, C. Nicolet, *Rendre à César: économie et société dans la Rome antique*, Gallimard, Paris, 1988, pp. 16–17.

28 See L. Dumont, *Homo aequalis: genèse et épanouissement de l'idéologie économique*, Gallimard, Paris, 1977, pp. 83–104.

29 There is a considerable bibliography: see, in particular, Ehrard, *L'Idée de la nature*, vol. II, pp. 378–81, 595–8; Rose de Labriolle, 'Le pour et le contre et son temps, II', *Studies on Voltaire*, vol. XXXV, Geneva, 1965, pp. 531–7; E. Ross, 'Mandeville, Melon and Voltaire: The Origins of the Luxury Controversy in France', *Studies on Voltaire*, vol. CLV, Geneva, 1976, pp. 1897–912; Cambiano, 'Montesquieu e le antiche repubbliche greche', pp. 131–44; on Melon, see the dissertation by F. Megnet, *Jean-François Melon, 1675 bis 1738: Ein origineller Vertreter der vorphysiokratischen Ökonomen Frankreichs*, L. G. Keller, Winterthur, 1955. Maxime Rodinson has drawn my attention, apropos Melon, to the following reference: M. I. Dufrenoy, *L'Orient romanesque en France, 1704–1789*, vol. III, Rodopi N.V., Amsterdam, 1975, pp. 321–83.

30 J.-F. Melon, *Essai politique sur le commerce*, n.p., n.d., [1734], p. 139.

31 See for example 'Sur la réponse qui a été faite à son discours [sur les sciences et les arts]', *Oeuvres complètes*, Bernard Gagnebin and Marcel Raymond (eds), vol. III, Pléiade, Paris, 1966, pp. 49–53.

32 Melon, *Essai politique*, pp. 96–98.

33 Ibid., pp. 107, 113, 115–16; see, in general, M. Foucault, *Discipline and Punish*, Penguin, Harmondsworth, 1979.

34 See for example in 'Mes Pensées', n° 1228, *Oeuvres*, vol. I, Pléiade, Paris, 1949, p. 1306–1307.

35 *The Complete Works of M. de Montesquieu*, Dublin, 1777, vol. II, bk XX, ch. VII, pp. 33–34; see Cambiano, 'Montesquieu e le antiche repubbliche greche', pp. 133–5.

36 See 'On the Populousness of Ancient Nations' (1752), in D. Hume, *Essays, Literary, Moral and Political*, London, 1894, pp. 245, (on Thucydides) p. 248; compare this with the much more optimistic remarks in the earlier treatise, 'On Commerce', ibid., pp. 149–158; on the originality of D. Hume, see M. I. Finley, *The Ancient Economy*, Chatto & Windus, London, 1973, pp. 21–2, 2nd edn 1985.

37 The first edition is entitled: *The Spirit of Athens: Being a Political and Philosophical Investigation of the History of that Republic*; the second edition is entitled: *The History of Athens Politically and Philosophically Considered with a View to an Investigation of the Immediate Causes of Elevation and of Decline, Operative in a Free and Commercial State*; the third edition, which appeared after the Revolution, is called: *The History of Athens, Including a Commentary on the Principles, Policy and Practice of Republican Government, and on the Causes of Elevation and Decline, which Operate in every Free and Commercial State*. Only the second edition was accessible to us, but our friend Simon Pembroke was kind enough to undertake a systematic comparison between the first and the second editions and, apart from the title, found no significant difference with respect to the importance of the theme of commerce.

38 *The History of Athens*, p. 63; see, for the reference to Montesquieu, p. XI.

39 Chastellux, *De la félicité publique ou considérations sur le sort de l'homme dans les différentes époques de l'histoire*, Amsterdam, 1772. We cite this book partly because, against Rousseau, Chastellux declared himself to be a theorist of representative government in terms which prefigure Constant: 'For myself, I believe that there will be no solid and lasting liberty except amongst peoples where everything will be done through representation' (p. 43), and partly because it contains a relatively rare example of a critique addressed against both Athens and Sparta, prefiguring Volney (see pp. 22–49).

40 *Voyages de M. le marquis de Chastellux dans l'Amérique septentrionale dans les années 1780, 1781 and 1782*, 2 vols, Paris, 1784.

41 At first they marvelled, then, after the Revolution, they waxed indignant. On the *oeuvre* of Abbé Barthélemy, published in Paris at the end of 1788, see the thesis by M. Badolle, *L'Abbé Jean-Jacques Barthélemy (1716–1795) et l'hellénisme en France dans la seconde moitié du XVIII* siècle*, PUF, 1927; on the reaction after the Revolution, see R. Canat, *L'Hellénisme des romantiques*, vol. I, Didier, Paris, 1951, pp. 115f: typical is the letter from P.-L. Courier to Chlewaski (27 February 1799): 'I think that all books of this kind, half-history, half-novel, in which modern *mores* are mixed up with ancient ones, do less than justice to both, purveying very false ideas about everything and affronting both taste and scholarship' (*Oeuvres*, vol. II, p. 662).

42 On de Pauw, a few details may be found in C. Becdelièvre, *Biographie liégoise*, vol. II, 1835, n° 1799, pp. 531–36, which has on occasion simply been copied (see Michaud, *Biographie universelle*, 2nd ed., vol. XXXII, Paris, 1861, pp. 321–2); see also G. Avenel, *Anacharsis Cloots*, Paris, 1865, and on his work, the information provided above, n. 13 and below, n. 44. Our attention was drawn to de Pauw by a 'mémoire de maîtrise' devoted to Barthélemy and defended in 1976 by Alain Chauvet. We cite de Paux from the second edition of Year III.

43 N. Broc, *La Géographie des philosophes*, p. 457. This 'protestant' was in fact ordained as a sub-deacon and became the canon of Xanten.

44 A commentary is provided by M. Duchet, *Anthropologie et histoire au siècle des Lumières*, Maspero, Paris, 1972; see the index.

45 On these themes in the eighteenth century, see, as well as N Broc, H. Baudet, *Paradise on Earth: Some Thoughts on European Images of Non-European Man*, tr. E. Wentholt, Yale University Press, New Haven and London, 1965, pp. 37–55.

46 J. de Guignes, *Mémoire dans laquelle on prouve que les Chinois sont une colonie égyptienne*, Paris, 1758; the thesis had already been put forward by P. D. Huet in his *Histoire du commerce*. This work provoked a whole polemic, the references for which are of no importance here (vol. I, pp. 166–7).

47 C. de Pauw, *Oeuvres*, Paris, Year III (1795), vol. VI, pp. i–iv.

48 Ibid., p. ix.

49 De Pauw, *Oeuvres*, vol. VI, p. 16.

50 We cite the translation of R. Martin, *L'Urbanisme dans la Grèce antique*, Picard, Paris, 1956, p. 26.

51 De Pauw, *Oeuvres*, vol. VI, p. 20f.

52 Ibid., pp. 64–5, 156.

53 Athenaeus, VI, 272 c; de Pauw, *Oeuvres*, vol. VI, p. 156 and vol. VII, pp. 305f.

54 De Pauw, *Oeuvres*, vol. VII, pp. 153–5, 201, 215–16; on democracy, he bases his remarks on Plutarch, *Life of Aristides*, XXII, 1.

55 Ibid., p. 358.

56 We are thinking of, for example, B. A. Van Groningen, who wrote the preface to the Belles-Lettres edition, Paris, 1968.

57 See Mona Ozouf, *Festivals and the French Revolution*, Harvard University Press, Cambridge, Mass. and London, 1988; a report by Talleyrand reproduced in B. Baczko, *Une Éducation pour la démocratie: textes*, Garnier, Paris, 1962, pp. 109–73, in particular pp. 162–4, shows that Barthélemy and de Pauw were two of the authors consulted for inspiration in the organization of the revolutionary festivals.

58 We will mention only the most important book, H. T. Parker, *The Cult of Antiquity and the French Revolutionaries*, Chicago University Press, Chicago, 1937.

59 Prince de Ligne, *Mémoires et mélanges historiques et littéraires*, vol. I, 1827, p. 25.

60 A good chapter of synthesis is to be found in S. Moravia, *Il tramonto dell'illuminismo*, pp. 315–444; we have consulted the works of F. Ponteil, *Histoire de l'enseignement 1789–1965*, Sirey, Paris, 1966; E. Allain, *L'Oeuvre scolaire*

de la Révolution, Firmin-Didot, Paris, 1891; the collections of C. Hippeau, *L'Instruction publique en France pendant la Révolution*, vols I and II, *Débats législatifs, discours et rapports*, Didier; and J. Guillaume, *Procès-verbaux du Comité d'instruction publique de l'Assemblée législative*, Paris, 1889, and *de la Convention nationale*, 6 vols, Paris, 1891–1917; also B. Baczko, *Une éducation pour la démocratie*.

61 Mirabeau, 'De l'éducation publique', in Baczko, *Une éducation pour la démocratie*, pp. 69–91, first speech, cited from p. 82.

62 G. Romme, 'Rapport sur l'instruction publique considérée dans son ensemble' (December 1792), ibid., pp. 267–92, cited from p. 269; Condorcet, 'Rapport sur l'instruction publique considérée dans son ensemble' (December 1792), ibid., pp. 181–218, in particular pp. 192–4.

63 Le Peletier, 'Plan d'éducation nationale, présenté par Robespierre' (13 July 1793), ibid., pp. 347–87.

64 Fourcroy, in Hippeau, *L'Instruction publique en France pendant la Révolution*, vol. I, cited from pp. 389, 397.

65 Ibid., vol. II, p. 99.

66 See, as well as the works cited above, the fine article by L. C. Pearce Williams, 'Science, Education and the French Revolution', *Isis*, 44, 1953, pp. 311–30.

67 Rouziès, *Tableau analytique des études de l'École centrale du département du Lot*, Paris, Year VIII, p. 13.

68 Lakanal, 'Rapport sur les Écoles centrales', (26 Frimaire, Year III), in Baczko, op. cit. (see n. 57), pp. 490–6, cited from p. 494.

69 Allain, *L'Oeuvre scolaire de la Révolution*, pp. 116–19.

70 See A. Prost, *Histoire de l'enseignement en France, 1800–1967*, A. Colin, Paris, 1968, pp. 52–6.

71 Daunou's report can be found in Condorcet, *Oeuvres*, A. Condorcet O'Connor (ed.), vol. VI, Paris, 1847, pp. 3–5.

72 There is a good chapter on Condorcet in Manuel, *The Prophets of Paris*, pp. 53–102; a rich collection of material on Condorcet is also to be found in the special number devoted to him by the *Cahiers de Fontenay, 5, Philosophie*, December 1976. On Condorcet, see also Manuela Albertone, *Una Scuola per la Rivoluzione, Condorcet e il dibattito sull' istruzione, 1792–1794*, Guida, Naples, 1979; E. and R. Badinter, *Condorcet: 1743–1794: un intellectuel en politique*, Fayard, Paris, 1988.

73 Bonald called it 'the apocalypse of the new Gospel', cited by Manuel, *The Prophets of Paris*, p. 61; on J. de Maistre, see above, pp. 104–6; on Chateaubriand, see J. Dagen, 'L'"Essai sur les révolutions" ou les mémoires d'outre-histoire', *Annales publiés par la faculté des lettres de Toulouse, Littératures*, 14, 1967, pp. 19–42.

74 Original edition, Agasse, Year III (1795). We cite the *Esquisse d'un tableau historique des progrès de l'esprit humain*, from the Garnier-Flammarion edition, Paris, 1988 (Introduction, Chronology and Bibliography by A. Pons, followed by *Fragment sur l'Atlantide*). The references to the English translation used, *Sketch for a Historical Picture of the Progress of the Human Mind*, tr. J. Barraclough, London, 1955, are given in brackets following the references to the French edition.

75 *Esquisse*, p. 81 (*Sketch*, p. 4).

76 Ibid., pp. 123–37 (pp. 41–54). The same idea is to be found in *Fragments de la quatrième époque*, which was not reprinted in the latest French edition of the *Esquisse*, but it is to be found following the *Tableau historique*, Bureau de la bibliothèque choisie, Paris, 1829, pp. 291–382.

77 *Esquisse*, p. 134 (p. 52).

78 In his 'Projet de décret sur l'instruction publique', presented to the Legislative Assembly, in Baczko, op. cit., pp. 193–4.

79 *Esquisse*, p. 133 (p. 51).

80 *Fragments*, p. 366.

81 Ibid., p. 292. The italics are ours.

82 Ibid., pp. 380–1.

83 *Esquisse*, p. 125 (p. 43): 'Out of the obscurity of these systems, two felicitous ideas shine forth, ideas which will appear again in more enlightened ages.'

84 On Volney, the essential book is by J. Gaulmier, *L'Idéologue Volney (1757–1820)*, impr. catholique, Beirut, 1951; Gaulmier summarized it in *Un grand témoin de la Révolution et de l'empire, Volney*, Hachette, 1959; for the intellectual framework, see the above-cited book by Moravia, *Il tramonto dell'illuminismo*. See chapter 5 below, pp. 141–169.

85 We cite the *Voyage* from the critical edition by J. Gaulmier, Paris, The Hague, 1959. The references to the English translation, *Travels through Syria and Egypt* (tr. G. G. J. and J. Robinson, London, 1838) are given in brackets after the French references; the *Oeuvres complètes* are cited from the Firmin-Didot edition of 1838 (1843 on the first page).

86 In our view, this point is not sufficiently emphasized in the pages devoted to Volney in the above-cited study on Volney by Moravia, 'Philosophie et géographie à la fin du XVIIIe siècle'; Chateaubriand's *Itinéraire* was to be, in large part, a dialogue with Volney: see J. Gaulmier, 'Chateaubriand et Volney', *Annales de Bretagne*, 75, 1968, pp. 570–8.

87 See J. Gaulmier in his edition, pp. 8–9.

88 Volney, *Voyage*, p. 26 (*Travels*, vol. I, pp. 3–4).

89 Volney, *Les Ruines*, Slatkine, Paris, Geneva, 1979. The English translation used is *Volney's Ruins*, Garland Publishing Inc., New York and London, 1979 (facsimile of the translation published by Levrault, Paris, 1802). The references for the English translation are given in brackets after the references to the French edition. Gaulmier, *L'Idéologue Volney*, p. 220. Gaulmier cites, p. 221, a letter from Volney, dated 26 December 1814, attacking 'Bossuet's Roman Jew, so highly exalted'; see also, on *The Ruins*, Moravia, *Il tramonto dell'illuminismo*, pp. 163–8.

90 Volney, *Les Ruines*, p. 86 (*Volney's Ruins*, p. 134).

91 On Volney's place in the history of orientalism, see M. Rodinson, *La Fascination de l'Islam*, Maspero, Paris, 1980, p. 74. On his attempts to write Arabic and Hebrew in Latin characters, see Gaulmier, *L'Idéologue Volney*, pp. 543–7.

92 Volney also visited another country which 'through its physical constitution, and the *mores* and character of its inhabitants, is totally different from the rest of France' and has about it something of 'the wild state and a civilization that has

hardly begun': Corsica; see his 'Précis de l'état de la Corse', published in *Le Moniteur* on 20 and 21 March 1793, and *Oeuvres*, p. 738.

93 *Oeuvres*, p. 728; a whole section of this book constitutes a polemic against Chateaubriand; see Gaulmier, 'Chateaubriand et Volney' and the 'Tableau du climat et du sol des États-Unis', pp. 630–98 in the *Oeuvres complètes*.

94 See above, p. 100.

95 *Oeuvres*, p. 725.

96 Ibid., pp. 724–5.

97 Ibid., p. 725, based on Thucydides, I, 2, 5–6; but when, on this same page, Volney cites the famous description of a ruined Sparta (Thucydides, I, 10, 2), he suppresses the parallel with Athens.

98 We cite the *Leçons* from J. Gaulmier's *La Loi naturelle; leçons d'histoire*, Garnier, coll. Classiques de la politique, 1980, pp. 83–146. On the École normale, see Moravia, *Il tramonto dell'illuminismo*, pp. 380–91.

99 *Leçons*, pp. 140–1. This may be compared to the comment of J. de Lolme, the Genevese theorist of the representative regime, in his *Constitution d'Angleterre* (1778), new ed., Geneva, 1793, vol. II, p. 22, n. 1: 'Even in Athens, which is the only ancient republic where there appears to have been liberty, the magistrates are seen to proceed more or less as happens these days amongst the Turks.'

100 Volney, *Leçons*, pp. 141–2.

101 Note the opposite responses of Sir Ronald Syme and Arnaldo Momigliano in Ducrey (ed.), *Gibbon et Rome*, pp. 47–72.

102 *Essai historique, politique et moral sur les révolutions anciennes et modernes, considérées dans leurs rapports avec la Révolution française, London 1797.* Mindful of J. Mourot's warning that one needs to use the edition of 1797 (J. Mourot, *Études sur les premières oeuvres de Chateaubriand*, Éd. de Minuit, Paris, 1962, pp. 37–179, in particular p. 88), we have systematically made sure that the texts cited are not significantly different from the original edition. All the references to the *Essai* and the *Génie du christianisme* are for the volume produced in the Pléiade collection, Paris, 1978. The English translation used is *An historical, political and moral essay on revolutions ancient and modern*, Henry Colburn, London, 1815, which is an abridged edition. The page references (where available) are given in brackets, after the French.

103 Introduction, p. 43. 'The trouble, the great trouble, is that we do not belong to our own age' etc., p. 42.

104 Sainte-Beuve, *Chateaubriand et son groupe littéraire*, 2nd ed., Garnier, Paris, 1861, vol. I, pp. 147, 153.

105 The tone is set in the Preface, p. 15 ('a detestable and altogether ridiculous book'); the 1826 notes were designed to hammer home the – totally ambiguous – proof; on these notes designed to 'keep the upper hand' and 'act as a lightning conductor' against the original text, which Chateaubriand tried to incorporate in the *Génie du christianisme*, see Mourot, *Études*, p. 94, and Dagen, 'L'"Essai sur les révolutions" ou les mémoires d'outre-histoire', p. 20.

106 We have borrowed this expression from Dagen, 'L'"Essai sur les révolutions" ', p. 22.

107 Compare Saint-Just's exclamation: 'The world has been empty since the Romans', *Oeuvres complètes*, C. Vellay (ed.), Fasquelle, Paris, 1908, vol. II, p. 331. On the surprising absence of the Middle Ages from the *Essai*, see F. Engel-Janosi, 'Chateaubriand as a Historical Writer', *Four Studies in French Romantic Historical Writing, The Johns Hopkins University Studies in Historical and Political Science*, LXXI, 2, 1955, 31–56, in particular p. 35.

108 Chateaubriand's protestations of serious scholarship (see Introduction, p. 44, note B, and I, ch. LXX, pp. 262–3) do not impress M. Badolle (*L'Abbé Jean-Jacques Barthélemy*, pp. 366–70), in whose view Chateaubriand plagiarized *Le Jeune Anacharsis*; Mourot, *Études*, pp. 66, 87–8, 91, is of a similar opinion. A much more qualified view is expressed by F. Letessier, 'Une source de Chateaubriand: "Le Voyage du jeune Anacharsis"', *Revue d'histoire littéraire de la France*, 59, 1959, pp. 180 203 (a file on the whole matter).

109 'The remarkable aesthetic sense with which he was endowed was not based on solid scholarship' (*L'Avenir de la science*, Calmann-Lévy, Paris, 1890, p. 295); in note 133 (ibid.), Renan even goes so far as to accuse Chateaubriand of having lined Calypso's cave 'with lilacs', through a misreading of the word λιλαιομένη (*Odyssey*, I, 15). As a result of not having checked the validity of this assertion in the passage from the *Génie du christianisme* (II, IV, ch. I, p. 718) to which Renan inaccurately alludes, C. R. Hart (*Chateaubriand and Homer*, Johns Hopkins University Press, PUF, Baltimore and Paris, 1928, p. 101) perpetuates this legend which literary critics, shortly after, set about destroying; see the demonstration in the articles on 'Renan et Chateaubriand' by G. Moulinier, *Journal des débats*, 15 May 1935; M. Duchemin, *Chateaubriand, Essais de critique et d'histoire littéraire*, Vrin, Paris, 1938, pp. 455–61; and R. Lebègue, *Revue d'histoire littéraire de la France*, 59, 1959, pp. 39–49.

110 As is recognized even by F. Letessier, 'Une source de Chateaubriand', p. 203.

111 I, ch. VII, pp. 70–1; it is worth noting that, in his review of the *Essai*, Montlosier, one of Chateaubriand's earliest readers, cites this chapter as an example 'of the spirit and tone of this work' (*Journal de France et d'Angleterre*, fascicule of 22 April 1797, p. 318). On this review, published by Montlosier in London between 6 January and 29 July 1797, and on the review of the *Essai*, see P. Christophorov, *Sur les pas de Chateaubriand en exil*, Éd. de Minuit, Paris, 1960, pp. 203–5, 216; A. Andrewes procured us a copy of this article, unobtainable outside the Bodleian Library, Oxford, and we are most grateful to him for doing so.

112 One might add: the Seven Sages and the Encyclopédistes (I, ch. XXIV, p. 120), the Scythian bowmen and the Swiss guards of the kings of France (I, ch. XLIX, p. 192) etc.

113 I, ch. XXV, p. 130. See the note to p. 221 (n. B, ch. LX), in which Chateaubriand announces that 'from now on speaking of Persia and Germany together', he will simply indicate by a dash 'the switch from one empire to the other', and, between p. 260 and p. 261, the table showing the forces marshalled on each side.

114 I, ch. VI, p. 69; see also pp. 67, 69, 71, 89, 231, 269 etc.

115 Montlosier, *Journal de France et d'Angleterre*, p. 317, speaks of comparisons that are 'piquant'; 'insignificant, puerile, inexact, forced' are the adjectives used

by the modern critics (for example Canat, *L'Hellénisme des romantiques*, vol. I, p. 53); see, however, on these comparisons as the key to the entire work, the remarks of Sainte-Beuve, *Chateaubriand et son groupe littéraire*, p. 153, and Dagen, 'L'"Essai sur les révolutions" ', p. 21.

116 Montlosier, *Journal de France et d'Angleterre*.

117 See I, ch. V, p. 65 ('the Athenians who in so many respects resemble the French'), I, ch. XLIX, p. 192 (p. 23), and above all I, ch. XVIII (ch. XIV) (The character of the Athenians and the French), a chapter whose theme is repeated almost word for word in *Le Génie du christianisme* (III, III, ch. V, pp. 842–3).

118 In this respect, Montlosier's critique of Chateaubriand is interesting (*Journal de France et d'Angleterre*, pp. 317–18): Chateaubriand did not see the difference between an ancient society, in which slavery 'purified' the atmosphere of political government because 'all those known today as *sans-culottes* were in servitude', and the French Revolution, which 'set in movement a class of barbarians and savages whom modern societies take into their embrace'.

119 I, ch. XXVII, p. 133 (p. 102); see also I, ch. LXVIII, p. 253–5 (Athens or Cleopatra's nose). Montlosier was not taken in ('One laughs to see the events of Attica compared . . . to those of France', *Journal de France et d'Angleterre*, p. 317). On the construction of the *Essai* around Athens, see Dagen, 'L'"Essai sur les révolutions" ', p. 32.

120 I, ch. XXVI, p. 132 (p. 100), where 'the Greeks' twice refers to the Athenians; I, ch. LXII, p. 229 (p. 210). This may be considered a direct effect of the equivalence, implicit in the *Essai*, between 'the French' and 'Paris', but that presupposes that Athens is thought of as a kind of capital of Greece.

121 Athens, on the other hand, is saved by a chronological break which puts all the 'good things' on the side of the 'Persian War' (that is to say, for Chateaubriand, from 504 to the peace of Artaxerxes) and all the 'bad' on the side of the imperialist 'passion for conquest'.

122 As is clearly seen by P. Barberis, who speaks of 'fascination' ('Chateaubriand et le préromanticisme', *Colloque de Rennes [Bicentenaire de la naissance de Chateaubriand]) Annales de Bretagne*, 75, 1968, pp. 547–58, cited from p. 552.

123 See ch. XIII to XVII and above all p. 79 (p. 39), p. 83 (p. 44) (and the 1826 note), pp. 87, 89 (n. B), 90 (conclusion).

124 On the reception of the *Essai*, see Christophorov, *Sur les pas de Chateaubriand*, pp. 201–10.

125 There has been and may still be disagreement over the date of the original edition, as some authors and certain catalogues claim that there were either one or two editions in Lausanne in 1796. Robert Triomphe, in his long monograph, *Joseph de Maistre: étude sur la vie et sur la doctrine d'un matérialiste mystique*, Droz, Geneva, 1968, does not resolve the question, as he adopts the earliest date in the chronology (p. 602) and the most recent in the text (pp. 170–4). For our part, we have followed the conclusions of the edition produced by R. Johannet and F. Vermale, Vrin, Paris, 1936. We cite the *Considérations* from the edition by J. Tulard, Garnier, Paris, 1980, and *L'Étude sur la souveraineté* from book I of the *Oeuvres complètes*, 14 books in 7 volumes, Slatkine, Vitte and Perrussel,

Paris, 1884–1886), pp. 309–554. The *Considérations sur la France* were also republished in Brussels, Éd. Complexe, 1988, followed by the *Essai sur le principe générateur des constitutions politiques et autres institutions humaines*.

126 Burke, *Reflections on the Revolution in France*, ed. C. C. O'Brien, Penguin, Harmondsworth, 1976.

127 Triomphe, *Joseph de Maistre*, pp. 375–485; the text from Juvenal, *Satires*, X, 174–5, '*quidquid Graecia mendax audet in historia*' is cited in *Soirées de Saint-Petersbourg*, in *Oeuvres complètes*, vol. IV, Lyons, 1884, p. 81.

128 Reproduced in *Oeuvres complètes*, vol. I, Lyons, 1884, pp. 309–554.

129 Ibid., pp. 187–220.

130 On Lycurgus, see *Étude sur la souveraineté*, I, pp. 333–41, 346 (together with Moses, Servius, Numa, Charlemagne, Saint Louis), 361–362; *Considérations*, pp. 51, 58 (together with Numa, Moses, Mahommed), 63, and in the *Fragments*, vol. I, p. 205.

131 L. de Bonald, *Théorie du pouvoir politique et religieux dans la société civile démontrée par le raisonnement et par l'histoire*, Constance, 1796, in *Oeuvres complètes*; a facsimile copy of the Paris edition, A. Le Clère, 1843, was published by Slatkine, Paris and Geneva, 1982, 15 books in 7 volumes. Books I and II of the *Théorie du pouvoir politique et religieux* are respectively in books XII–XIII and XIV–XV in the Slatkine edition; we cite from II, pp. 93, 454.

132 I, p. 163.

133 I, p. 169.

134 I, p. 165.

135 Johannet and Vermale, *Considérations*, p. XVIII.

136 *Considérations*, p. 63: the idea is partly suggested by Plato's *Phaedrus*, which J. de Maistre was to cite later, in 1814; see *Oeuvres complètes*, book I, p. 255.

137 For a reading of Mitford and Young, see Triomphe, *Joseph de Maistre*, p. 381. On Mitford's *History of Greece*, London 1784–1810, see A. Momigliano, *Studies in Historiography*.

138 *Étude sur la souveraineté*, book I, p. 486.

139 Ibid., p. 346.

140 Ibid., p. 347; *Considérations*, p. 63.

141 See Johannet and Vermale, *Considérations*, pp. XXII–XXIII.

142 *Étude sur la souveraineté*, book I, pp. 321–2.

143 Ibid., pp. 380, 449, 453.

144 *Considérations*, p. 48.

145 Ibid., p. 48. In a remarkable sophism, J. de Maistre immediately adds: 'The age of Augustus *followed* immediately upon the civil war and the proscriptions'; see also p. 48: 'extreme carnage often accompanies extreme density of population, as has been seen above all in the ancient Greek republics'.

146 Ibid., p. 48.

147 See Gaulmier, *L'Idéologue Volney*, p. 380 (Volney was then in America).

148 1795: the date of the creation of the Institute, after the vacation represented by the revolutionary period; 1803: the date of the dissolution of the class of moral and political sciences by Napoleon, who was hostile to the ideologues and much

preferred to re-establish the old Académie des inscriptions under the name 'Classe d'histoire et de littérature ancienne' (on the history of the Académie des inscriptions between 1789 and 1832, see the Preface to the *Table générale et méthodique des mémoires de l'Académie des inscriptions et belles-lettres* by E. de Rozière and E. Châtel, A. Durand, Paris, 1856, pp. XI–XVI). On the ideologues at the Institut, see Moravia, *Il tramonto dell'illuminismo*, pp. 425, 439.

149 On Louis-Sébastien Mercier before 1789, see L. Béclard, *Sébastien Mercier, sa vie, son oeuvre, son temps d'après des documents inédits*, Paris, 1903, and above all pp. 153–88, on the *Essai sur l'art dramatique* (1773), in which Mercier spiritedly attacked the imitation of the Ancients and pleaded for a 'new theatre that related to the nation before which it spoke'; on Mercier at the Institut and on his relations with the ideologues, see Moravia, *Il tramonto dell'illuminismo*, pp. 97, 423, 425, 435–8.

150 Daunou, who summarizes this 'Appréciation de l'histoire ancienne' in the *Notice des travaux de la Classe des sciences morales et politiques de l'Institut (nivôse-ventôse an X)*, Paris, n.d., pp. 15–16, observes that Mercier's assertions did not 'prevent the Class from applying itself, during this term, above all to the historical sciences'.

151 *Notice de travaux . . . pendant le dernier trimestre de l'an X*, Paris, n.d., p. 3: 'Mémoire sur l'histoire, comme science et comme art', by citizen Lévesque.

152 On Bon-Joseph Dacier, the permanent secretary to the Académie des inscriptions 'with which he had, so to speak, identified', see the Preface to the *Biographie générale Michaud*, Paris, 1885. The *Rapport* was published in Paris in 1810; we would refer the reader to its recent republication under the title *Histoire et littérature ancienne*, Preface by D. Wonoroff, Introduction and Notes by F. Hartog, Belin, Paris, 1989.

153 See his declarations in the respective prefaces to *Histoire de Thucydide, fils d'Olorus*, Paris, 1795, book I, p. III, *Histoire critique de la République romaine*, Paris, 1807, p. 1, *Études d'histoire ancienne et de celle de la Grèce*, Paris, 1811, book I, pp. X, XV.

154 'Considérations sur les trois poètes tragiques de la Grèce', 'Mémoire sur Aristophane', *Mémoires de l'Institut national des sciences et arts, Classe des sciences morales et politiques*, book I, Paris, 1798, pp. 305–44, 345–73 (= *Études*, book V, pp. 48–80); Mémoires 'sur Hésiode', 'sur Homère', 'sur les moeurs et usages des Grecs du temps d'Homère', presented in 1796 and 1797, *Mémoires*, book II, pp. 1–21, 22–37, 38–67 (= *Études*, book IV, pp. 454–85, 486–507; II, pp. 131–75); and above all Mémoires 'sur la Constitution de la république de Sparte' and 'sur la Constitution de la république d'Athènes', delivered between 1799 and 1801, published in *Mémoires*, book III, Paris, 1801, pp. 347–81, and book IV, Paris, 1803, pp. 113–277, and reprinted in *Études*, book II, pp. 282–330 (Sparta) and book IV, pp. 257–387 (Athens). A systematic comparison of the 'Mémoires' and the *Études* proves that, from 1799–1800 to 1811, Lévesque made very few changes to his passages on Sparta and Athens: a few stylistic corrections, the omission of a few over-precise allusions to the revolutionary period, the removal of a number of critical discussions (in particular the polemic with de

Pauw, judged to be too much of a friend to Athens, *Mémoires*, book IV, pp. 181, 203–11, 264, 265–6, disappears in the *Études*).

155 On the life of P.-C. Lévesque, see B.-J. Dacier, 'Notice historique sur la vie et les ouvrages de M. Lévesque', *Histoire et Mémoires de l'Institut royal de France*, Paris, 1821, book V, pp. 162–78. So far as we know, no study has as yet been devoted to P.-C. Lévesque, the historian of Greece. On Lévesque's life and activities as a historian in Russia, see A. Mazon, 'P.-C. Lévesque, humaniste, historien et moraliste', *Revue des études slaves*, 42, 1963, pp. 7–66.

156 Lévesque was 'recruited' by Diderot for Catherine: see the examination of the contract in Mazon, 'P.-C. Lévesque', pp. 18–23.

157 Preface to the *Histoire des différents peuples*, p. III.

158 *L'Homme moral ou l'Homme considéré tant dans l'état de pure nature que dans la société*, Amsterdam, 1775; *L'Homme pensant ou Essai sur l'histoire de l'esprit humain*, Amsterdam, 1779. To judge from the numerous pirated further editions of these two works, they must have enjoyed quite a success. Lévesque himself reproduced these essays in the form of *Mémoires*: 'Considérations sur l'homme observé dans la vie sauvage, dans la vie pastorale et dans la vie policée', 'Considérations sur les obstacles que les Anciens ont apportés aux progrès de la saine philosophie', Paris, 1796, *Mémoires*, book 1.

159 *Études*, book I, Preface, p. XII.

160 *Histoire de Russie*, book I, p. 73.

161 On the quality of his *Histoire de Russie*, which was long to remain 'the only enterprise of this kind undertaken by a Frenchman', see M. Cadot, *L'Histoire de la Russie dans la vie intellectuelle française (1839–1856)*, Fayard, Paris, 1967, pp. 382 (quotation), 542, and also Mazon, 'P.-C. Lévesque', pp. 41–3.

162 The mirage of Peter the Great: see the remarks of A. Lortholary, *Le Mirage russe en France au XVIIIᵉ siècle*, Boivin, Paris, 1951, n. 155, p. 303, and n. 222, p. 306; Lévesque implicitly criticizes the myth orchestrated by Voltaire: see also Mazon, 'P.-C. Lévesque', pp. 38–40, 43. The mirage of Frankish 'democracy', so dear to Abbé de Mably: see the introduction to *La France sous les cinq premiers Valois*, pp. 45–6, and the 'Mémoire sur le gouvernement de la France sous les deux premiers dynasties', *Mémoires*, book V, Paris, 1804, pp. 244, 279; on p. 315, he writes 'Let us give up the illusion of hoping to find a good government amongst ignorant and barbaric peoples.' The mirage of the Roman Republic, or to be more precise the illusion of the French who have imitated Rome and, 'through the crazy pretension of becoming Roman citizens have become bad citizens': see *Histoire critique*, Preface, p. XXXVII. The Spartan mirage: see below, pp. 141–169: 'The place of Greece in the imaginary representations of the men of the Revolution.' It should be added that as early as *L'Homme pensant* (p. 3), Lévesque had expressed his distrust of imaginary representations.

163 That is the work's essential theme (see Preface, p. XXXIV), but there are others: on Lévesque as a forerunner of Niebuhr, see Rytkönen, *Niebuhr*, p. 57.

164 Comparison between Russia and Greece: *Histoire de la Russie*, book III, pp. 81–3, 88, 93 etc.; on the 'classicism' of the *Histoire*, see C. Wilberger, 'French Scholarship on Russian Literature', *Eighteenth Century*, 5, 1971–1972,

pp. 503–26, in particular pp. 515–18. Comparison between Greece and Russia: 'Mémoire sur les moeurs et usages des Grecs du temps d'Homère', *Mémoires*, book II, pp. 46, 52–3, 56, 65; 'Mémoire sur Hésiode' (in which Lévesque compares the myths of Pandora and the races with a sacred book of the Kalmouks, which he had read in a Russian translation).

165 See the two excursus, 'on the primitive identity of the Greek language with one of the most ancient languages of the North', 'on the northern origin . . . proved by . . . religious rites', in books II and III of the translation of Thucydides, pp. 315–63, 278–322, and also *Études*, book II, pp. 77–89.

166 Preface to *Études*, p. III; the same idea resurfaces, two years later, in the *Essai sur les révolutions*, book I, ch. XXXVIII, pp. 170–2. Egger's work, *L'Hellénisme en France*, purveys the same historicism, devoting considerable space to 'the introduction of hellenism in France through Marseilles' (book I, pp. 24–39), after having commented at length upon the affinity between the Gallic genius and the Greek spirit (with a comparison between the Athenian funeral oration and the military poetry of the Gauls: book I, pp. 11–14).

167 See *Études*, book II, pp. 238–67 (the mythical kings of Athens and 'Theseus' democracy'), 280 (the Athenians were from the start 'in love with pure democracy'). On Lévesque as a critic of Abbé Barthélemy, see however the remarks of Malte-Brun, 'Éloge de feu M. Lévesque', *Histoire de Russie*, 4th ed., Paris 1812, p. XXII.

168 *Études*, III, p. 25.

169 *Études*, Preface, p. XX.

170 *Histoire de Thucydide*, Preface, p. XXVII.

171 The disappearance of the lawgiver: *Études*, book II, pp. 102, 366–7. One of us has already underlined the importance of the translation of Thucydides in 1795 (Vidal-Naquet, 'Tradition de la démocratie grecque', p. 34).

172 *Histoire de Thucydide*, Preface, p. XXVII.

173 *Études*, book III, pp. 54–5 (commentary on Thucydides, III, 73–4).

174 See G. Lefebvre, *La Révolution française*, 6th ed., PUF, Paris, 1968, p. 361, and Paule-Marie Duhet, *Les Femmes et la Révolution, 1789–1794*, Gallimard, Julliard, Paris, 1977, pp. 129–31, 135–60; see chapter 5 below, pp. 141–169.

175 *Études*, book II, pp. 375–6. It will be remembered that Pisistratus is the leader of the 'Montagnards': the prefiguration is complete.

176 *Études*, book II, pp. 306–7. Conversely, studying 'France under the two first dynasties', Lévesque refers to Sparta (*La France sous les cinq premiers Valois*, pp. 46, 86; *Mémoires*, book IV, pp. 254, 258): the existence of the 'servitude of the plebs' makes it possible to compare the Franks and the *Homoioi*, and the serfs and the helots.

177 On Sparta, see *Études*, book II, pp. 286, 295, 303–8, 322–4, 328, and Lévesque's explanatory notes to the *epitaphios* of Pericles (*ad Thucydidem*, II, 37, 2; 29, 1; 40, 2).

178 *Études*, book II, pp. 291–2; see also pp. 293–4 (the Spartans as 'savages of Greece'; Sparta's golden age is nothing but a dark age).

179 *Études*, book II, pp. 237–8; see also p. 461.

180 *L'Homme pensant*, ch. XVII, pp. 74–6: 'One should pity peoples amongst whom the warrior is more important than all other citizens simply because he is a warrior.'

181 *Études*, book II, pp. 318, 324.

182 *L'Homme moral*, p. 163. This idea may be contrasted to Danton's declaration during the debate on Le Peletier's plan for teaching: 'I am a father; but my son is not mine; he belongs to the Republic' (cited by Ponteil, *Histoire de l'enseignement en France*, p. 68).

183 *Études*, book II, pp. 283, 281.

184 *Études*, book I, Preface, p. IX; book II, pp. 237–8; book III, p. 2 ('One imagines the whole of humanity to have an interest in the preservation of this people which is an honour to humanity').

185 Property: *Études*, book II, p. 363 (on Solon. see *L'Homme moral*, p. 70, and the *Observations et discussions sur quelques parties des ouvrages de l'abbé de Mably*, Paris, 1787, pp. 77–8). Private life: *Études*, book II, pp. 360–1 (on Solon). Commerce: ibid. book II, p. 320 ('How nations poor by nature entered into commerce'); *a contrario*, on the Spartans, see the *Éloge historique de l'abbé de Mably*, Paris, 1787, p. 59. Work and industry: *Études*, book II, pp. 364–5 (still on Solon).

186 *Histoire de Thucydide*, book I, Preface, p. VI; *Études*, book III, p. 180. The same theme appears in the 3rd edition (1804) of Young's work (see above, note 37).

187 *Études*, book III, p. 186, which may be compared to Xenophon, *Hellenica*, II, 4, 42.

188 *Études*, book III, p. 363.

189 *Études*, book III, p. 143 (democracy is responsible for the defeat in Sicily); book IV, pp. 258–62 (Cleisthenes); it will be noted that, on the subject of Cleisthenes, the *Études* are less forceful than the earlier mémoire; compare *Mémoires*, book IV, p. 121, and *Études*, the cited passage; book IV, p. 375 (popular justice).

190 *Études*, book III, p. 25.

191 *Études*, book IV, p. 387. This peroration, in which the themes of the 'quarrel between the Ancients and the Moderns' resurface, returns, without appreciable changes, to that of the mémoires presented to the Institut.

192 We know of no work of synthesis on B. Constant and the ancient world. See however a few pages in Canat, *L'Hellénisme des romantiques*, book I, pp. 44–59; see also, by the same author, his Latin thesis: *Quae de Graecis Mme de Staël scripserit*, Paris, 1904. The general work, Paul Bastid, *Benjamin Constant et sa doctrine*, 2 books, A. Colin, Paris, 1966, is very disappointing from this point of view. On Constant's general attitude, we have profited from reading B. C. Fink, 'Benjamin Constant and the Enlightenment', in H. S. Pagliaro (ed.), *Studies in Eighteenth Century Culture*, book III, London, 1973, pp. 67–81; R. Mortier, 'Constant et les Lumières', *Europe*, 467, March 1968, pp. 5–18; P. Thompson, 'Constant et les vertus révolutionnaires', ibid., pp. 49–62; the collection edited by D. Verrey and A.-L. Delacrétaz, *Benjamin Constant et la Révolution française, 1789–1799*, Droz, Geneva, 1989, though useful in itself, contributes nothing on his relations with Antiquity.

193 See Momigliano, *Studies in Historiography*, p. 49.

194 *Journal*, in *Oeuvres*, A. Roulin (ed.), Pléiade, Paris, 1964, p. 359.

195 On Constant's education and his relations with German scholarship, see the old book by G. Rudler, *La Jeunesse de Benjamin Constant*, Paris, 1909, and, more recently, P. Deguise, *Benjamin Constant méconnu*, Droz, Geneva, 1966 (which concentrates particularly on *De la religion*). In the present study, we shall be concentrating on the political dimension to Constant's relations with Greece, leaving altogether aside his works on ancient religions, despite the fact that he was involved in these right up to his death.

196 Letter cited by P. Bastid, *Benjamin Constant*, book I, p. 109.

197 *De la force du gouvernement actuel de la France et de la nécessité de s'y rallier* (1796); *Des réactions politiques* followed by *Des effets de la Terreur* (1797); *Discours prononcés au cercle constitutionel pour la plantation de l'arbre de la liberté* (30 Fructidor Year V); all these texts are collected together in C. Cordié (ed.), *Gli scritti politici giovanili di Benjamin Constant*, Marzorati, Como, 1944, and also, with one exception, in the edition by P. Raynaud, Flammarion, coll. 'Champs', Paris, 1988; the most complete study on this period in Constant's life is, however: B. Jasinski, *L'Engagement de Benjamin Constant: amour et politique (1794–1796)*, Paris, 1971. See also chapter 5 below, pp. 141–169 and nn. 114, 115.

198 *De la force*, in *Gli scritti politici*, p. 45 = ed. Raynaud, p. 175.

199 *Des effets de la Terreur*, ibid., p. 114 = ed. Raynaud, p. 175.

200 *Discours*, ibid., p. 229.

201 Nouvelles Acquisitions françaises (NAF), 14358–14364; on the importance of these manuscripts, see, for example, Fink, 'Benjamin Constant and the Enlightenment', and the Preface and Notes by O. Pozzo di Borgo to his edition of the *Écrits et discours politiques de Benjamin Constant*. See also the edition published by E. Hofmann, *Les Principes de politique*, Droz, Geneva and Paris, 1980, II. We give the references to the manuscript only where we have not been able to find them in E. Hofmann's publication. See also below, pp. 159–160.

202 *Considérations*, p. 42.

203 See the edition presented by M. Gauchet, *De la liberté chez les modernes*, Hachette, coll. 'Pluriel', Paris, 1989.

204 See D. Janicaud, *Hegel et le destin de la Grèce*, Vrin, Paris, 1975, 'La constitution de l'idéal de la belle totalité', pp. 27–48.

205 *Mélanges de littérature et de politique*, Paris, 1829, pp. 469–72; analogous formulae, for example, in an article from *Minerve française*, 51, 1818, reproduced in B. Constant, *Recueil d'articles: le Mercure, la Minerve et la renommée*, E. Harpaz (ed.), Droz, Geneva, 1972, p. 494.

206 *De la perfectibilité de l'espèce humaine*, NAF, 14362, f° 76r; to which may be opposed what he said in 1819: 'The individual was kept in much more subjection to the supremacy of the social body in Athens than he is nowadays in any free State in Europe' (*De la liberté des Anciens comparée à la liberté des Modernes*, M. Gauchet,ed., p. 501).

207 Ibid., f° 76r. The Greeks of Antiquity had lived through the collapse of theocracy.

208 *De la liberté des Anciens*, p. 499.

209 Chapters VI–VIII of the pamphlet *De l'usurpation* (*Oeuvres*, pp. 1010–23) reproduce or summarize several chapters from the *Principes de politique*, XVI, NAF, 14360, ff[os] 2–27, which may be found in Hofmann, pp. 419–55.

210 *Principes de politique*, f° 10, Hofmann (ed.), p. 427; references to de Pauw are several times cited in this connection.

211 *De l'usurpation*, in *Oeuvres*, p. 1011, reproducing NAF, 14360, ff[os] 10–11, Hofmann (ed.), p. 42; M. Gauchet (ed.), p. 183.

212 *Principes de politique*, f° 10, Hofmann (ed.), p. 427; de Pauw is several times cited as a reference in this connection.

213 We have found no proof that Constant had read Melon. He bases his remarks principally on the work of his former colleague in the Tribunat, Charles Ganilh, *Essai politique sur le revenu public des peuples de l'Antiquité, du Moyen Age, des siècles modernes* (2 books, Paris, 1806) who also makes use of these concepts (see book I, p. 47–9) and also cites (NAF, 14360, ff[os] 9–10, n. G, p. 445, in the Hofmann ed.), the *Essai sur l'histoire de l'espéce humaine* by C. A. Wailkenaer, Paris, 1798, who devotes pp. 251–368, a whole section of his work, to the consequences of 'the introduction of factories and commerce', although it is not made clear at which point in History this happened.

214 *Esprit de conquête*, in *Oeuvres*, pp. 959–60, reproducing NAF, 14360, f° 9; Hofmann (ed.), p. 425; M. Gauchet (ed.), p. 118.

215 *Esprit de conquête*, ibid., p. 960, and NAF, 14360, f° 10; England's victory thus has nothing to do with this remark; Hofmann (ed.), p. 427; M. Gauchet (ed.), p. 119.

216 We are thinking in particular, amongst apologists of the representative system, of the marquis de Chastellux, *De la félicité publique*; also of another citizen of Geneva, J. de Lolme, to whom H. Pappé has drawn our attention; see his *Constitution de l'Angleterre*, book II, pp. 14f.

217 See above, pp. 116–120.

218 Sismondi, *Histoire* . . . , book IV, Zurich, 1808, p. 369; the text is cited in NAF, 14364, f° 79, and *De l'usurpation*, in *Oeuvres*, p. 1011 (with a slight pagination error); also in M. Gauchet (ed.) on p. 183.

219 Ibid., p. 1010; M. Gauchet (ed.), p. 182.

220 Ibid., p. 1013; M. Gauchet (ed.), p. 184.

221 NAF, 14360, f° 18; Hofmann (ed.), p. 435.

222 *De l'usurpation*, in *Oeuvres*, p. 1012.

223 What is called 'a form of his modern man's bad faith' by Thompson, 'Constant et les vertus révolutionnaires', p. 55.

224 *Oeuvres*, p. 1013, and NAF, 14360, f° 12, and Hofmann (ed.), p. 430: 'The word illusion is a word the equivalent of which is found in no ancient language.'

225 Ibid., p. 1012.

226 Ibid., p. 1014; NAF, 14360, f° 16, and Hofmann (ed.), p. 434, read as follows: 'No more Lycurgus, no more Numa, *no more Muhammad*'.

227 *De la liberté des Anciens*, p. 502.

228 *De l'usurpation*, in *Oeuvres*, pp. 993–4, partially reproduced (the last sentence) from NAF, 14360, f° 2; Hofmann (ed.), p. 419.

229 The second edition appeared in 1862, with substantial additions and significant corrections: between 1851 and 1862, Duruy had read Grote and the Empire had been established.

230 We should point out that, until not so long ago, Duruy's *Histoire grecque* was still considered one of the books most in demand in the Bibliothèque nationale!

231 For example, Glotz's pages on Pericles' 'work of social mutual assistance and preservation', *La Cité grecque*, 2nd ed., Albin Michel, Paris, 1968, pp. 142–3, may be compared to those which Duruy devotes to 'Pericles' measures to ensure the well-being of the people', *Histoire grecque*, Hachette, Paris, 1851, pp. 284–5; as a rule, we shall systematically be citing from that first edition.

232 See G. Monod, 'Victor Duruy', *Revue internationale de l'enseignement*, 28, 1894, pp. 481–9, and E. Lavisse, *Un ministre, Victor Duruy*, A. Colin, Paris, 1895, pp. 164–5; see, more recently, the remarks of P. Gerbod, *La Condition universitaire en France au XIXe siècle*, PUF, Paris, 1965, p. 442, on the 'pedagogical revolution' brought about by the appearance of the first volume of the *Histoire des Romains* in 1843.

233 Circular of 1 October 1864, cited by D. Rohr, *Victor Duruy, ministre de Napoléon III: essai sur la politique de l'Instruction publique au temps de l'empire libéral*, Librairie générale de droit et de jurisprudence, Paris, 1967, p. 112. It is worth remembering that, as Minister of Public Instruction from 1863 to 1869, Duruy, at the same time as introducing a clear-cut distinction between research (with the creation of the École des hautes études) and teaching, did make a special effort to make teaching relate more to life: see Ponteil, *Histoire de l'enseignement*, pp. 248, 263, and Gerbod, *La Condition universitaire*, pp. 443, 451–62.

234 In which he differed from other students of Michelet's, such as Wallon, who soon turned to research, and Ravaisson, who lost no time in aiming for the upper echelons of University administration.

235 Gerbod, *La Condition universitaire*, p. 400 (citing an article in the *Revue de l'Instruction publique*).

236 The third and fourth volumes of the *Histoire des Romains* were ready in 1850, 'but in them Duruy pleaded the cause of the Empire and was unwilling to publish them until 1872' (Lavisse, *Un ministre, Victor Duruy*, p. 22).

237 'In the year 1851, there was an orthodox and official version of history. . . . It was not permitted . . . not to admire the Spartans absolutely and without reservations. . . . The moral greatness of Sparta was one of the ornaments of the gilded cardboard palace that the university set up for the admiration of its students' (Lavisse, ibid.).

238 Review of the *Histoire grecque* by M. Victor Duruy, teacher of history at the Lycée Saint-Louis, *Journal général de l'Instruction publique et des cultes*, Paris, 1851, pp. 557–60; Duruy's reply, pp. 606–7. Charles Nisard was the brother of the famous university professor Désiré Nisard – whom Victor Hugo described in *Toute la lyre* (VIII, 25), as 'a true bourgeois / an ass in literature and a hare in politics'. Charles Nisard specialized in popular French literature and produced many articles for governmental reviews: see the entry in the *Biographie Firmin-Didot*, also Gerbod, *La Condition universitaire*, pp. 390, 397, and the thesis by

J. Malavie, *Un Bourgeois de Louis-Philippe: Désiré Nisard dans la crise de 1848*, Champion, Lille, 1972, p. 18.

239 Where Sparta was concerned, demonstration was a delicate matter, so Nisard summoned to his aid two 'oligarchies' that had lasted, Rome and Venice; his conclusion was simple: Athenian democracy had, in contrast, 'died of exhaustion after eighty years of glory'.

240 Essentially, the reign of the ambitious, such as Alcibiades, or, even worse, of 'the lazy, the needy' – in other words, the people – 'the incompetents and the dema-gogues'. Nisard has no sympathy for anything other than Solon's 'democracy', and shows indulgence only for democracy in the form in which it was restored after 403.

241 In the extremely official *Précis de l'histoire* by Porson and Cayx, Paris, 1827, we are told that the people 'compromised the welfare of the State by its furious decisions' (p. 70) and that Solon's constitution was the cause of the short-lived . . . greatness of Athens (p. 77). See also pp. 148 (Cimon, the greatest of the Athenians), 149 (Athenian ambition), 154 (Pericles debased Solon's constitution forever), 178 (Socrates, the supporter of 'moderate aristocracy'), 238 (Phocion). In the *Histoire ancienne* by T. Burette, Dumont, Paris, 1835, Cahiers d'histoire universelle à l'usage des collèges . . . under the direction of Messrs Dumont, Gaillardin, Wallon and Duruy – already – there is a passage in praise of Lycurgus who 'formulated these principles under the influence of the Doric genius' (4th *cahier*, p. 13), one in praise of Cimon (5th *cahier*, p. 79) and the usual remarks about demagogues and the fickle temperament of the Athenians (5th *cahier*, pp. 69, 80).

242 Burette, *Histoire ancienne*, 6th *cahier*, p. 76. The 10th edition of Porson and Cayx (1846) is also much more measured in its critique of Athens.

243 Duruy writes: 'That, sir, is why, in the century following the Persian Wars, I am definitely in favour of Athenian democracy, whose hour had come, and against the oligarchy, whose moment had passed' (*Histoire grecque*, p. 607).

244 Ibid., Preface, p. XIV.

245 Ibid.

246 Duruy's 'errors' have been noted by C. Lescoeur, 'Le droit privé des Romains dans l'*Histoire* de M. Duruy', *Bulletin de l'Institut catholique de Paris*, Paris, 1895, pp. 3–30. Duruy tries to minimize the gap that separated slaves from free men (*Histoire grecque*, pp. 6, 10, 13, 22) and women from men (ibid., pp. 19–20), and takes the *jus commercii* to be the right to engage in commerce (ibid., p. 11).

247 The programme of contemporary history for the philosophy class (24 September 1863) was drawn up by Duruy; extracts are to be found in Rohr, *Victor Duruy*, pp. 181–4.

248 Reply to C. Nisard, *Histoire grecque*, p. 607.

249 *Histoire grecque*, pp. 5–7, 46, 67, 83; see also the *Histoire de la Grèce ancienne*, Paris, 1862, pp. 2–4, 9.

250 *Histoire grecque*, Preface, p. XVI; on the opposition between the East and the West, see ibid., pp. 28, 37, 236, 302 etc.

251 Ibid., Preface, p. VII.

252 Duruy alludes to the history of the Achaean League between 272 and 221; see *Histoire grecque*, pp. 609–31, and passages in the *Histoire des Romains*, book I, Hachette, Paris, 1843, p. 478.

253 *Histoire grecque*, Preface, pp. XVII–XVIII; in the *Histoire des Romains*, book II, Hachette, Paris, 1970, p. 40, Duruy maintains that Rome's strength lay in its middle class.

254 *Histoire grecque*, Preface, p. XII, and pp. 58–9, 63, 65–7.

255 Ibid., Preface, p. x. In the 1862 edition, Duruy refers to the *Menexenus* (249 a–b), unbothered by the disparity between his 'maternal' Athens and the Athens of Plato, which, faced with orphans, assumes the role of a *father*. It is a significant disparity: at all costs, Duruy was determined to ensure the promotion of women in Athens!

256 Ibid., Preface, p. X.

257 *Histoire grecque*, Preface to the edition of 1862, p. x; see *Histoire grecque*, pp. 437, 474 (Duruy against Plato) and, in the 1862 edition, a strange addition (book II, p. 138) on Socrates as the defender of 'the sanctity of the family and work' (?).

258 Ibid., pp. 204, 242–3, 246–7, 272, 284, 293, 400.

259 Ibid., p. 281; Preface, p. IX ('That domination which ensured safety on the seas, promoted industry and commerce, spread well-being and encouraged intelligence, was Greece's happiest moment, and the most brilliant in the life of the human race').

260 Ibid., p. 394, on the Thirty.

261 Ibid., p. 246; same idea p. 293.

262 Ibid., p. 258.

263 Ibid., p. 379. For a declared sympathy for Athens, see also pp. 271–2, 285, 296.

264 Ibid., p. 280, where Duruy swiftly obscures agrarian wealth by liquidity. Yet he certainly recognizes the importance of land when Rome is at issue: 'In the Middle Ages, to own land meant entering the ranks of the nobility; in Rome, it meant truly becoming a citizen, it was real wealth . . . and, furthermore, the only form of wealth which Rome, without industry or commerce, knew and respected' (*Histoire des Romains*, book I, p. 170). We may conclude that, for Duruy, agrarian wealth disappeared with the advent of industry and commerce!

265 *Histoire grecque*, p. 141; see also the 1862 addition (I, p. 255).

266 Ibid., pp. 181–3.

267 Ibid., p. 265.

268 Ibid., p. 275.

269 Ibid., p. 285.

270 Ibid., p. 293.

5

The Place of Greece in the Imaginary Representations of the Men of the Revolution

━━━━━◦◦◦◉⦗⧼⧽⧽⦘◉◦◦◦━━━━━

Two hundred years have now passed since the French Revolution and it seems a good time to reflect upon the first hundred. It is a hundred years since the death of Fustel de Coulanges, whose works the counter-revolutionaries saw fit to commemorate above all else. In 1864, as a young professor at the University of Strasbourg, this historian, who by the time of his death had won renown, had published *The Ancient City*. The latest editor of this famous text, François Hartog,[1] writes in his Introduction that Fustel's purpose 'was perfectly explicit and [that] the book could well be subtitled: 'Let us have done with imitating the Ancients.'[2]

At the very start of his book, Fustel stresses the difference between *them* (the Ancients) and *us*:[3]

> We have some difficulty in considering them as foreign nations; it is almost always ourselves that we see in them. Hence spring many errors . . . Now, errors of this kind are not without danger. The ideas which the moderns have had of Greece and Rome have often been in their way. Having imperfectly observed the institutions of the ancient city, men have dreamed of reviving them among us. They have deceived themselves about the liberty of the ancients, and on this very account liberty among the moderns has been put in peril. *The last eighty years*[4] have clearly shown that one of the great difficulties which impede the march of modern society is the habit which it has of always keeping Greek and Roman antiquity before its eyes.

This paper was first presented in the Sorbonne, to the members of the French Philosophy Society, on 31 May 1989.

'The last eighty years' – broadly speaking that, of course, takes us back to the time of the Revolution.

Amongst Fustel's contemporaries there were some who were radical democrats, or even socialists, and at the same time clung to the model of the Greek city with all its transparency, if necessary tacking on polytheism. One such was Louis Ménard (1822–1901), who became a *normalien* in 1842. He was a witness and historian of the 'June Days', the author of an *apologia* on Greek polytheism, published in 1863, and a fervent admirer of the Greek city as an example of government that cost the community virtually nothing.[5] Fustel must have read Ménard, but he could not have read *L'Avenir de la science*, which Renan had written in 1848 but did not publish until 1890. In this text[6] Renan, who was a young philosophy graduate, produced an *apologia* for an Athenian city even more violently revolutionary than the France of 1793, yet at the same time responsible for creating the serenity of the Parthenon and the Propylaea: a classic example of identification. There were others of the same period who saw things differently: Edgar Quinet, for example, for his part blamed the men of the Convention of Year II for having drawn their inspiration from Moses rather than the Ancients.[7]

Fustel was clearly not the first to denounce this *imitatio perversa*. In 1845 Marx, in a famous passage in *The Holy Family*, had criticized Robespierre and Saint-Just for having

> confused the ancient realistic-democratic commonweal based on real slavery with the *modern spiritualistic-democratic representative state*, which is based on emancipated slavery, bourgeois society. What a terrible illusion it is to have to recognize and sanction in the *rights of man* modern bourgeois society, the society of industry, of universal competition, of private interest freely pursuing its aims, of anarchy, of self-estranged natural and spiritual individuality, and at the same time to want afterwards to annul the manifestations of the life of this society in particular individuals and simultaneously to want to model the political head of that society in the manner of antiquity.[8]

Marx – and there can be no doubt that he had read Benjamin Constant[9] – considered it all to have been a tragic illusion, not on the part of the revolutionaries themselves, but on that of the men of the Terror, the men of 1793 and the early months of 1794.

But we need to go back much further than Constant, much further than the French Revolution itself, to find what I believe to be the first decisive thinking on the absurdity of members of a modern city taking themselves to be citizens of the Roman Republic, Athens or Sparta. The year is 1764, a whole century before *The Ancient City*, and the author I am about to cite was addressing the inhabitants – or to be more exact the citizens, a small minority – of the republic of Geneva:

> Remain yourselves and do not blind yourselves to your position. The ancient peoples are no longer a model for the moderns; they are too alien in every respect. You, above all, people of Geneva, keep to your place and do not aim for elevated objectives which are set up before you in order to conceal the abyss being dug before you. You are neither Romans nor Spartans; you are not even Athenians. Leave aside those great names which do not suit you. You are merchants, artisans, bourgeois, always concerned with your own private interests, people for whom liberty itself is simply a means of acquiring possessions without let or hindrance and possessing them in security.

Who wrote those words? The style is unmistakable: Jean Jacques Rousseau, in the ninth of his *Lettres écrites de la Montagne*,[10] Rousseau who, in an argument that was to follow the Terror, the distant echoes of which are detectable in the texts of Fustel and Marx cited above, was, along with Mably, to become Public Enemy no. 1.[11] It is true that this particular text was not produced at just any moment of the author's life. In 1763 he had renounced his rights as a bourgeois of Geneva, so in a sense what he was destroying was his own childhood, nurtured on Plutarch and the value of his position as a citizen of Geneva. But both before and after this dramatic break he always was faithful to the antithesis reflected in his thinking:[12] on the one hand man as nature made him, who would never reappear, however great the nostalgia for him, on the other the citizen whose very existence was a challenge to history, of whom Sparta had provided an example, if not a model that could be imitated.

At any rate, that was the text that, a whole century earlier, had resolved the argument which Fustel believed he was clinching with *The Ancient City*.

With that somewhat epistemological preamble out of the way, we must now tackle the Revolution itself. The subject is certainly not new: there has been no lack of either analyses or syntheses and there are even a few statistics available.[13] Nor, of course, was the argument new at the time of the opening of the Estates General. The '*philosophes*' had already clashed over Sparta and Athens. It will come as no surprise to learn that Voltaire, who was not really very interested in the Greeks, preferred Athens, Rousseau Sparta.[14]

More fundamentally, it has been suggested – for instance in the central thesis of Peter Gay's famous work[15] – that the Enlightenment movement as a whole, in its ideological attack on society and Christian ideology, constituted a 'neo-paganism', and drew upon both space and time to set up its counter-models. Athens and Sparta played their part in this endeavour and there gradually emerged the antithesis which was to operate in the nineteenth century, in France, and also in the Franco-German debate: the antithesis between a bourgeois, cultivated Athens, a 'liberal' model, set in opposition to a virtuous and military Sparta.

In this domain, where everything depends on details, I shall nevertheless not go into details but simply note a few major points.

1 The chief figure to emerge from the discourse of the Age of Enlightenment, whether Greek or Roman, Athenian or Spartan, or even Russian or Indian, was that of the lawgiver. As J.-L. Quantin shows, it was he who made possible a double transition, the shift from barbarity to civilization and the passage from primitive anarchy to the beginnings of a State. A lawgiver in the shape of either a man or a god. Rousseau suggested that 'it would take the gods to give men laws'. 'He divided [society] into classes, groups and orders and established a system of signs, that is to say interlocking representations.'[16] Three lines written by Alfieri for André Chénier, on 12 April 1789, sum up the impact made by this figure well enough:

> *Uomini e donne, militari e abati,*
> *Tutti Soloneggiando i Parigini,*
> *Non s'ode altro gridar che: Stati, Stati.*
> (From men and women, soldiers and priests,
> With all the Parisians playing at Solon,
> The only cry heard is: 'States! States!')[17]

2 The model which emerged from tradition, an extremely mixed tradition, was not so much that of the politician at grips with the dark realities of choice, rather that of the hero,[18] as provided by, for example, Plutarch, who had filled the dreams of the little Jean Jacques Rousseau, but also the hero whom, despite the Enlightenment, centuries of Christianity had likened to the martyrs. That was exactly how Saint-Just saw himself, Saint-Just who was so supremely possessed by what Jaurès called 'the dizzying vision of sacrifice and the dangerous intoxication of death'.[19] Even Robespierre, on 8 Thermidor Year II, referred to himself as 'the Republic's living martyr'.[20] And Camille Desmoulins, describing his childhood, tells us that, like so many others, he was 'in despair at not being Greek or Roman'.[21] Naturally, that heroic model implied an anti-model – the tyrant; and it also implied a kind of division in the temporal world: on the one hand the heroic times, on the other the times of decadence. Of

course, this kind of time is not historical; and even if Abbé Barthélemy's Young Anacharsis (1788) arrives in Athens from his far-off Scythia at a precise point in the fourth century, what he discovers there is a culture, that of classicism, not history, let alone politics.

Since 1750 art had been neo-classical, or rather had been becoming so; David's *Death of Socrates* was painted in 1785. In Jean Starobinski's words,[22] This art 'translated and transformed the passion for the beginning into nostalgia for a new beginning'. That equivocation is central to the two words that dominate the period: 'revolution', 'regeneration'. Mona Ozouf has made some crucial observations on this point.[23] More than an abstraction which men revered, revolution was a *return*, and Antiquity was the chief instrument of that return, which was often conceived as bringing about a reappearance of the 'fine days of Greece and Rome'.[24] By no means the least paradoxical aspect of the word 'revolution' is the fact that, at one and the same time, it meant both an aspiration which can only be described as apocalyptic, and also a single day, a particular moment of crisis and violence. July 14 was one revolution;[25] 9 Thermidor was another.

On the one hand there was the riot-revolution, on the other the regeneration-revolution, and the word 'regeneration' was so trendy that when Toulon was captured by the royalists, who handed it over to the English in 1793, they dated their decrees 'in Year I of the regeneration of the French monarchy'.[26]

Now let us try to address ourselves directly to this Revolution and to describe the Greek apparel in which it was clothed. I realize that that is a somewhat arbitrary thing to say since, despite Hugo's famous line of poetry, Rome did not 'replace Sparta'; it accompanied it, for what the *Republic*, which had itself become *consular*, was replaced by was the *empire*. Nevertheless, let us now address ourselves to this Revolution and immediately mark out a few limits, for it should not, after all, be imagined that the entire French people began to speak the language of Plutarch's heroes as translated by first Dacier, then Ricard,[27] or that in every village the new-born children were named Anacharsis or Brutus.[28] It has not been possible to go through all the records, so I have used four main sources of information: the selection of archival documents recently put together by la Documentation française,[29] the twofold collection published by the CNRS on revolutionary and counter-revolutionary caricatures,[30] the catalogue of the exhibition on the same theme recently organized at the Bibliothèque nationale,[31] and the five volumes in which Michel Vovelle presents the revolution in images.[32]

What conclusions may be drawn from these soundings, themselves clearly sifted out from a process of selection? There are whole domains where Antiquity hardly creeps in at all. In the world of the figurative arts, while painting and prints with lofty subjects draw upon Greece quite as much as upon Rome, if need be with the encouragement of the public authorities, and while Brutus is depicted on playing cards, other whole areas of art entirely or almost entirely eluded the supposed tyranny of the gods and themes of Antiquity. Caricature was one of these: it is true that the Hydra of Aristocracy was a common theme.[33] But when Mercury, the god of commerce, is represented by opponents to the emancipation of the American Blacks, it is Friar Chabot who is contained in the huge casse-role he is depicted as carrying.[34] Louis XVI is caricatured as a pig, as Gargantua, as a cuckold, as a devil or (by the counter-revolutionaries) as Christ.[35] At the very most he occasionally appears as Janus or Medusa but never, so far as I know, as Nero, Caligula or Pisistratus. The religious repertory taken from the Old and New Testaments is by no means the sole preserve of the royalists: the tablets of the Declaration of Human rights and the Constitution are everywhere represented as the tablets of Moses or the words of Jesus.[36]

And what of revolutionary heroes? So far as I know, there was no Robespierre-Lycurgus; however, in the summer of 1793, there was a Marat represented as a friend of Diogenes by Villeneuve (although this was an exception). It shows Diogenes, lantern in hand, no longer needing to seek for his man: he has found him, in the person of 'sans-culotte comrade' Marat, who has just crushed the Hydra of Aristocracy.[37] Publications which followed the news closely, day by day, do not seem to have developed themes taken from Antiquity.[38] In contrast, as well as in painting, which was closely monitored by the authorities, and in sculpture and prints, Antiquity was overwhelmingly ubiquitous in parliamentary speeches,[39] the press, the theatre[40] and, of course, the festivals which were supposed to give expression to a unanimous nation,[41] in the lyrics of the songs that celebrated them, in funeral ceremonies, in fact in all the domains in which the cultivated bourgeoisie could express its culture and its own ideology. An example is provided by the festival of the Supreme Being at Lons-le-Saunier,[42] where the following words were sung to the tune of the *Marseillaise:*

> First of all principles, supreme being,
> God of Socrates and Plato,
> O you, the one whose extreme power
> Created both the elephant and the mite . . .

In these areas the ancient gods *were* present, in particular Hercules who, as J.-C. Benzaken had recently observed, 'after centuries spent in good and loyal service to the king of France', rallied to the Revolution

Figure 4 Villeneuve, *Marat, the defeater of the aristocracy*, caricature from the revolutionary period. *Taking Liberties*, Satirical Prints of the French Revolution, Dublin. Chester Beatty Library, 1989, no. 128.

and later, in fact, also to the Counter-Revolution. That went for texts as well as images, for in June 1793 the Jacobins of Limoges, in an address to those in Paris, declared that they had 'always recognized in the people of Paris that same Hercules who, born in a town of a hundred gates, while still in the cradle, on 14 July tore apart the two snakes sent by Juno to strangle him'. They then proceeded to enumerate the other eleven labours of Hercules.[43]

The anthems composed to mark festivals or commemorations are clearly a mine of assorted ancient references. Here, as a late example, is part of the anthem composed to mark the sixth anniversary of the execution of Louis XVI at the festival of Mesnil-Jourdain (Eure). Its particular target was the Austrian General Mack:[44]

> Against our ten thousand
> Who emulate the Greeks,
> His eighty thousand
> On all sides come to grief.

Those who composed the speeches, for the most part written in official-ese, which reached the Convention or other organs set up in Year III, also made the most of references to Antiquity. The communication to the Directory, after the Coup d'État of 18 Fructidor Year V (16 September 1797), composed by the republican 'friends of order and humanity in Léré in the Cher department',[45] ran as follows:

Allow us to inform you that amongst your number we believe we can spy just as many of those Solons and Lycurguses who, in the days of those ancient republics, deemed it their duty to expound the Laws to their fellow-citizens. We fancy ourselves to be in the Lyceum [*sic*] of Athens, putting into practice the philosophical lessons of all those Xenocrateses and Platos.

Another area infiltrated by Antiquity was that of naming,[46] previously a religious domain, both for children and for towns and villages. Famous though the cases of Anacharsis Cloots and Anaxagoras Chaumette may be, the influence of Rome was in general greater than that of Greece. From 1793, Brutus was naturally overwhelmingly preponderant; but there was also, for example, a Pericles in Montpellier in Year IV and in Corbeil an Epaminondas, one of the few Greek heroes known at the time of the Revolution who was neither Athenian nor Spartan.

The matter of name changes was raised in the Convention on 7 Nivôse Year II (27 December 1793), in connection with a ruling by the administrators of Langres, who had forbidden an official to add the name Socrates to his patronym. Nor was this a solitary case. As Danton remarked, 'Since the saints have been ousted from paradise, it is of course possible no longer to be called George or Peter, but it seems excessive to take the names of great men of Antiquity without possessing their virtues.'[47] In Year III, Baboeuf raised the question of forenames as follows: 'My own forename Gracchus still comes under attack. Is it not decreed that worship may be free? Who can oblige me to take a Christian hero as model? What harm can there be in taking as my godfather a great man rather than an insignificant one?'[48] No large town that was renamed adopted a name from Antiquity: neither Marseilles (*Sans-nom*), nor Lyons (*Commune-Affranchie*), nor Toulon (*Port-la-Montagne*); but at the village level, there was a spate of Brutuses and Scaevolas, a Themistocles in the Allier department, a Sparta (Ham) in the Nord department and even two Marathons, which was a way of recalling to mind both the battle and the 'people's friend'. That was explicitly the case at Saint-Maximin, in the Var department, where the leader of the local *sans-culottes* was none other than Lucien Bonaparte.[49]

Nor was it simply a matter of children and villages. There were statues too. A Saint Scholastica by Houdon was thus renamed and became a statue of Philosophy.[50] A song-writer of Year VIII commented humorously upon this ubiquitous presence of Greek Antiquity:

> Myriagramme, Panthoon,
> Metre, kilometre, oxygen,
> Litre, centilitre, Odeon,
> Prytaneum, hectare, hydrogen.
> The Greeks hold so many charms for us
> That nowadays, to understand
> And comprehend French properly,
> It's Greek that we must learn.[51]

You could think that it was Boileau criticizing Ronsard – or Colette writing *L'Enfant et les sortilèges* for Ravel. But here again, we should mark out the limits. Antiquity was in competition with the language of the most traditional Judaeo-Christianity, which remained a powerful influence. Its presence sometimes remained more or less masked, however, as for example when the Declaration of Human Rights was, as I have mentioned above, represented as the Tablets of the Law.

But in this area, there were many gradations of nuance: in Brumaire Year II, Aveyron organized a 'festival of the poor', a kind of Saturnalia in which, for a day, the rich waited upon the poor in celebration of 'the maxim recorded by our legislators: do as you would be done by'.[52] It is a sentiment which, despite the eminently philosophical context, does not have a particularly Greek ring to it.

That Christian presence could well be mixed in with references to Antiquity. In *Le Vieux Cordelier* (The Old Friar) – to which I shall be returning – Camille Desmoulins intermingled praise of Athens with a reference to the prophet Isaiah and an apologia for the figure whom, following Hébert, he calls 'the *sans-culotte* Jesus'.

It should be added that references to Antiquity were used above all in rhetorical preambles and very seldom played any part in the actual body of legislation. As for 'human rights', it was not possible to base them on any reference to Antiquity; or rather, to be more precise, only one such reference appears in the Declaration of 26 August 1789, namely the word 'citizen'.[53] In 1791 Saint-Just observed: 'the ancient lawgivers did everything for the republic, France has done everything for humanity. Human rights would have been the undoing of Athens and Sparta. There, all they knew about was the beloved motherland; that was what one sacrificed oneself for.'[54]

One proposal for a Constitution, elaborated by J.-M. Rouzet, the representative of the Haute-Garonne department, submitted on 18 April 1793, suggested introducing ephors, an Areopagus and the institution of ostracism.[55] But nobody took it seriously. The Constitution of Year III included a Council of Five-Hundred and a Council of Elders; both were reminiscent of the Athenian *Boulē*, the former by virtue of the number of its members, the latter through the respect shown to 'the principle of age'. The *Tribunat* of Year VIII, with its consuls and its Tribuneship, made use of an obviously Roman vocabulary, but there was never any question of the consuls, particularly the First Consul, being appointed annually.

Ever since Taine, much ridicule has been poured upon the letter from Hérault de Séchelles to the curator of the department of printed archives of the Bibliothèque nationale, asking him to obtain for him 'immediately' – this was 17 June 1793 – the text of the laws of Minos, which were needed urgently for his work as the author of a constitutional text.[56] So far as I know, B. Hemmerdinger has been the only person to propose a solution to his problem, by suggesting retrospectively that this member of the Convention might have consulted Aristotle's *Politics*.[57] As I have pointed out elsewhere,[58] when the Convention, purely theoretically, abolished slavery, not a single orator on that 4 February made any reference to ancient slavery. The contrast between the adulation of Sparta and the memory of the Helots would have been altogether too stark.

G. Glotz made an implicit comparison, in his *Histoire grecque*,[59] between the creation of the departments under the Constituent Assembly and the reforms of Cleisthenes, with their demes, *trittyes* and *phylai*, but it was in vain that I combed through the debates for the slightest reference to that Athenian legislator, who was, it is true, not at all well known at the time.

The domain in which it was very tempting to take the Ancients, particularly the Greeks, as models was without doubt that of education. And indeed, the minutes of the successive committees responsible for such matters, from the Legislative Assembly to the Convention, published between 1889 and 1907 by the anarchist James Guillaume,[60] are an extraordinary mine of information containing plenty of references to Lycurgus and Plato. But, typically enough, in the plan Robespierre himself put forward on 13 July 1793, in the name of the proto-martyr of the Convention,

Michel Le Peletier, a plan which concerned all male children between the ages of five and twelve, the following passage appears:

> To prolong this public institution until the end of adolescence is a fine dream; on occasion we have read with enthusiasm of this being done in the annals of Sparta; on occasion we have seen an insipid caricature of this in our own colleges; but Plato formed only philosophers, Lycurgus formed only soldiers, our professors formed only schoolboys. The French Republic, whose splendour resides in trade and agriculture, needs men of every kind: so we must no longer shut them up in schools.[61]

Clearly, even a Jacobin who was supposed to be an extremist was not unfamiliar with bourgeois values.

But even that pronouncement was too much for Abbé Grégoire, who remarked dryly on 31 July that

> it is not enough that a system be presented surrounded by famous names, with Minos, Plato, Lycurgus and Le Peletier as its patrons; the first thing to do is to recognize fully the immense difference between the little city of Sparta . . . and a vast empire, between a people which, wholly preoccupied with arms, left its agriculture to the Helots, and a people which is engaged, not only in military operations but also in agriculture, manufacturing and trade.[62]

In other words, even at a time when Spartomania was at its height, there were plenty of calls for a return to reality.

Let us now pick out a few of the high points and also a few of the low ones for the Greek presence in these imaginary representations, the broad lines and limits of which I have tried to indicate. Reading the principal orators of the Constituent Assembly,[63] one soon realizes that what Greek Antiquity amounted to was essentially a collection of *exempla* which could easily be associated with modern *exempla*. For example, in 1791 Mirabeau pointed out that gold and silver are not the only materials that can be used for coins. Was there not a currency of iron in Sparta?[64] On 31 August 1789, Lally-Tollendal, the most brilliant partisan of the institution of two chambers, argued for the future creation of a Senate, recalling the example of Sparta: 'In Sparta, authority was divided into three branches and the Spartans were long known as the happiest people on earth,[65] whereas ten years after the laws of Solon, the Athenians were already tired of the divisions between the Areopagus and the assemblies of the people.'[66] Similarly, on 5 September, Mounier drew upon *The Young Anacharsis* to

remind his listeners that in Athens there was a *Boulē* alongside the assembly of the people, a *Boulē* composed of elders, hence a Senate.[67] What
one orator found in Sparta another found in Athens. On 18 May 1790,
Abbé Maury, the leader of an extreme traditionalist group even invoked
Cadmos and the Spartoi of Thebes.[68] Many of these examples were in fact
counter-examples. Whether it was a matter of authorizing assemblies
instead of a king, or of declaring war or peace, on 21 May 1790 Barnave,
a man with a genuinely historical mind, who systematically rejected the
model of Antiquity, argued that the National Assembly had nothing to do
with 'the democracy of the public meeting-place in Athens';[69] and in answer
to those who rejected the idea of an electoral census and the very principle of a representative regime, he protested at those – and they did exist
– who

> constantly point to the models provided by the governments of Athens
> and Sparta! Quite apart from the difference in population and area
> and the political disparities between those States and ourselves, have
> they really forgotten that pure democracy only ever existed in those
> little republics and in Rome, when its liberty was declining, by virtue
> of an institution – I mean slavery – more vicious than anything for
> which a representative government can be reproached?[70]

That was the argument which was to resurface in Year III; and I could
continue playing this game of quotations for a long time. Occasionally in
the nineteenth century,[71] and frequently today, the conflict between the
Gironde and the Mountain has been represented as a struggle between
Athens and Sparta. There is some truth in the idea. Condorcet was an
admirer of Athens, which, in his historical system, occupied the place
Sparta held in Rousseau's.[72] On 11 May 1793, the Convention heard
Vergniaud denounce those who sought to feed the French with the gruel
of Sparta and remind his audience what that model implied: the division
of land, the destruction of industry and the constitution of a Helot people.
However, Vergniaud did not on that account rally to the Athenians, whom
Billaud-Varennes, on Floréal Year II (20 April 1794) denounced as follows: 'Citizens, in Sparta the inflexible austerity of Lycurgus became the
unshakeable basis for the republic; the weak and trustful nature of Solon
plunged Athens back into slavery. This parallel contains all the science of
government.' Robespierre did, on occasion, cite, if not Athens, at least the
Athenians. Thus, on 28 December 1792, during the trial of the king, he
declared: 'Truth has always been in the minority on earth.[73] Had it not
been so, would the earth be full of tyrants and slaves? . . . All your Critiases,
Anytuses, Caesars and Claudiuses were the majority; but Socrates was in
the minority, for it was he who drank the hemlock; and Cato was in the

minority, for he disembowelled himself.'[74] And a few months later, he explained that he would have liked 'to be the son of Aristides – just as much as the heir presumptive to Xerxes'. As for Saint-Just, in the speech that he was prevented from delivering on 9 Thermidor, he referred to the conflict between Philip and Demosthenes: 'Was Demosthenes a tyrant? If he was, it was tyranny that preserved the liberty of the whole of Greece for many years.' But that being said, whatever the qualifications that may be introduced, the ideological identification of the Montagnard leaders with Sparta (and Rome) during the period in which they held power on their own, between June 1793 and July 1794, cannot be in doubt. What was the nature of this identification? How was it that Robespierre could declare, in his major report delivered on 18 Floréal Year II (7 May 1794): 'The centuries and the earth were apportioned to crime and tyranny; for barely an instant did liberty and virtue alight upon one or two spots on the globe. Sparta shines like a flash of lightning amid huge shadows'? What was it that made Saint-Just, in the speech in which he accused Danton, on 11 Germinal Year II (31 March 1794) exclaim: 'Since the Romans, the world has been empty and it is their memory that fills it and still *prophesies* liberty'? A religious and apocalyptic text, if ever there was one.[75]

Three words provide me with the answers to those questions.[76] The first is 'virtue', the virtue which, according to Montesquieu, was the guiding principle of republicans, and which Robespierre claimed to have always been a quality possessed by a minority. In his report of 17 Pluviôse Year II (5 February 1794) 'on the principles of political morality which must guide the National Convention', Robespierre, drawing upon Montesquieu himself, but obliterating all historical distance,[77] put that very question and produced the following reply: 'What is the fundamental principle of a democratic and popular government, that is to say the essential mainspring which supports and motivates it? It is virtue: I mean the public virtue which brought about so many marvels in Greece and Rome and which must produce even more astonishing ones in republican France.' So the Republic meant a return in force of marvels, after all the shadows from which Sparta had shone out.

The second word is, of course, 'equality', since the Montagnards had been misled by that old misunderstanding, which resulted in *hoi homoioi* – which was how the Spartan 'peers', aristocrats if ever there were, were known – being translated as 'the equal ones'.

The third word, a modern one this time, is 'transparency'.[78] The model is Sparta, through which Robespierre and Saint-Just saw their own society as transparent, ideally united, a society whose very essence repelled conflict between different classes, interests and parties, conflict that was the sole preserve of traitors and rascals whom it was perfectly legitimate to eliminate, in the name of those 'pure men' of whom Robespierre was still speaking on 9 Thermidor. The Sparta of Robespierre and Saint-Just embodied at once a rejection of history and a desperate rejection of politics. The day would come when their fate would be to stand themselves as models of that twofold rejection,[79] which would in turn itself masquerade as profound historical thought.

It was a frozen image, which one man, Camille Desmoulins, would try to destroy, with the help of the counter-model of Athens; in the process he himself would be destroyed. It is advisedly that I single out Camille Desmoulins, for Danton, with whom he is generally associated in the group which the partisans of Robespierre dubbed 'the Indulgent faction', could not have cared less about either Athens or Sparta. Upon working through the entire body of his speeches it transpires that he did, it is true, pay ritual homage to Solon and Lycurgus, introducing both of them into the hall in which the Convention gathered.[80] But there was only one occasion on which he mentioned the name of Athens – in a debate on the idea of setting up a human stud farm, in which he recalled that, after a long and decimating war, the legislators of Athens, 'to repair the State's loss of citizens, ordered those who remained to take several wives'.[81] But Camille Desmoulins and Greece – now, that is a subject well worth treating at length, although in the present context I will mention only the campaign conducted in *Le Vieux Cordelier*, six numbers of which were published between 5 December 1793 and 25 January 1794, the seventh being at proof stage when, on 17 March, the printer of this journal was arrested. His arrest was soon followed (30 March) by that of Camille Desmoulins himself, who on 5 April was taken to his execution in the very same tumbril as Danton.[82] We should not be misled or overimpressed by the symmetry between the two factions, on the one hand the Hébertistes, on the other the *Indulgents*, which Robespierre lumped together and liquidated in quick succession. Camille Desmoulins had written of Hébert: 'Instead of blaspheming against the freedom of the press, let him give thanks to that undefined freedom which alone is responsible for the fact that he has not been brought before the Revolutionary Tribunal and that the only guillotine to which he will be led is that of public opinion.'[83] Nevertheless, in truth he was partly responsible for the liquidation of Hébert, against whom he had vainly tried to form an offensive alliance with Robespierre. However, the problems that he set out were fundamental ones. Under the Terror and the dictatorship of virtue, Camille strove to restore the very idea of politics, drawing for support upon Tacitus and Machiavelli.[84]

It was a dramatic struggle involving a number of parties, in which

Athens played a major role, in opposition to Sparta of course, but also to the Caesars, who were discreetly compared, in no. 3 of *Le Vieux Cordelier*, to the leaders of the Committee of Public Safety. What was needed was to escape from 'this violent and terrible state'[85] without seeking to establish the 'reign of Astraea' on earth. Whatever Montesquieu may have said, virtue was not the basis of a republic. 'What does the form of government matter if all the citizens are virtuous?'[86] So it was that Athens was mobilized against Sparta.[87] The theme is fully developed in no. 6, in which Camille recalls, somewhat unfairly, his polemics against Brissot: 'What are you trying to say with your black gruel and your Spartan freedom? Some legislator, that Lycurgus! All he was capable of doing was imposing upon his fellow-citizens privations which made them all equal in the same way that a storm makes equals of all those who are shipwrecked!'[88] It was an argument that was very much in the air and must have struck home, for it was clearly to Camille that Robespierre was replying in that same report of 17 Pluviôse Year II (5 February 1794), cited above: 'We are not trying to cast the French Republic in the mould of the republic of Sparta, we are not trying to impose upon it either austerity or the corruption of the cloister.'

Camille returned to the subject in no. 7, the proofs of which were circulated. The true Republic was not Sparta, nor was it Rome – despite the fact that Camille and Lucile Desmoulins had named their son Horace. 'The real republicans, the lasting democrats, on principle and by instinct, were the Athenians.'[89] Athens was the paradigm of what, for Camille, was the most fundamental liberty of all, freedom of the press: 'Read Aristophanes, who was writing comedies three thousand years ago [*sic*] and you will be amazed at the strange resemblance between democratic Athens and democratic France.' A strange resemblance indeed, for a few lines later Camille was declaring that today Aristophanes would go straight to the guillotine, an Aristophanes whom Camille hastened to exonerate from all responsibility in the death of Socrates.[90] Yes, it was indeed a 'delightful democracy', that of the *sans-culottes* of Athens, where Solon was free to enjoy 'wine, women and song'.[91]

Freedom of the press was what Camille called 'the right to be wrong',[92] the theoretical basis of what we today call political pluralism. The Athenian example to which Desmoulins repeatedly returned was that of the amnesty granted by vote to the accomplices of the thirty tyrants, after the return of Thrasybulos and the restoration of democracy, the amnesty which imposed, upon pain of death, what Nicole Loraux calls 'amnesia within the city'.[93] That example was to prosper. Chateaubriand returned to it in 1797 in his *Essai sur les révolutions*,[94] as did many others after him, for better or worse.

But it was not always favourable examples that Camille Desmoulins took from Athens, in the first place because he knew perfectly well that tolerance had not always reigned there;[95] and secondly because Athens had also been that direct democracy which Camille, faithful in this respect to what the Jacobins shared with the Girondins, rejected in the name of representative democracy. He maintained that it was not at all politic to close temples and theatres and

> at the same time to multiply popular societies and, by setting them up in every section, to group the whole of Paris, with everybody in his own quarter, around the tribunes erected in all the public squares; and through the sudden appearance of these fifty-three clubs, never heard of until today yet now promoting revolution in Paris, to work hard to propagate an epidemic of this craze for governing, the very sectarian spirit which caused the downfall of Rome and Athens, when everyone wanted to be an active part[96] of the people-king and such groups were permanent fixtures in the Pnyx and the forum.[97]

These were words that Camille was never able to publish and they did not appear publicly until June 1795, one year after Thermidor, which is what I now wish to consider.

The day 9 Thermidor was mainly engineered by a particularly blood-thirsty group of terrorists – Billaud-Varennes, Collot d'Herbois, Fouché, Tallien; at first it was also, as the latest historian of the period following Robespierre's fall has commented, an event 'in search of political meaning'.[98] It was society, in all its weariness and with all its power, that came down on the side of a radical change rather than a 'revolution' like all those that had taken place since 14 July 1789 and, in particular, since 2 June 1793. What were to be the consequences of this change as regards what interests us, namely Greece? They were of capital importance, for it was at this point that *our* vision of Greece emerged or rather, to a certain degree, re-emerged and developed.[99] I shall call upon three important witnesses here, but will try to limit myself to what is essential.

The first is Pierre-Charles Lévesque. He was born in 1736, so could by this time already be accounted an old historian of France and Russia. He had already, before the Revolution, translated a number of Greek texts for Didot's collection of *Moralistes anciens*, but it was not on that account that he gained his place in the Académie des inscriptions et belles-lettres in 1789 and at the Collège de France in 1791.

One of the translations he produced was that of Plutarch's *Apophthegmata Laconica*, which seems to have escaped the notice of the authors of studies devoted to him.[100] The preface with which the book begins explains its pertinence: 'At a time when our now liberated nation resolves to consecrate itself to virtue, which alone can guarantee the preservation of its liberty', Plutarch's text could not fail to be useful since 'it diffuses a love of liberty combined with the most ardent courage'. Every word has a Robespierrist ring to it. Imagine, then, the reader's surprise upon perusing the opening piece, *On the political constitution of the Lacedaemonians*. For this short treatise is little more than a violent indictment in which Sparta clearly serves as a pretext for settling immediate political scores. Sparta 'did not even have laws'; it lived 'in the same state of barbarity in which our fathers languished, when the feudal regime was still in force'. Most Lacedaemonians, whether Helots or not, lived in 'humiliation under the rule of these lords', for that is what the so-called 'Equals' should be called. In short, Sparta was no democracy – which is what Athens, in contrast, undeniably was – but was an aristocracy which constituted a threat to the whole of Greece, and was illiterate to boot.[101] There was perhaps nothing new in this. It had all been said before Lévesque and Lévesque had himself already said it in his *Éloge de M. de Mably*.[102] But the date of the publication of these *Apophthegmata* is both of crucial importance and at the same time somewhat mysterious. The next volume in the collection was announced to be 'at the press' and eventually appeared in Year III. The volume with which we are here concerned was dated both 1794 and Year II. Was it prepared under Robespierre and published, with a number of revisions, between 9 Thermidor (27 July 1794) and the end of Year II (21 September)? That seems a reasonable enough assumption and, if it could be confirmed, would constitute the first sign of an evolution in France that would shift Sparta from, so to speak, the extreme left to the extreme right of the political spectrum. Three years later, Joseph de Maistre, in his *Considérations sur la France* was to hail Lycurgus' constitution as 'the most vigorous institution of secular Antiquity'.[103] At any rate, Lévesque himself clearly aligned himself with a parliamentary regime. His attack on Sparta is all the more significant given that he was, at the time, working on his translation of Thucydides, an author not at all well known to the generation of 1789. Lévesque defended its relevance as follows:

> Of all the historians, Thucydides is the one who must be studied the most in countries where one day all the citizens may play a part in government. A most enlightened member of the Parliament of England has said that there could arise no question upon which light would not be shed by Thucydides.[104]

In other words, Thucydides is essential reading if one lives in a parliamentary regime. In a parliament one does not set up a reign of virtue; one talks politics.

My second witness is Volney,[105] an orientalist and the discoverer of the wretchedness of the East, or what we would today call the third world, who was proud of his own Western superiority. In 1789 he had been a revolutionary; in 1793 he wrote a 'citizen's catechism'; in the November of that same year he had been imprisoned for mixing business with politics over the purchase of a property in Corsica; when released, following Thermidor, Volney acquired a post teaching history at the École normale of Year III, which was inaugurated on 21 January 1795, the third anniversary of the death of Louis XVI.

His six *Leçons d'histoire*[106] not only constituted a course on relativism – obviously enough – but also were a means of showing that 'history takes on the character of the periods and times in which it is written'.[107] The history of the Greeks is not our history, either as a piece of writing or as a sequence of events. History can be lethal – witness the Bible – but it can also heal, after making a diagnosis. The *Leçons d'histoire* were intended to be clinical in the same sense that medicine was then becoming clinical.[108] What Volney's audience needed to be cured of was precisely that 'superstitious adoration . . . of the Greeks and the Romans' which new apostles had inculcated into those willing to believe them, forgetting that Sparta and Athens were cities with slave-based economies:

> Our ancestors swore by Jerusalem and the Bible, and a new sect has sworn by Sparta, Athens and Livy. What is strange in this new kind of religion is that its apostles have not even had any clear idea of the doctrine they were preaching, or that the models they have suggested for us are diametrically opposed to their statements and intentions. They have praised the liberty of Rome and Greece, forgetting that in Sparta an aristocracy of thirty thousand nobles held down six hundred thousand serfs under an atrocious yoke; that to prevent these – as it were – blacks from becoming too numerous, the young Spartans would go out hunting Helots at night, as though for wild animals; and that in Athens, that sanctuary of all liberties, there were four slaves for every free citizen.[109]

This time Athens, as well as Sparta, was swept away in the storm or, as it was beginning to be called at this time, the reaction.[110] Not even the Acropolis found favour in Volney's eyes:

> Those who love the arts have been seduced by the glory of their masterpieces, and it has been forgotten that it was these buildings and temples of Athens that were the primary cause of its downfall, the first symptom of its decadence; because they were the fruit of a

system of extortion and plunder, they provoked both resentment and jealousy in its allies.

The Acropolis was for Athens what the Louvre and Versailles were for France, a cause of ruin and debt, an obstacle to the useful works which could give rise to a representative bourgeois regime in the future. 'Ah! let us cease to admire those Ancients whose only constitutions were oligarchies, whose only politics were exclusive rights for citizens, whose only morality was the law of the strongest and hatred of all foreigners.'[111]

My third and last witness, one more reflective and above all more political than Lévesque, and less extreme than Volney, was Benjamin Constant. He was twenty-two in 1789 and it was in June 1795 that he arrived in Paris in Madame de Staël's luggage, with very definite financial and political ambitions. He was equipped with a solid classical education acquired in the universities of Erlangen and Edinburgh and in 1803 would even rub shoulders, in Göttingen, with the first of the German 'philologists'. In 1787 he had translated part of the *Greek History* by the Scot John Gillies.[112] At the time when Volney was fulminating with anathemas against the new religion, Constant, who in fact was always to retain his admiration and even affection for Greece and the Greek cities and would devote years of his life to writing an apologia for polytheism, was voicing far more classical sentiments, in which his own personal ambitions could also be detected. He declared, for example: 'The ancient Republics produced men who were illustrious in every field. Miltiades, Aristides and Xenophon cultivated learning, were army commanders and attracted crowds to the tribune: already such glorious examples are reappearing amongst us.'[113] Constant did enter the Tribuneship, the only place of political discussion tolerated by the consular Republic, but in 1802 was ejected from it, as an ideologue.

It was during and after this political experience that Constant reflected upon 'the liberty of the Ancients compared to that of the Moderns', to quote the text of a famous lecture delivered in 1819 at the Athénée Royal in Paris.[114]

In point of fact – as has long been known but has become better known since the publication of Constant's main manuscripts preserved in copies in the Bibliothèque nationale and the Bibliothèque cantonale universitaire de Lausanne, under the title *Principes de politique*[115] – it was in 1806 that Constant's thought fixed upon these points, after long years of reflection and study. It is true that by this date, the revolutionary years *stricto sensu* had been left behind, but reflection upon the Terror had begun as early as 1795 and Constant's *oeuvre* provides the last word on the Greek mirage of the French Revolution.

The whole of Book XVI of this manuscript is devoted to the differences between the Ancients and the moderns, and the last chapter in this book is entitled 'On the modern imitators of the republics of Antiquity'. In Book III already, Constant had written: 'Imbued with their principles, the leaders of the French Revolution believed themselves to be Lycurguses, Solons, Numas, and Charlemagnes; even today, despite the depressing result of their efforts, it is the lack of skill of the entrepreneurs, rather than the nature of the enterprise itself, that is blamed.'

In opposition to Mably[116] and Rousseau, as he understood them, and to their revolutionary disciples, Constant proceeded to set out an argument which, by no means fortuitously, prefigured that of Marx, one of the starting points for this study. The liberty of the Ancients was opposed to that of the moderns, as impulse to calculation, war to trade, participation to enjoyment, the immediate to the deferred and, finally, the slavery of the majority to the individual liberty of all. Constant more or less copied the following passage from a manuscript of Madame de Staël, written in 1800, and it summarizes his ideas: 'The liberty of ancient times consisted in all that assured the citizens of the greatest share in the exercise of social power. The liberty of modern times consists in all that guarantees the independence of citizens against the authorities.'[117] In this dichotomy, it goes without saying that participation in power concerns only a tiny number of people; what concerns everyone is civil liberty. And, needless to say, Constant hates 'that huge monastery, Sparta'.[118] The difficulty lies in understanding the status of Athens, a city with an economy based on slavery, like every Greek city. Commenting upon Lysias' περί τραύματος (*On the Wounding*),[119] Constant writes: 'It is difficult for us to conceive of a social state so ferocious that such a plea could be pronounced',[120] yet there is a truly modern dimension to Athens: 'In Athens one enjoyed much greater individual liberty than in Sparta, because Athens was a trading city as well as a warlike one, whereas Sparta was exclusively concerned with war'; and he also remarked: 'If the thoroughly modern character of the Athenians has not been sufficiently noticed, that is because the general spirit of the age influenced the philosophers and they always wrote in reaction to the national *mores*.'[121] Here, Constant shows himself to be well aware of what we nowadays call the 'Spartan mirage', that invention of the Athenian intellectuals. But are we, today, altogether free of the ambiguous Athens of Benjamin Constant's thinking at the beginning of the last century?

Benjamin Constant brings me to the end of my overview of the revolutionary period, for we have arrived at the point of the establishment of the ideological bases of what P. Rosanvallon has called the 'Guizot Moment',[122] the moment of the generation of 1814, which was to elaborate the theory of a monarchy based on a census. This was the intellectual generation which reckoned that the French Revolution was over and done with, although there is perhaps room for doubts on that score, given what is currently happening in China.[123] However, I should like to add a few words touching upon a question that is both very distant from and very close to those so far considered in this study.

While the Revolution was indulging in its Greek and Roman extravaganzas, another Greece, whose inhabitants were, incidentally, known as 'Romans', was living and changing under Turkish occupation. Not much was said about that Greece in the string of assemblies of the time. All the same, Grégoire, in his famous report on 'dialects and the use of the French language', produced on 16 Prairial Year II (4 June 1794), saw fit to state that the Greeks of the present day 'brilliantly preserve the dance described, three thousand years ago, by Homer, on his shield of Achilles',[124] that is to say in Book XVIII of the *Iliad*.

The meeting between modern Greece and the French Revolution took place slightly later, to be precise on 10 Messidor Year V (28 June 1797), when the troops led by General Gentilly[125] arrived from Venice to occupy the island of Corfu. This event was described by General Buonaparte, in his report dated 14 Thermidor (1 August), published in *Le Moniteur* of 21 Thermidor (8 August), as follows:[126]

A huge crowd was on the shore to greet our troops with the cries of joy and enthusiasm which animate peoples whenever they recover their liberty. At the head of this great throng was the *papas*, or local religious leader, that is to say the Orthodox archpriest of Corfu – a learned man of advanced years. He approached General Gentilly and said to him: 'Frenchman, on this island you will find a people ignorant in the sciences and arts in which most nations distinguish themselves. But do not despise it on that account. It can still become what it once was: by reading this book, learn to respect it.' Filled with curiosity, the general opened the book which the *papas* handed him and was considerably surprised to see that it was Homer's *Odyssey*.

Buonaparte goes on to report that 'according to Homer, the island of Corcyra was the land of Princess Nausicaa' and that Captain Arnaud, 'who enjoyed a well deserved reputation' as a man of letters, immediately set sail 'for Ithaca, to raise the tricolour flag over the remains of the palace of Ulysses'.

Notes

1 His edition of *La Cité antique* was published by Flammarion in 1984. Since then, F. Hartog has published *Le XIXe Siècle et l'histoire: le cas Fustel de Coulanges*, PUF, Paris, 1988. The English translation used here is by W. Small, Doubleday Anchor Books, Garden City, NY, 1956.

2 F. Hartog, ed., *La Cité antique*, op. cit., p. xiv.

3 Ibid., pp. 1–2.

4 My italics.

5 On Louis Ménard, see H. Peyre, *Louis Ménard (1822–1907)*, Yale University Press, New Haven, 1931; the two works by Ménard to which I allude are *Prologue d'une révolution*, Paris, 1849, reprinted in *Cahiers de la quinzaine*, 1904, and *Du polythéisme hellénique*, Charpentier, Paris, 1863.

6 I refer to the passages reproduced in *Oeuvres complètes*, III, H. Psichari (ed.), Calmann-Lévy, Paris, 1949, pp. 1063–4. I cite and comment extensively upon this text in my paper 'Renan et le miracle grec', presented on 18 May 1989 at the colloquium on 'Le miracle grec' (University of Nice) and reproduced below, pp. 177–199.

7 See E. Quinet, *La Révolution*, 1865, reprinted with a preface by C. Lefort, Belin, Paris, 1987: see pp. 465–7; see F. Furet, *La Gauche et la Révolution au milieu du XIXe siècle: Edgar Quinet et la question du jacobinisme*, Hachette, Paris, 1986.

8 See F. Furet, *Marx and the French Revolution*, texts by Marx presented and collected by Lucien Calvié and translated into English by D. K. Furet, The University of Chicago Press, Chicago and London, 1988, p. 138; see also p. 142; for a comparison with Benjamin Constant: see pp. 24, 33. Marx's italics. See also M. Löwy, 'La poésie du passé, Marx et la Révolution française' in D. Bensaïd et al., *Permanence de la Révolution, pour un autre bicentenaire*, La Brèche, Paris, 1989, pp. 233–51.

9 On Constant, see below, pp. 159–160.

10 I am citing from *Oeuvres complètes*, Pléiade, III, Paris, 1964, pp. 880–1 (the letters are edited by J.-D. Candaux).

11 On Rousseau, Antiquity and Geneva, see, rather than D. Leduc-Lafayette's *Jean-Jacques Rousseau et le mythe de l'Antiquité*, the fine essay by R. A. Leigh, 'Jean-Jacques Rousseau and the Myth of Antiquity in the Eighteenth Century', in R. R. Bolgar (ed.), *Classical Influences*, pp. 155–68 and Y. Touchefeu, 'Le sauvage et le citoyen: le mythe des origines dans le système de Rousseau', in C. Grell and C. Michel (ed.), *Primitivisme et mythe des origines dans la France des Lumières, 1680–1820*, Presses de l'Université de Sorbonne, Paris, 1989, pp. 177–91. Touchefeu's thesis on this subject is due to be published in 1994. There is also much to be gleaned from L. Guerci, *Libertà degli Antichi e libertà dei Moderni: Sparta, Atene e i 'philosophes' nella Francia del 700*, Guida, Naples, 1979.

12 Well analysed in the above-mentioned work by Y. Touchefeu.

13 H. T. Parker, *The Cult of Antiquity and the French Revolutionaries*, Chicago University Press, 1937; F. Diaz Plaja, *Griegos y Romanos en la Revolución francesa: revista de Occidente*, Madrid, 1960; M. N. Bourguet, *La Référence à*

l'Antiquité chez Robespierre et Saint-Just, a *mémoire de maîtrise* supervised by Albert Soboul, université de Paris I, 1971; P. Vidal-Naquet, Preface to the French translation of M. I. Finley's *Democracy Ancient and Modern, Tradition de la démocratie grecque*, Payot, Paris, 1976; L. Canfora, 'Il classicismo della politica jacobina', *Ideologia del classicismo*, Einaudi, Turin, 1980, pp. 11–19; J. Bouineau, *Les Toges du pouvoir ou la Révolution de droit antique*, Université de Toulouse-le-Mirail and Éd. Eché, Paris, 1986; Myriam Revault d'Allonnes, *D'une mort à l'autre: précipices de la Révolution*, Seuil, Paris, 1989. The statistics appear in J. Bouineau's work, which contains data put together from the *Archives parlementaires*.

14 It is L. Guerci's book, cited above, that constitutes the starting point for all contemporary research. Chantal Grell's thesis casts general historical light on this question It is to be published by the Studies on Voltaire series, Oxford.

15 *The Enlightenment: An Interpretation*, I, *The Rise of Modern Paganism*; for essays of synthesis, apart from Guerci's book, N. Loraux and P. Vidal-Naquet, see chapter 4 above, pp. 82–140.

16 J.-L. Quantin, 'Le mythe de législateur au XVIII° siècle', in C. Grell and C. Michel, op. cit., pp. 153–64, quotation from p. 156; my quotation from Rousseau comes from the *Social Contract*, in *Political Writings*, tr. and ed. F. Watkins, Nelson, London, 1953, p. 41.

17 *Rime*, F. Maggini (ed.), Florence, Le Monnier, 1933, p. 260 ('Capitolo al signor André Chénier', l. 24–31).

18 See Miguel Abensour, 'Saint-Just ou les paradoxes de l'héroïsme révolutionnaire', *Esprit*, February 1989, pp. 60–81; see also C. Mossé, op. cit., p. 62; on martyrs, see also A. Schnapper, 'À propos de David et des martyrs de la Révolution', in M. Vovelle (ed.), *Les Images de la Révolution française*, Presses de l'université de Sorbonne, Paris, 1988, pp. 109–130.

19 *Histoire socialiste; La Convention*, II, Rouff, n.d., Paris, [1903], p. 915.

20 Taine cites this remark in *Les Origines de la France contemporaine*, VII, Hachette, Paris, 1899, p. 246, n. 1, but gives an incorrect reference. His speech, discovered amongst Robespierre's papers, after his arrest, was published after his death.

21 *La France libre*, 1789, in *Oeuvres complètes*, ed., with a Preface, A. Soboul, Kraus Reprint, I, Munich, 1980, p. 71; in May 1793, Camille also wrote as follows: 'We were brought up in the schools of Rome and Athens and amid pride of the republic, only to live abjectly under the monarchy and the sign of Claudius and Vitellius', *Histoire des Brissotins*, in *Oeuvres complètes*, I, p. 521, n. 1.

22 J. Starobinski, *1789, les emblèmes de la raison*, Flammarion, coll. 'Champs', 1979, p. 137.

23 In F. Furet, M. Ozouf, *Dictionnaire critique de la Révolution française*, Flammarion, Paris, 1988, pp. 821–30, 847–58; I am by no means entirely in agreement with the spirit of this book; but all the more reason to cite it and to use it. Mona Ozouf has also seen fit to give the title *L'Homme régénéré* to an essay on the French Revolution published by Gallimard in 1989.

24 See, amongst many other examples, those collected by D. Laredo in Montpellier, in M. Vovelle (ed.), op. cit., pp. 151–5. On the meaning and evolution of the

word 'revolution', see Alain Rey, *'Révolution', histoire d'un mot*, Gallimard, Paris 1989.

25 See document n° 11 in the collection, *La Révolution française à travers les archives, Documentation française*, Paris 1988; it refers to an anonymous police record dating from the second half of July 1789, found after 10 August 1792 in the Tuileries: 'Le départ de M. Necker a fait commencer la révolution' (*sic*). I shall henceforward cite: *Documentation française*.

26 See the *Mémoires* of Barras, G. Duruy (ed.), Hachette, Paris, 1895, I, p. 109. This point was not made in M. Vovelle's chapter on the Revolution in *Histoire de Toulon*, M. Agulhon (ed.), Privat, Toulouse, 1980.

27 See J.-L. Quantin, 'Traduire Plutarque d'Amyot à Ricard; contribution à l'étude du mythe de Sparte au XVIIIᵉ siècle', *Histoire, Économie et Société*, Paris, 1988, pp. 243–59.

28 The archives of a Provençal village which I know well have recently been catalogued and analysed; see Cercle d'études et de recherches sur l'histoire de Fayence, *La Révolution française à Fayence*, Fayence town hall, 1989; I have not found a single reference to Antiquity here.

29 I have already cited this admirable collection at note 25.

30 A. de Baecque, *La Caricature révolutionnaire*, CNRS, 1988; C. Langlois, *La Caricature contre-révolutionnaire*, CNRS, 1988; I shall henceforward cite de Baecque or Langlois.

31 C. Burlingham, J. Cuno, *Politique et polémique: la caricature française et la révolution*, BN, Paris, 1989; I shall henceforward cite BN; an exhibition with a similar theme was organized at the end of 1989 at the Collège des Irlandais in Paris (cf. n. 37 below). In contrast to caricatures, pamphlets were prone to make use of ancient mythology: see Chantal Thomas, *La Reine scélérate*, Seuil, Paris, 1989.

32 *La Révolution: images et récits*, 5 vols, Messidor, Paris, 1985–8; I shall henceforward cite: Vovelle.

33 For example Langlois, p. 137; BN, nᵒˢ 25, 26.

34 De Baecque, pp. 78, 120. It was quite natural that Mercury should appear on the first telegrams. I have also noted the presence of Charon and Chronos (BN, nᵒˢ 92, 19). See *Documentation française*, nᵒˢ 246, 251.

35 For Christ, see, for example, Vovelle, II, p. 58, Langlois, p. 194; BN, p. 53 (the same document).

36 See, for example, Vovelle, I, pp. 301, 306, 307; II, pp. 33ff.; IV, pp. 140–1, with the following legend: 'The republican constitution, resembling the Tablets of the Law of Moses, emerges from the bosom of the Mountain amid thunder and lighting.'

37 I am grateful to Jean-Paul Pittion, of Trinity College, Dublin, for drawing my attention to this rare document and thank him most warmly. He has since published it in *Taking Liberties, Satirical Prints of the French Revolution*, Chester Beatty Library, Dublin, 1989, n° 128.

38 They are absent from the examples collected in Vovelle's five volumes.

39 The work by J. Bouineau contains an analysis which seems very scrupulous.

40 J. Bouineau, op. cit., pp. 61–4.

41 See the classic book by Mona Ozouf, *La Fête révolutionnaire*, Gallimard, Paris, 1976.

42 *Documentation française*, n° 122.

43 The address of the Jacobins of Limoges has been published in *Journal de la Montagne*, 23 July 1793. It is cited by A. Aulard, *Études et leçons sur la Révolution française*, IV, Alcan, 1908, p. 14; J.-C. Benzaken, 'Hercule dans la Révolution française (1789–1799) ou les Nouveaux Travaux d'Hercule' in M. Vovelle (ed.) op. cit., pp. 203–14.

44 *Documentation française*, n° 236.

45 *Documentation française*, n° 230.

46 See J. Bouineau, op. cit., pp. 50–7.

47 *Discours*, A. Fribourg (ed.), Cornély, Paris, 1910, p. 628.

48 *Documentation française*, n° 225.

49 See *Tradition de la démocratie grecque* (cited above, n. 13), p. 16.

50 *Documentation française*, n° 205.

51 Cited by J. Bouineau, op. cit., p. 50.

52 *Documentation française*, n° 153; this maxim from the Gospels appears in the following form in the Declaration of Human Rights of 29 May 1793, article 5: 'Do not unto others that which you would not have them do unto you' and, similarly, in article 6 of the Declaration preceding the *Acte constitutionnel* of 24 June 1793: 'Do not to another that which you would not have him do to you'; see M. Gauchet, *La Révolution des droits de l'homme*, Gallimard, Paris, 1989, pp. 327, 332.

53 It is with good reason that the ancient reference is not analysed in the above-cited book by M. Gauchet.

54 *Esprit de la Révolution et de la Constitution (1791)*, in *Oeuvres*, Champ libre, Paris, 1984, p. 287.

55 See J. Bouineau, op. cit., pp. 189–92, and C. Mossé, op. cit., pp. 100–1.

56 See P. Vidal-Naquet, *Tradition de la démocratie grecque*, p. 16 and n. 25.

57 *Belfagor*, 31, 1976, pp. 355–8.

58 *Tradition de la démocratie grecque*, p. 33.

59 G. Glotz (with the collaboration of R. Cohen), *Histoire grecque*, I, *Des origines aux guerres médiques*, PUF, Paris, 1925, p. 476.

60 Most of this material has been reproduced in the above-cited collection by B. Baczko, *Une éducation pour la démocratie*. See also D. Julia, *Les Trois Couleurs du tableau noir*, Belin, Paris, 1983.

61 B. Baczko, op. cit., p. 353.

62 *Procès-Verbaux du Comité d'instruction publique de la Convention*, II, J. Guillaume (ed.), Impr. Nationale, Paris, 1894, p. 174.

63 The volume published in May 1989 in the Pléiade series, *Orateurs de la Révolution française*, I, *Les Constituants*, by F. Furet and R. Halévi, can serve as a catalogue. The index will appear in vol. III (*Les Conventionnels*); The book is organized in a perfectly reasonable fashion: this volume collects together orators who were principally active from 1789 to 1791, which means, for example, that Robespierre does not figure in it.

64 *Archives parlementaires*, XX, p. 221, cited by J. Bouineau, op. cit., p. 364.

65 *Les Constituants*, p. 376. A note reads: see Plato, Xenophon, etc.
66 Ibid.
67 Ibid., p. 904.
68 Ibid., p. 587.
69 Ibid., p. 21.
70 Ibid., p. 43.
71 That was the case for Louis Ménard.
72 See the texts cited above, pp. 95–96.
73 An observation which elicited from Marat the exclamation: 'All that is simply charlatanism.'
74 This text has frequently been reproduced and commented upon, for example by Jaurès, *La Convention*, II, p. 912; most recently by M. Waltzer, *Regicide and Revolution: Speeches at the Trial of Louis XVI*, tr. M. Rothstein, Cambridge University Press, Cambridge, 1974, p. 178.
75 I have italicized the verb *prophesies*, so as to stress the religious overtone. A work by Miguel Abensour tackles this question.
76 On a number of points I have been helped by M. Revault d'Allonnes, *D'une mort à l'autre* (cited above, n. 13), in particular pp. 100–10.
77 The text in question is Montesquieu, *L'Esprit des lois*, IV, 5.
78 See *Tradition de la démocratie grecque*, p. 29. My remarks are based principally upon the fundamental essay by Marc Richir, 'Révolution et transparence sociale', which is used as a Preface to the new edition of J.-G. Fichte's *Considérations sur la Révolution française*, Payot, coll. 'Critique de la politique', 1974; see also N. Loraux, 'Aux origines de la démocratie: sur la transparence démocratique', *Raison présente*, 49, 1979, pp. 3–13.
79 See Tamara Kondratieva, *Bolcheviks et Jacobins: itinéraire des analogies*, Payot, Paris, 1989.
80 Speech of 18 May 1793. The wounded Lycurgus offers his house as a refuge; A. Fribourg (ed.), p. 432; Lycurgus, Solon and Brutus, 'the honour and support of their countries', 29 May 1793, ibid., p. 463.
81 Intervention on 4 March 1794 (Fribourg, p. 685); Danton's source, probably indirectly, is Diogenes Laertius, *Lives of the Philosophers*, II, 26; in point of fact, it was not a matter of marriage, rather of 'making children' with other women.
82 All the quotations from *Le Vieux Cordelier* are taken from the edition produced by P. Pachet, Belin, 1987, which makes it at last possible to read n° 7 in a text that is philologically accurate. On Camille Desmoulins and his wife, see J.-P. Bertaud, *Camille et Lucille Desmoulins: un couple dans la tourmente*, Presses de la renaissance, Paris, 1986.
83 *Le Vieux Cordelier*, n° 4, Pachet (ed.), p. 89.
84 Ibid., n° 1, p. 40; n° 4, p. 67; n° 5, p. 87.
85 Ibid., n° 3, p. 49.
86 Ibid., n° 7, p. 142; this was an old theme of Camille's. In *L'Histoire des Brissotins*, he had written: 'The immortal glory of this society is to have created the Republic with vices' (*Oeuvres complètes*, I, p. 523).
87 Setting Sparta in opposition to Athens was another of Camille's old themes; it was used in his very first pamphlet, *La France libre*, in 1789. His thesis is the

following: there were two separate orders in Sparta, the Spartans and the Helots; in Athens there was a single order; see *Oeuvres complètes*, I, pp. 25–6; Desmoulins quite simply forgot about the slaves.

88 Ibid., n° 6, p. 102; in February 1792 Desmoulins had clashed with Brissot in this polemic over clients of Desmoulins, who ran a gaming house. In the course of this polemic, also recorded in, for example, Buchez and Roux, *Histoire parlementaire de la Révolution française*, XIII, Paulin, 1834, pp. 181–214, Camille certainly maintained that he supported a republic that showed tolerance in respect of social *mores*, but the role played by Sparta in this affair was no more than minimal. See however p. 191, and *Oeuvres complètes*, I, p. 358.

89 Ibid., n° 7, p. 124.

90 Ibid., pp. 124–6.

91 Ibid., p. 126.

92 Ibid., n° 6, p. 96.

93 N. Loraux, 'L'oubli dans la cité', *Le Temps de la réflexion*, I, 1980, pp. 213–42, and in the volume *Usages de l'oubli*, Seuil, Paris, 1988, 'De l'amnistie et de son contraire', pp. 23–48. References to Thrasybulus in *le Vieux Cordelier*, n° 4, pp. 64–7; n° 5, p. 79.

94 *Essai*, II, ch. VIII, pp. 288–9, M. Regard (ed.), Pléiade, Paris, 1980.

95 *Le Vieux Cordelier*, n° 7, p. 130.

96 It is hard not to think at this point of the distinction between active citizens and passive citizens.

97 Ibid., pp. 138–9.

98 B. Baczko, *Comment sortir de la Terreur: Thermidor et la Révolution*, Gallimard, Paris, 1989, p. 48.

99 I am here returning to themes sketched in or developed in *Tradition de la démocratie grecque* and in the essay written with N. Loraux, 'The formation of bourgeois Athens', see above, pp. 82–140.

100 I am indebted to François Hartog, who drew this text and its importance to my attention and I thank him most warmly. The translation of the *Apophthegmata* was published by Didot, in Year II, in the 'Moralistes anciens' collection.

101 I am citing pp. 2–17 of the Introduction.

102 *Éloge historique de M. l'abbé de Mably*, Guillot, Paris, 1787; the funerary encomium is followed by 'Observations et discussions sur quelques parties des ouvrages de l'abbé de Mably'; on Lycurgus, see pp. 59–62; against Lycurgus, Lévesque takes up the defence of Solon.

103 The oldest extant edition is that of 1797, but it is sometimes claimed, albeit without serious evidence, that there was also an edition dated 1796. *Considérations*, p. 95 of the 1789 edition; J. Tulard (ed.), Garnier, Paris, 1980, p. 63.

104 *Histoire de Thucydide fils d'Olorus*, tr. P.-C. Lévesque, Year IV, Paris, 1795, 4 vols; see in particular pp. iii, xi, xii and xxvii of the Preface.

105 On Volney, I refer the reader essentially to the bibliography cited in the notes to 'The formation of bourgeois Athens' and in particular to the works of J. Gaulmier.

106 C.-F. Volney, *La Loi naturelle* and *Leçons d'histoire*, introduced by J. Gaulmier, Garnier, Paris, 1981; on this text and its context, see also M. Raskolnikoff, 'Volney et les idéologues: le refus de Rome', *Revue historique*, 167, 1982, pp. 357–73.

107 Volney, op. cit., p. 99.

108 See Michel Foucault, *The Birth of the Clinic*, London, 1973; the comparison with clinical medicine is made by Volney in the fifth lesson, p. 123, in which he considers 'the physiological science of government'. Although he may have been unaware of the fact, Volney was, on this point, a disciple of Thucydides.

109 Volney, op. cit., pp. 140–1; J. Gaulmier writes, in connection with this passage, p. 157, n. 21: 'this was a courageous remark to make in Year III'; but he seems to be forgetting that Year III was not Year II.

110 See F. Furet, 'Une polémique thermidorienne sur la Terreur: autour de Benjamin Constant', *Passé-Présent*, 2, 1983, pp. 44–55.

111 Volney, op. cit, pp. 142–3.

112 On which see A. Momigliano, *Problèmes d'historiographie ancienne et moderne*, pp. 363–6.

113 'Discours prononcé au cercle constitutionnnel pour la plantation de l'arbre de la liberté, 30 fructidor an V', a text which may be found in C. Cordié (ed.), *Gli Scritti politici giovanili di B.C.*, p. 229.

114 The text may be found in B. Constant, *De la liberté chez les modernes*, a collection of texts with a long and useful preface by M. Gauchet; by the same author, see also the article 'Constant', in the *Dictionnaire critique*, cited above, pp. 943–50.

115 *Principes de politique*, E. Hofmann (ed.); on the themes tackled here, see in particular I, pp. 345–54; Constant's texts are edited in volume II; N. Loraux and I commented at length on these manuscripts, then unpublished, in our study of 1979, 'The Formation of Bourgeois Athens' (see chapter 4 above, pp. 82–140).

116 See the studies of E. Harpaz, 'Mably et ses contemporains', *Revue des sciences humaines*, 1955, pp. 351–66, and 'Mably et la postérité', ibid., 1954, pp. 25–40; however, the essential work is T. Schleich, *Aufklärung und Revolution: Die Wirkungsgeschichte Gabriel Bonnot de Mablys in Frankreich (1740–1914)*, Klett-Cotta, Stuttgart, 1981. On Rousseau's Thermidorian critique, see J. Roussel, *Jean-Jacques Rousseau en France après la Révolution, 1795–1830*, A. Colin, Paris, 1972, and in particular pp. 489–522, which are devoted to Benjamin Constant.

117 *Des circonstances actuelles qui peuvent terminer la Révolution et des principes qui doivent fonder la république en France*, Lucia Omacini (ed.), Droz, Paris and Geneva, 1979, pp. 111–12, see E. Hofmann, op. cit., II, p. 432, n. 45; Mme de Staël's precise words were: 'The liberty of the present time lies in all that guarantees the independence of citizens against the power of the government. The liberty of ancient times lay in all that assured citizens of the greatest share in the exercise of power'.

118 See E. Hofmann, op. cit., II, p. 439.

119 Speech n° 4.

120 E. Hofmann, op. cit., II, p. 427.

121 Ibid., pp. 427–8.

122 Gallimard, Paris, 1985.

123 I should point out that this paper was first delivered on 31 May 1989.

124 This report is reprinted in M. de Certeau, D. Julia, J. Revel, *Une politique de la langue: la Révolution française et les patois*, Gallimard, Paris, 1975, pp.

300–17, quotation p. 308. The source for Grégoire is P. A. Guys (1720–99), the author of a *Voyage littéraire de la Grèce*, Paris, 1771, 2 vols, to be precise I, pp. 181–2.

125 Or Gentili; the spelling of this officer's name varies greatly in the sources of the period.

126 I mentioned this episode in my introduction to Makryannis' *Mémoires*, tr. D. Kohler, Albin Michel, Paris, 1986. Napoleon did not refer to it in the memoirs that he dictated in Saint-Helena.

6

From Paris to Athens and Back

On 23 August 1806, M. de Chateaubriand, who had spent the previous night at Eleusis, made his entry into Athens: 'We proceeded in silence along the Sacred Way; and never did the most devout of the initiates experience transports equal to mine.'[1] With Fauvel,[2] a famous expert, as his guide, Chateaubriand saw all there was to see, although his visit of three days was a short one for those times, when tourists were in no hurry. The visit to Athens followed a trip to Sparta and his exclamation there of 'Leonidas, Leonidas!', which died away without echo, except perhaps for the repetitions provided by Chateaubriand himself. Once again, the parallel which has been haunting our world of imaginary representations ever since Thucydides presented itself, and Chateaubriand made his choice: 'As I passed from the ruins of Sparta to the ruins of Athens, I felt that I should have liked to die with Leonidas and live with Pericles.'[3] Why was he so carried away and why did he make that choice?

Much later that century, another Breton, Ernest Renan, who was also to pray on the Acropolis before devoting the rest of his life to Jerusalem, was to declare that 'true admiration is historical': an equivocal statement, for there is no such thing as pure history and even in the London and Paris of today it is by no means the case that Greek classical culture is simply one of many cultures; but also a remark of essential profundity, for it presupposed a distance between the admirer and whatever he was admiring and also that he was conscious of that distance.

Was that the case with Chateaubriand? Let us try to understand his position at the particular crossroads where he stood. Chateaubriand, a historian? At first one is tempted to laugh the idea out of court, at the thought

This chapter is an abridged version of the text published in Yannis Tsiomis (ed.), *Athènes, ville capitale*, Athens, Caisse des fonds archéologiques, 1985; the text is dedicated to him.

of this traveller who carried with him nothing but a cross-referenced Homer, Racine and Tasso, and who was to make a tour of the walls of Jerusalem (dating from the time of Suleiman the Magnificent) in order to check out the accuracy of the description of the Holy City provided by the author of *Jerusalem Delivered*. Yet in a sense he *was* a historian, in that he was sensitive to breaks in continuity. In the Introduction to his *Itinéraire* (*Travels*), he speaks of 'history's long silence concerning the most famous country in the universe', a silence that continued for seven centuries during which Athens was lost to view. And he tried to repair that silence by giving his own account of the history of Sparta and Athens from the age of Augustus to his own day. Amongst the authorities whom he consulted were the great Greek scholar Boissonade, who reviewed the proofs of his *Les Martyrs* and the *Itinéraire* from the point of view of a critical historian, and François Guizot, a young Protestant historian who had translated Gibbon and who was later to be described as 'the Gramsci of the bourgeoisie'.[4]

What makes Chateaubriand's experience so fascinating is that it condenses the aspirations and contradictions of two whole centuries. He was a man of the Enlightenment through his early education and, after he had returned from emigration, through his links with the old '*philosophe*' Delisle de Sales who, it must be said, was also the mentor of the occultist Fabre d'Olivet.[5] In 1797 he wrote his *Essai historique sur les religions*, according to which the French Revolution made it possible to reinterpret and understand the revolutions of Antiquity,[6] and first and foremost 'the establishment of republics in Greece'. He travelled in America too, where, in one go, he discovered on the one hand savages in a state of nature and, on the other, a modern republic. 'An Epicurean with a Catholic imagination', to quote Sainte-Beuve, Chateaubriand, in the shadow of Buonaparte, was one of those who restored Catholic worship in France. For him, Athens was but a staging post on the way to Jerusalem, yet Greece was scattered with deserts that recalled America to him and, between Eleusis and Athens, he had passed, without stopping, alongside the magical Byzantine monastery of Daphni, 'erected on the ruins of the temple of Apollo'.[7]

Then he came to the Pnyx. He did not regard the Athenian republic as a model of transparency. Although he loathed despotism, he did not idealize democracy: 'The vices of the Athenian government paved the way to the victory of Sparta. A purely democratic State is the worst of all governments when it has to contend with a powerful enemy and one single will is necessary for the safety of the country.[8]

But the text that sprang to his mind when he found himself on the very spot where the Ecclesia took its decisions was the famous description

of the Athenians which the Corinthians vouchsafed in Thucydides: 'The
Corinthian envoys told the Spartans – "they are given to innovation and
quick to form plans and put their decisions into execution; they are bold
beyond their strength" '.[9] It is a text, if ever there was one, that is stamped
with a sense of history as the *modus vivendi* of a particular people.

Politics was inextricably mixed with aesthetics for Chateaubriand. Was
that a legacy from the Age of Enlightenment? The distant past had been
used as a war machine to 'crush the infamous', that is to say the myth of
Judaeo-Christianity, a distant past which of course included the Graeco-
Roman world, although that was not all that had been called upon. For the
men of the Enlightenment, all times and all places, from India to the
mythical Atlantis, could be used to produce fantasies in which security
and autonomy could be sought. Sparta and Lycurgus appeared in the
forefront of myths about legislators, it is true, but Athens, an Athens that
already appeared almost as a bourgeois city – a trading, liberal city with
a taste for beauty – also had its partisans, first and foremost Voltaire.[10]

In this domain, the Revolution invented nothing, but it did operate a
choice. The cult of Antiquity, the identification with Antiquity, meant a
cult first of Sparta and then of Rome. In 1802, to borrow Victor Hugo's
words, 'Rome took the place of Sparta.'

Actually, this period of paroxysmal millenarianism did not last long.
Athens only figured in it as a contrast and as an indication of rebellion:
for Camille Desmoulins, who in *Le Vieux Cordelier*[11] condemned
Robespierre's Sparta in the name of Athenian liberty, Thermidor, the fall
of Robespierre and of a democracy that claimed to be radical but really
promoted an essentially bourgeois kind of freedom, thus marked a transition, even a total break. The Thermidorean intellectuals salvaged what
they could from the legacy of the Age of Enlightenment: Athens as opposed
to Sparta, liberty as opposed to State slavery; but they also distanced
themselves. There was nothing really new about all this: Rousseau in
particular had been accused, along with Mably, of being at the origin of
the French Revolution's mistaken self-identifications, but in 1794, in the
ninth of his *Lettres écrites sur la Montagne*, he had addressed the Genevese,
who were sometimes inclined – not very successfully – to cast themselves
in the role of ancient republicans, as follows:

> The ancient peoples are no longer a model for the moderns. They are
> too alien in every respect. You, above all, people of Geneva, keep
> to your place . . . You are neither Romans nor Spartans; you are not
> even Athenians. Leave aside those great names which do not suit
> you. You are merchants, artisans, bourgeois, always concerned with
> your own private interests, your work, your trade, your profit; people

for whom liberty itself is simply a means of acquiring possessions without let or hindrance and possessing them in security.[12]

After Thermidor it was possible to be bourgeois, acknowledge the fact and proclaim it without shame. It was only after the revolutionary crisis that modern discourse on Ancient Greece got going and that gradually, between 1795 and 1830 and thereafter, a compromise was elaborated, which filled the school textbooks with all those chapters on the East (including Israel), Greece and Rome. In them, Athens triumphed over a Sparta to which, somewhat paradoxically, nobody was loyal apart from intellectuals of the right or extreme right. As we have seen, Chateaubriand had himself been in two minds about the matter.

But in the context of this resolutely bourgeois world what part did the ideologues play? And I use that term advisedly, in two senses: the one, modern since Marx, meaning those who, in their discourse, disguise the violent realities of the social world, and also that of the sect embodied by the last generation of the Age of Enlightenment, grouped around Cabanis and Destutt de Tracy, Mme Helvétius and Sophie de Condorcet, the sect which took the name, precisely, of 'Idéologues'.

All were in agreement in rejecting, as fundamentally distant, the model of the ancient city, in particular that of Sparta, which during the Terror of Year II had functioned as a myth of social transparency; but not everyone situated Antiquity at exactly the same distance.[13]

Camille Desmoulins, followed by Volney, Mme de Staël and Benjamin Constant,[14] had each in their own fashion criticized that identification, and Desmoulins even paid with his head for that rejection. When Volney went to America he was impressed not by the apparent analogy between Washington and Athens, which so delighted many intellectuals of the young Republic,[15] but rather by the resemblance of Athens and Sparta to the cities of the 'redskins', the American Indians.[16] His travels in the East, mentioned above,[17] had already acquainted him with poverty and backwardness and, on the eve of the Revolution, had confirmed his pride as a Westerner and a Frenchman.

The fact remains that Chateaubriand, for his part, was travelling to the East, an East that was both the East of origins, but in this case those of Christianity, and Volney's East; but he reached it by way of Greece, the status of which was not, nor could be, comparable to that of Egypt and Syria: Greece was a Christian country, the place of, not all our origins, since *Le Génie du christianisme* and *Les Martyrs* had reawakened a different sense of beauty, but certainly a political and aesthetic culture that Chateaubriand had absolutely no intention of rejecting.

To be sure, his *Itinéraire* provided him with a dichotomy which made it possible to spare the Greeks of the present day and ascribe all their poverty, in every sense of the term, solely to the Turkish occupiers of their land. He seldom felt any aesthetic emotion in the presence of Turkish monuments. But he did like their cemeteries, since the Turks who lay there were dead: 'I had one consolation in beholding the tombs of the Turks: they showed me that the barbarian conquerors of Greece had also found their end in this country which they have ravaged.' But he immediately added:

> In other respects, these tombs were a pleasing object. The rose-laurel there grew at the foot of the cypresses, which resembled large black obelisks; white turtle-doves and blue pigeons fluttered and cooed among their branches; the grass waved about the small funeral columns crowned with turbans . . . Fain would I have lingered awhile in this cemetery, where the laurels of Greece, overtopped by the cypress of the East, seem to renew the memory of the two nations whose ashes repose in this spot.[18]

And when he reached Athens, the diversity or *poikilia* of the spectacle moved him: '[There] appeared Athens itself. Its flat roofs interspersed with minarets, cypresses, ruins, detached columns and the domes of its mosques crowned with the large nests of storks produced a pleasing effect in the sun's rays.' But he quickly reconsidered: 'But if Athens might yet be recognized by its ruins, it was obvious at the same time, from the general appearance of its architecture, and the character of its edifices, that the city of Minerva was no longer inhabited by her people.'[19]

Recognize Athens? Since, precisely, no one had ever seen it before, how could anyone do that? But if the Greeks were victims of the Turks and their crushing despotism, they also shared in the poverty which Volney had described and which allowed a Western observer to savour his own superiority, as can be seen from details noted by Chateaubriand, which sometimes border on the ridiculous: 'Some honey from Mount Hymettus was brought to table; but it had a strong taste, which I disliked; and in my opinion, the honey of Chamouni (Chamonix) is far preferable.'[20]

In truth, the astonishing thing is that amongst the travellers of 1806, we find all the themes that were to resurface amongst not only Western philhellenes but also the builders of the Greek State and its capital 'so foreign to itself'[21] and likewise the ideologues of a purified Greek language:

> The indifference of the Greeks relative to their country is equally deplorable and disgraceful; they are not only ignorant of its history,

but almost all of them are such utter strangers to the language which constitutes their glory, that we have seen an Englishman, impelled by a holy zeal, propose to settle at Athens, for the purpose of teaching ancient Greek.[22]

Athens' return to Athens was thus to be mediated by foreigners or, to be more specific, Westerners.

And Athens was to take the form of, not the ancient city, but the national State. Chateaubriand was certainly not the first to preach national unity to the ancient Greeks but at this point, at the beginning of the nineteenth century, the lesson took on a particular meaning. As a result of the clash between them, Athens and Sparta were both dead: 'Athens ceased to exist as a State the moment that it was taken by the Lacedaemonians.'[23] As for Sparta, after taking Athens, it had missed its chance to become Rome. 'Had the Spartans, after the humiliation of Athens, reduced Greece to a Lacedaemonian province, they would perhaps have made themselves the masters of the universe.' Philip would have been 'crushed in his cradle', 'and Alexander, instead of being born under a monarchy, would have sprung, like Caesar, from the bosom of a republic'.[24]

It is perhaps not too far-fetched to think that it was this retrospective myth that was later to give birth, in Greece, to the dream of a massively expanded territory known as the Great Idea (*Megali idea*).

Notes

1 *Travels in Greece, Palestine, Egypt and Barbary*, tr. Frederic Shoberl, London, 1812, vol. I, p. 185.

2 On the groups of people encountered by Chateaubriand and in particular on the character of Fauvel, see W. Saint-Clair, *Lord Elgin and the Marbles*, Oxford University Press, Oxford, 1983.

3 *Travels*, p. 188.

4 This is the title of the Preface by P. Rosanvallon to F. Guizot, *Histoire de la civilisation en Europe*, Hachette, Paris, 1985; see idem, *Le Moment Guizot*, Gallimard, Paris, 1985.

5 On these two figures, see my article: 'Hérodote et l'Atlantide', *Quaderni di Storia*, pp. 30–7, and the study by Pierre Malandin, *Jean-Claude Izouard dit Delisle de Sales (1741–1816), philosophe de la nature*, J. Touzot, Studies on Voltaire, The Voltaire Foundation at the Taylor Institution, Oxford, 1982, pp. 203–204.

6 See above, pp. 100–104.

7 *Travels*, p. 185.

8 Ibid., p. 259.

9 Ibid., p. 200, citing Thucydides, I, 70.

10 See above, p. 87.
11 Repr. P. Pachet, Belin, 1987.
12 See above, p. 143.
13 See above, pp. 152–153.
14 Ibid., pp. 153–160.
15 See J. W. Eadie (ed.), *Classical Tradition in Early America*, University of Michigan Press, 1976; M. Reinhold (ed.), *The Classic Pages, Classical Readings of Eighteenth Century Americans*, American Philological Association, Pennsylvania State University, 1975; idem, 'Eighteenth-Century American Political Thought', in R. R. Bolgar (ed.), *Classical Influences*, pp. 223–43.
16 'Tableau du climat et du sol des États-Unis', Paris, 1803, in *Oeuvres complètes*, Paris, 1838, pp. 724–5.
17 See above, p. 97.
18 *Travels*, pp. 87–8.
19 Ibid., pp. 186–7.
20 Ibid., p. 194; to be fair to Chateaubriand, he did later note that he found an excellent honey in Turkey, near Pergamum.
21 'Athènes étrangère à elle-même', the title of the thesis defended at the université de Paris X by Yannis Tsiomis, 1983.
22 *Travels*, pp. 182–3. Chateaubriand adds that there were some glorious exceptions, such as Koraes.
23 Ibid., p. 258.
24 Ibid., p. 260.

7

Renan and the Greek Miracle

————⊶•◦●◖⫷⫸◗●◦••⊶————

In memoriam: Henriette Psichari

The 'Greek miracle' is a good subject for a colloquium or a conference, as it makes it possible to combine talks upon a variety of themes or even contrasting ones, yet is not an altogether meaningless concept. A few years ago the intellectual heirs of Louis Gernet – the eponymous hero of the research centre to which I belong – decided to publish a collection of little-known texts by this sociologist and Greek scholar. Quite the best title for this collection of papers, suggested by Riccardo di Donato, was *Les Grecs sans miracle* (The Greeks without a miracle).[1] As J.-P. Vernant explains,

> what interested Gernet and what he sought, using in particular Greek legends, were the means to understand the transition, at all levels, from what may be termed, from a social and mental point of view, a prehistory of Greece over to the city civilization. The development of law, the creation of a currency, the institution of politics, the emergence of ethics, the birth of philosophy, history, science and tragedy: all these testify to one and the same 'revolution'.[2]

A revolution is not the same as a miracle. In fact, the two concepts are antithetical. But even if the 'Greek miracle' has no place in history, any more than does the resurrection of Christ, to take an example which is of crucial importance to Renan, the idea of a 'Greek miracle' certainly does stem from our intellectual disciplines. The facts that it first appeared in the issue of the *Revue des deux mondes* of 1 December 1876, then in the Introduction to the *Prayer on the Acropolis*, then again, in 1883, in his *Memoirs* (*Souvenirs d'enfance et de jeunesse*), that the way was paved for

This paper was first presented on 18 May 1989 at the colloquium on 'Le Miracle grec', organized at the University of Nice by Antoine Thivel.

it in all Renan's earlier writings and that it continued to pervade all that he wrote throughout the rest of his life (born in 1823, he died in October 1892) make it worth our while to reflect upon it and explore this area of his thought even if it has already been probed by other scholars.[3]

In the second half of the nineteenth century, Renan's influence was that of a kind of intellectual king, the impact of which is hard to imagine today. He was at once a private scholar, a member of the Académie des inscriptions et belles-lettres at the age of thirty-three, the director of a scholarly project as important as the *Corpus inscriptionum semiticarum* and a man renowned for his editorials, leading articles and public appearances, the most famous of which was his inaugural lecture as Professor of Hebrew at the Collège de France on 11 January 1862. In this he denied the divinity of Jesus Christ (as a result of which his appointment was first suspended, then revoked), speaking as one of the oracles of the liberal bourgeoisie and as what he had always wanted to be, namely the prophet of a new scientific age.

He had emerged from a seminary in 1845, and in 1848 considered himself a socialist, even a revolutionary (this was when he was writing *The Future of Science*). But he subsequently rallied to the Empire and in 1861 accepted an archaeological mission in Phoenicia. He was appalled by the Commune and regarded the Franco-Prussian conflict as a civil war. The Republic showered upon him even more honours than the clerical party had denied him under the Empire, but he never considered it anything better than a second-best: the government of a Caliban grown wise, such as he evoked in one of his 'philosophical dramas' (1878).[4]

It was towards the end of his life that – not counting the clerical party, of course – an ironical counterpoint to the adulation that surrounded him first made itself heard, through the insolent remarks of the young Barrès.[5] A little later, a book such as *Le Système historique de Renan* (1906) rudely suggested that the eminent scholar should stick to literature: 'Today many people would like to conceal the close relationship that exists between the novel and history, but we should not be taken in by the scholarly declarations of the pedants of our time', and claimed that his work had been ruled by 'aesthetic reasons'.[6]

It is not easy to situate the text of 1876 within Renan's *oeuvre*, for he was a by no means simple character and was perfectly prepared to make himself seem even more complicated. In his letter to Buloz, the editor of *La Revue des deux mondes*, which was originally supposed to accompany the *Prayer*, Renan described himself as follows:

> Willy-nilly and despite all my conscientious strivings in the opposite direction, I was predestined to be what I am, a Romantic protesting

against Romanticism, a Utopian striving unsuccessfully to seem bourgeois, a tissue of contradictions reminiscent of scholasticism's *hircocervus*, with its two different natures. One half of me ought to spend its time devouring the other half, like Ctesias' fabulous creature which consumed its own paws without realizing it.[7]

The *Prayer* was presented, in 1876, as a powerful surge of memory, the precise moment when Renan's past surfaced in his thoughts: 'Strangely enough, it was in Athens, in 1865, that I felt myself, for the first time, powerfully drawn to the past.[8] It was like a cool, penetrating breeze coming from regions very far away.' The entire *Prayer* is presented as not only an invocation to the goddess but also a recollection of his clerical Breton childhood. But Renan's preface is not devoted solely to memory, for the whole text oscillates, so to speak, between the Platonic *idea* and Romantic *memory*:

> There is one place where perfection exists and only one. It is there. I had never imagined the like of it ... For a long time past I had ceased to believe in miracles in the strict sense of the word. Nevertheless, the unique destiny of the Jewish race, whence proceeded Jesus and Christianity, seemed to my mind something altogether apart. But here, side by side with the miracle of the Jews, was the Greek miracle, a thing which existed once, which had never been seen before and will never be again, but which will live on in its effects for ever. And by that I mean as a type of eternal beauty, transcending every frontier of nation or of place.

After this, Renan proceeded to confess his 'sins' towards Athena: the sin of being a historian of the Jewish world while beauty lay in Greece; and he emerged strengthened from this experience, claiming to have rediscovered amongst his 'travel notes' an 'old paper' which constituted the text of his famous *Prayer*.

Mine was probably the last generation in France to be made, in early childhood, to read this text as a prime model of great French prose. Today the *Prayer* is no longer considered a masterpiece and Greek art itself has ceased to be a norm or even the inaccessible model that it was for one of Renan's contemporaries born only five years before him, namely Karl Marx.[9]

All – or almost all – that there is to say on the genesis and sources of this famous text has already been said by Jean Pommier,[10] Henriette Psichari and Simone Fraisse.[11] There can be no doubt that it was a 'literary fiction', even – some would say – a hoax. It may be true that a few notes made in Athens were used in the composition of the text (the alexandrine with which the *Prayer* closes, '*dans le linceul de pourpre où dorment les dieux morts*: in the purple shroud wherein the dead gods sleep' even goes back as far as 1862[12]); it may true that it was in a letter from Athens that Renan first used the word 'miracle' in connection with the Acropolis, albeit in a different sense,[13] and it may also be true that, as his notebooks and correspondence indicate, Renan did experience a shock in February 1865 when he arrived in Athens from Alexandria, Beirut and Smyrna. However, the fact is that the published text was not composed until 1876, that is to say after the traumatic rift with Germany (as the text itself abundantly proves) and also after his return to the Collège de France. At this point Renan was close to completing his *Histoire des origines du christianisme*, which he had begun in 1863 with the *Life of Jesus*. The fifth book, *Les Évangiles et la seconde génération chrétienne* appeared in 1877.

With those chronological remarks out of the way, it must be said that the *Prayer on the Acropolis* is, in truth, a remarkable patchwork put together from the network of Renan's reading, the principal works involved being those of Guigniaut, the adapter of Creuzer, and Beulé, the author of a *L'Acropole d'Athènes*.[14] It even contains a number of extremely Christian echoes, which is hardly surprising on the part of a man who had been described as a 'disaffected cathedral':[15] 'Late, late I come to thee, O peerless Beauty' comes straight from Augustine's *Confessions*: '*Sero te amavi pulchritudo tam antiqua et tam nova*'.[16]

The text of the *Prayer* is written in a Franco-Romano-Greek dialect designed to be intelligible to the ancient deity to whom it is addressed. Lord Elgin is thus a 'Caledonian', the Latin name for a Scot, but was almost a Hyperborean, which would have been the Greek word. The first time the Jews are mentioned they are 'Syrians of Palestine'.[17] The story of Christ is that of the son of Cronos (Zeus!) 'who was said to have made a journey to the earth'. In the sixteenth century, Etienne Dolet had similarly refused, as a good Ciceronian, to speak of Christ and instead referred to him using the expression: the son of *Jupiter optimus maximus*. Bankers are, understandably, 'trapezites' and the Bretons become 'Cimmerians', which poses a few problems of historical geography.

But Athena herself, in the series of epithets which Renan generously showers upon her, is not purely Athenian and classical. Certainly she is 'Promachos, Archegetis, Erganè'; she is also Kora, the young girl (not Korè) and that makes her a Dorian; she is the daughter of Zeus but also of Jove and is related to Mars. Such was the language of the period and in particular of Guigniaut. And although she is also 'Democracy', with an unusual note at the bottom of the page giving the sole reference to Philippe Le Bas' collection of inscriptions,[18] Renan fails to make it clear that that particular inscription dated from the Roman period.

Athena even almost became a modern Greek, for in the manuscript she was called 'Sotira'; but this was later changed to '*la Salutaire*' (the 'Saving One').

To whom does the Athena of the *Prayer* stand in contrast? The fundamental opposition is clearly between Greece, symbolized by Athens, and Judaea. Renan evokes the journey made by Saint Paul, 'an ill-favoured little Jew speaking the Greek of the Syrians', who visited Athens 'with uncomprehending mind' and thought that in an unknown deity he had discovered his own God.

But within Greece itself Athens is set in opposition to the Sparta so revered by German scholarship, the Sparta that was 'a mistress of darksome error', just as the Galilee of Jesus is set in opposition to the Jerusalem of the Pharisees. And it is contrasted to Rhodes as spiritual to material richness. The fates of Rome and the East are sealed not in the *Prayer* itself but in its Preface, while the ancient barbarian world is also present and provides another contrast: 'There is poetry in the frozen Strymon and the drunkenness of Thrace.'

From the historical point of view it is the 'ill-favoured little Jew', who introduced another 'miracle', who won out up until the Renaissance: 'For a thousand years the world was a desert in which there blossomed not a single rose.'

In the whole of the last section, the text relativizes the 'Greek miracle', having previously exalted it: 'The world is bigger than thou thinkest. If thou hadst seen the polar snows or the wonders of the Austral sky, thy brow, O goddess, ever calm, would not be so serene; thy head, which would greater be, would embrace divers kinds of beauty.' Even if the temple of Athena is more solid than the Gothic churches,[19] Hagia Sophia, in Constantinople, also produces a 'divine effect' with its bricks and plaster. A few paragraphs earlier Renan had expressed his regret at having believed that 'beauty and ugliness, reason and folly are fused into one another by gradations as imperceptible as the hues on the neck of a dove' – in effect the theme of his unaugural lecture of 1862.[20] He then concludes with a return to relativism: 'The gods, like mortals, have their day and get them hence. It were not well that they should live forever.' Gods? Christ, to be sure, but also Athena.

To what extent did Renan really know this Greece which he idealized, albeit with subtle reservations? His familiarity with Greek literature has been questioned, in particular by his own Greek son-in-law Jean Psichari, one of the most valiant promoters of *dimotiki*, the popular Greek language, but also a somewhat violent and immoderate figure. He even declares that he himself always regarded the *Prayer* 'as not so much an invocation to the saviour-goddess, more a hymn to Celtic poetry'.[21] In Psichari's view, Renan appreciated only the plastic arts of Greece and 'maintained no close relations with any representative of Greek literature'.[22] 'All in all', he declares, 'Renan's Greek culture amounted to no more than that of any good senior schoolboy or any *licencié ès lettres.*' He goes on to draw a number of risky conclusions from the absence from Renan's catalogue of various works – Homer and even the Greek text of the New Testament. Psichari has the goddess in whose name he wrote a reply to Renan's *Prayer* remark: 'Even if you were no Greek scholar, at least you were a glorious philhellene.'[23]

There is a measure of truth in these claims. Jean Pommier has shown,[24] for example, that although Renan did occasionally turn to the Greek text of the Gospels – sometimes to trace a Hebrew expression[25] – he read them first and foremost in Latin; and the same went for authors as important to him as Flavius Josephus.

This was a relatively crucial period for the history of Greek studies in France. It was between 1840 and 1860 that, under the influence of German immigrants, some of them German Jews (Dindorf, Hase, Dübner, Henri Weil), they switched from a Romantic, literary admiration and eclecticism in the manner of Cousin to adopt, albeit ten years late, the methods of German philology.[26] History was an early beneficiary of these changes. Fustel de Coulanges' *The Ancient City* was published no more than a year before Renan's stay in Athens. Before leaving on his journey to the East, Renan had only had time to acknowledge receipt of the book.[27]

What was Renan's position amid these transformations? His youthful, clerical education was that of a good pupil at the church school of Tréguier and, as a young member of the seminary of Saint-Nicolas-du-Chardonnet in the Breton city, he had usually carried off the first prize for Greek prose composition.[28] At Saint-Sulpice he was, of course, a scholar of Hebrew rather than Greek. His *Cahiers de jeunesse* (1845–6) testify to a no more than run-of-the-mill admiration for Greek literature. Looking back on those years, he was himself to admit: 'All my visions of the antique world came to me through Fénelon's *Télémaque* and *Aristonoüs.*'[29] All the same, he did sing the praises of a Greece composed of artisans and farmers and protested against the slavish reproduction of the plots of the Greek tragic poets, pointing out that the heroes of Aeschylus and Sophocles 'are not our fathers'.[30] He also compared the 'sutures' of the *Iliad* to those of the Book of *Genesis.*[31]

Having left the seminary, in the course of the seven extraordinary years in which he won a whole gamut of academic qualifications and collected more manuscripts than most scholars do in a lifetime, it is true that Renan devoted most of his research to the structure of Semitic languages, to

Averroès – pointing out the latter's dearth of originality as compared with Aristotle[32] – and to writing *The Future of Science*, which remains the founding work of French historicism. But he also studied under Eugène Burnouf and Émile Egger, whose friend he became.[33] Egger, a Greek scholar and historian of Greek studies, an epigraphist and archaeologist, who was a disciple of Claude Fauriel, may, precisely, be regarded as epitomizing the generation that spanned the transition from Romanticism to positivism. It was also during this brief period that Renan composed a memorandum of over 700 pages for the Académie des inscriptions et belles-lettres, which had included its subject in its 1848 competition.[34] Renan's work was entitled *Histoire de l'étude de la langue grecque dans l'Occident de l'Europe depuis la fin du Vᵉ siècle jusqu'à celle du XIVᵉ* and it has yet to find a publisher.[35] It is a work which shows that Renan was familiar with the principal French sources of manuscripts but that at this date his knowledge of other European sources was still indirect.

Throughout the studies of those years Renan was forcefully struck by the disparity between philosophy and science on the one hand and literature and everything to do with beauty on the other. And it was beauty that had disappeared. In the whole body of the strictly medieval texts Renan discovered only *one* Homeric hemistich cited in Greek.

His conclusion to this book testifies to what now became his religion, a religion nurtured by philology: 'May the spirit of patient and laborious research never die amongst us! May we understand that science is a religion and that everything that concerns it is sacred. And when future Academicians propose the history of classical studies in what we call modern times, let them not imagine that the nineteenth century represents the limits of culture.'

This was without doubt the greatest contribution that Renan made to Greek studies; to which, in fairness, should be added his epigraphical work in his own archaeological field: Lebanon, as his *Mission de Phénicie* most abundantly testifies.

That being said, however, it is quite true that, although he published in the daily press (*Le Journal des débats*), produced reviews aimed at the general public (*La Revue des deux mondes*) and also wrote for scholarly journals on every possible subject imaginable (India as well as the Western Middle Ages, Iranian art as well as the Celts, the Caesars of Rome as well as the Egypt of the Pharaohs, all fields quite outside his own field of research), Renan wrote virtually nothing, apart from the *Prayer*, about the object of his worship: classical Greece.

It is as if, even before the discovery of Athens, for Renan Greece was an image to be admired and the object of a cult, even though his own scholarly interests lay in another direction. Certainly, as a linguist, a comparativist and a philologist, he was determined to transpose the lessons he had learned from Germany.[36] To him, German philological conferences seemed joyful councils of some religion of scholarship.[37] Throughout his life Renan remained convinced of this, and the work that he considered his most important on a scholarly level, namely his *Corpus des inscriptions sémitiques*, which in fact was not a success, is placed under the sign of Boeckh and Greek and Latin epigraphy.[38]

Typically enough, Renan admired everything to do with Greece except, precisely, the rhetorical and philological works.[39] So for him it remained a model rather than an object of direct scholarship. Renan was a Greek scholar in his heart but not in practice. In Freudian terms, we might say that, for him, Greece was connected with the 'principle of pleasure', the Semitic world with the 'principle of reality'.

But that was not the way Renan himself put it. In 1865, when he visited Athens, he glimpsed the phantom of another possible Renan, who might have devoted his life to Athens with joy and rapture. It was at this point that he thought of getting his friend Hippolyte Taine to embody his dream.[40] He returned repeatedly to the subject, right until the end of his life, always in terms of the pleasure involved. In 1887, for instance, in the preface to his *History of the People of Israel*, he wrote as follows:

Happy will be the man who shall, at the age of sixty, write this history *con amore*, after having spent his whole life in the study of works which so many learned schools have devoted to it. He will have for his recompense the greatest joy man can taste, that of following up the evolutions of life in the very centre of the divine egg within which life first began to palpitate.[41]

In his last public lecture, delivered on 5 May 1892 to the members of the Association for the Encouragement of Greek Studies, he repeated that view for the last time.[42] This does not mean that in 1848 Renan's Greece already possessed that somewhat frozen beauty that it acquired in his *Prayer*. At the point when he was writing *The Future of Science*, a book informed by a hatred of the bourgeois spirit that puts one in mind of Flaubert and that Renan, whatever his practice, was never to renounce entirely,[43] the entire Athenian people served as his model: 'What we require in the way of civilization is Greece, without the slave system.'[44] It was assuredly not a serene and tranquil people. Let me cite a little-known passage from this famous book, if only to counterbalance the *Prayer*. To situate the Renan of that period politically, it is worth recording that in his opinion 'a three-days revolution does more for the progress of the human mind than a generation of the Académie des inscriptions'.[45]

It is true that he did not become a member of that institution until 1856. Renan thus wrote as follows:

> The customary state of Athens was one of terror. Never were political habits more violent, or the security of the individual less. The enemy was always a few leagues off; not a year elapsed but what he appeared at the gates, but what it was necessary to go out and fight against him. And within, what an interminable series of revolutions! Today an exile, tomorrow sold as a slave or condemned to drink hemlock; then regretted, honoured as a god, liable each day to be dragged before the most pitiless revolutionary tribunal, the Athenian, who amid this life of rush and uncertainty was never sure of the morrow, produced with a spontaneousness which overwhelms us with surprise. Let us not forget that the Parthenon and the Propylaea, the statues of Phidias, the *Dialogues* of Plato, the stinging satires of Aristophanes, were the work of an epoch very similar to 1793, of a political state of things which entailed, in proportion to the number of people concerned, more violent deaths than our first revolution at its paroxysm. Where, in these masterpieces, do we find a trace of the terror?[46]

The image that Renan produced of the Greek miracle was full of contrasts, and the same goes for that other unique event equally full of contrasts, the coming of Christ: 'The appearance of Christ would be inexplicable in a logical and regular state of things; it is comprehensible during the singular crisis which at that period characterized the reasoning sense of Judaea.'[47]

For Renan in his maturity and old age, for the Renan who produced his great works of the late Second Empire and the Third Republic, there was both a 'Greek miracle' and a 'Jewish miracle'. The association and parallelism between them are a constant feature of his thought. Addressing the Société des études juives on 26 May 1882, he told a mainly Jewish audience: 'Your Parthenon, gentlemen, is – if you like – Jerusalem, but . . . your true Parthenon is the Bible.'[48] There can be miracles even within a general miracle. One such is the Acropolis within the history of Athens. Another is the phenomenon of prophecy within the history of Israel:

> The national god of Israel will be the absolute god, his worship must not be confined to inoffensive Panathenaea; to impose it is to impose a dogma, that is to say the one thing in the world least susceptible of being commanded. It is clear that the people were devoted to fanaticism, but fanaticism in its hands was not purely destructive as

in the case of Islam. By a miracle of which there is but one other example, viz. the Reformation of the fourteenth century, Jewish fanaticism at last ended in the most liberal creed ever seen in the world, in the religion of a god universally worshipped by the whole human race.[49]

That text dates from 1889; here is one written twenty years earlier:

Greece, a land of miracles, like Judaea and Sinai, flowered but once and can never flower again. It produced something unique which can never be repeated. It would seem that, when God reveals himself in a country, he dries it up for ever.[50]

Renan occasionally adds a third miracle to the Judaeo-Christian one that was renewed at the time of the Reformation: namely Rome. He does so in the preface (1887) to the *History of the People of Israel*: 'If there is such a thing as one miraculous history, there are at least three.' Judaea's lot was religion, Greece's truth and beauty, Rome's might. But when it comes to a hierarchy, Renan's choice is already made: 'In my opinion, the greatest miracle on record is Greece itself.'[51] The paradox is, however, that a few lines earlier Renan, as a good positivist historian, had rejected the very idea of miracles, starting with the best known of them all: the resurrection. And when he describes the doings of the prophets, he has nothing but scorn for 'miracles, with their usual accompaniment of imposture and affectation'.[52]

Indeed, the entire Introduction to *The Apostles*, which appeared in 1866 a few months after Renan's visit to Athens, is devoted to explaining why there is no such thing as a miracle. Having dealt with miracles of the physical kind, Renan tackles miracles of the moral kind, arguing that if one considers the birth of Christianity and the passion of its martyrs to be miracles, Buddhism, Babism and Islam have similar claims to make; and he goes on as follows: 'Let us allow that the foundation of Christianity is something utterly peculiar. Another equally peculiar thing is Hellenism. Hellenism, in other words, is as much a prodigy of beauty as Christianity is a prodigy of sanctity. A unique action or development is not necessarily miraculous.'[53] Prophecy, for example, was a 'unique institution' which, however, Renan compared to modern journalism.[54] But in 1892 still, at the banquet of the Association for the Encouragement of Greek Studies, he declared, having spoken of the Greek miracle, and it alone, 'What has happened only once is what I call a miracle.'[55]

This analysis may be considered somewhat simplistic, but it shows that 'miracle' is no more than a word, an exclamation, so to speak, simply a concession to the religious vocabulary into which Renan so easily slips. But whether it be a matter of Greece or Rome, the Reformation or Jesus, the history of the Jews or that of Athens, the word in no way constitutes a conceptual framework. That framework must clearly be sought elsewhere. Not only did Renan sometimes regret having been a historian of the Jewish world rather than a historian of Greece or of the French Revolution; he also regretted 'having preferred historical sciences to natural sciences, particularly comparative physiology'.[56]

There is nothing surprising about that temptation. This was the age of Geoffroy Saint-Hilaire and Claude Bernard, and also of Darwin, whose *On the Origin of Species* appeared in 1859; and even if Renan used a Darwinian vocabulary,[57] this amounted to no more than a temptation, a concession to the spirit of the age. But that temptation does explain the presence in Renan's *oeuvre* of a significant biological metaphor. We should remember that Marx regarded Greece as the childhood of modern humanity, a 'normal' childhood,[58] which implied that other cultures were, for their part, *not normal.* Already in *The Future of Science* Renan considered that some peoples are destined to an 'eternal youth'.[59] But that was not the case of the 'Aryas' and Renan was to declare in his inaugural lecture of 23 February 1862 that the primitive religion of the Indo-European race was 'charming and profound, as was the imagination of those peoples . . . It was a religion of children, full of naivety and poetry, but one which was destined to collapse as soon as thought became more demanding'.[60] By the time of Pisistratus, already, the Athenians were no longer children.

More precisely, what is Greece's position in this metaphor of the ages of life and civilizations? Cultures such as those of Egypt (and China) were 'born mature and almost decrepit and had always had that childlike and at the same time antiquated air noticeable in its monuments and history'. The text that I have just cited, an article on the Egypt of the Pharaohs,[61] which was published in *La Revue des deux mondes* of 1 April 1865, was, precisely, written in Athens, and in it Renan returned to the famous dialogue between Solon and the priest of Saïs, in the *Timaeus*. No, the Greeks were decidedly not children. Egypt, however, would always lack 'the divine youth of the *Yavanas*'; and Renan went on, imprudently for a philologist, to liken the *Yavanas* or *Iones* (Ionians) to *juvenes*, the young.[62] Once again this is only a metaphor, even if Renan does justify it with an unfortunate linguistic comment, but this metaphor points to what really is the key question, the question of *race* as Renan understood it.[63]

When Renan arrived in Athens in February 1865, the French ambassador there was Arthur de Gobineau (the self-styled Comte de Gobineau). His *Essai sur l'inégalité des races humaines* had been published in Paris in 1853–4. A copy was sent to Renan, who acknowledged this 'fine work', promising to comment on it one day (which he never did), but rejected the excessive nature of the book:

> A tiny quantity of noble blood circulating through a people is enough to ennoble it, at least so far as its historical effects are concerned: thus France, a nation altogether declined into a common condition, really does play the role of a gentleman in the world. Setting aside totally inferior races which, if mixed with the great races, would simply poison the human race, what I imagine for the future is a homogeneous human race in which all the original streams would mingle in one great river and in which all memory of diverse origins would be lost.[64]

Gobineau's Greece, a mythical creation if ever there was one, was the product of a mixture, sometimes fortunate, sometimes catastrophic, of 'Semites' and 'Aryans'. When Renan invoked his own 'blue-eyed goddess', there is no knowing whether he was inspired by Homer's *glaukôpis*, the statue of Athena with 'blue-green' eyes mentioned by Pausanias in connection with the Hephaesteion (or 'Theseion') of Athens[65] or 'the proud woman with golden hair, blue eyes and white arms' described by Gobineau.[66] It is hard for us today to credit that the greatest minds of the nineteenth century, whether or not they used the criterion of race consciously, were all – or almost all – convinced of the fundamental inequality of different peoples.[67]

Marx's East was a static place, the history of which amounted to no more than a 'history of religions'. For him, as for Engels, there existed 'peoples without a history', *geschichtslosen Völker*,[68] of whom the Czechs provided a paradigm. Renan thus arrived in Athens carrying in his luggage Michelet's *La Bible de l'humanité*, published in 1864. This was without doubt one source for the *Prayer*.[69] Now, this Bible compared all the 'sons of light', the Aryas, Indians, Persians and Greeks, whose 'inferior branches' were constituted by the Romans, Celts and Germanic peoples. It excluded from the human race the Chinese, with their 'attempts at life in the wild' and also the 'dark genius of the South', that is to say Egypt and Judaea. Greece was the quintessence of the 'Arya' world, but 'nothing lasts. The city, that sublime work of art, the city will pass away. And the gods too will pass away. Let us make man eternal.'[70]

So Renan is by no means isolated and while, from *The Future of Science* down to his last works, he clung firmly to the racist or 'racialist' paradigm,[71] it had in truth all been said already, in his *Histoire générale et système comparé des langues sémitiques*, published in 1855 but drafted as early as 1847. In contrast to the Indo-European languages, which were capable of progress and of creating and living history, the Semitic languages attained perfection in one go: 'The substance of Semitic philology . . . is metallic, if I may so put it, and ever since the earliest Antiquity, possibly ever since the first appearance of language, has preserved unchanged the most striking identity.'[72] This simplicity of the Semitic languages is not unconnected with the Semites' major invention, monotheism: 'The semitic race possesses those firm and sure intuitions which from the first freed the deity from its veils and, *without reflection or argument*, attained the purest religious form ever known to Antiquity.'[73] Such is Renan's racism (or racialism), an essentially linguistic variety. He rejected biological racism (amongst whites, at least), as was already clear in his reply to Gobineau. Nevertheless, that racism impregnates the whole of his *oeuvre*,[74] to such a degree that, for example, he describes Macedon and Thrace as a hearth of 'Aryan life'.[75]

Within his own particular discipline, Renan thus wrote history on two different levels, one of which was fantastical. While the Hebrews and subsequently the Jews represent the highest achievement attainable by Semitic peoples, they are confronted with the history of the Greek people, which, for its part, represents the most perfect expression of the Indo-European genius. For the former, monotheism,[76] but also egalitarian aspirations, even socialism: according to Renan, 'the first appearance of Socialism' was in about 622 BC, in *Deuteronomy*;[77] for the latter, beauty, truth, the State, a spirit of order and hierarchy,[78] with all that this implies in the way of both privileges for the best in society, and injustice: 'The State and even the *polis* (especially the latter) imply classes, hereditary privileges, injustices, abuses, liberty accorded to certain vices and a severe elimination of social questions.'[79] And Renan goes on: 'People were athirst for justice in Jerusalem, when at Athens and at Sparta no protest was raised against slavery, when the Greek conscience, in any embarrassing conjuncture, is satisfied with the peremptory reason: Διὸς δ'ἐτελείετο βουλή.[80]

In the conclusion to his last work, the *History of the People of Israel*, Renan declared both that Christianity and Judaism would disappear whereas 'the Greek achievement, that is to say science', 'will continue forever' and at the same time that 'the mark left by Israel will be eternal'.[81]

There remains the great, ultimate question which Renan felt bound to answer and did indeed attempt to do repeatedly throughout his life. Even if *linguistically* we, like all the great Indo-European peoples, are Aryas worthy to conquer the world – even Caliban learned the Aryan language[82] – *spiritually* we are Semites, since our god comes from Israel. How does Renan resolve this immense problem? His response is complex and, in

some respects, contradictory. He suggests that, in principle, 'things that
are too perfect do not affect one another'. 'The Hebraic genius and the
Greek genius of the fifth century could never establish a grip upon each
other.'[83] Even much later, when Saint Paul reached Athens in AD 53, an
Athens in a state of decadence despite the fact that 'the race had remained
quite pure', but where 'the monuments of the Acropolis were still intact',[84]
he beheld them without understanding them and was incapable of communicating with the Athenians.

Yet there were two places that did symbolize communication. First
Alexandria, in the Hellenistic period, Alexandria, 'that great humanitarian
town'.[85] It was no longer a city. 'The literary work of Greece was finished,
its scientific work was beginning.' What had been impossible and un-
thinkable in the fifth century was so no longer. 'A decadent Greece and
a decadent Hebraism could thus embrace.'[86] If it was true that 'Judaism
was simply the wild stock upon which the Aryan race produced its flower',[87]
that graft was effected in Alexandria. The Alexandrian who translated the
beginning of *Genesis* 'intuited the most sublime truth of history, namely
that the Hebrew genius would conquer the world through the Greek
language and in alliance with Hellenism'.[88] A twentieth-century scholar,
Elias Bickerman has said the same in different words: 'The Jews became
"people of the Book" when this Book was rendered into Greek.'[89]

The other place was Antioch, where, for the first time, the Christians
were actually called 'Christians'. According to Renan, the Renan of *The
Apostles* (1866), it was a den of 'moral putrefaction' and, situated on the
edge of both worlds, also 'the capital of all lies and the sink of every
description of infamy', the place where races intermingled and precisely
where, not despite that monstrosity but because of it, communication
could function. 'It was, then, on the shores of the Orontes that the religious fusion of races, dreamed of by Jesus or, to speak more fully, by six
centuries of prophets, became a reality.'[90] Dreamed of by Jesus? But was
Jesus himself the heir of the prophets or the heir of the 'Greek miracle',
as Simone Weil, in the wake of many others, believed?

On this slippery ground, Renan behaved more like a poet than a
historian, proceeding according to a logic of his own. That is to say he
was evasive. At first he wrote: 'Jesus was ignorant of the very name of
Buddha, of Zoroaster, of Plato; he had read no Greek book, no Buddhist
Sutra, yet notwithstanding there was in him more than one element which,
without his suspecting it, emanated from Buddhism, Parseeism or the
Greek wisdom.' What this seems to be discreetly leading up to is an
Aryan Jesus. Yet on the next page, we find the following words: 'What
the Golden Age was for secular art and literature, the age of Jesus was
for religion.' Here it is a matter not of a union between two decadent

cultures, but of one of those 'divine'[91] or 'miraculous' hours when it is possible for one world to overcome another.

There is one more question that I must raise. The text with which we started accompanied a prayer and so clearly presupposed a god and a religion. Is it the case that, having broken with Christianity, Renan was tempted to recreate, at the feet of the Greek goddess and around her, a kind of neo-paganism? The text of the *Prayer* itself shows that he was under no illusion and even if he did speak, on 5 May 1892, of that 'sacred soil where our acropolis is',[92] it is hard to take him entirely seriously, for he did, after all, also declare: 'The religion of Athena established no more of a hold on me than my childhood did.'[93] All the same, the question is not absurd. Following Peter Gay's work,[94] some scholars have spoken of a 'rise of paganism' in the Age of Enlightenment, in *philosophe* circles; and classical Antiquity, albeit Sparta and Rome more than Athens, were taken as models at the time of the Revolution, in opposition to the Christian model, which it was easy to assimilate to feudalism.[95] The Revolutionary calendar, for example, testifies to the neo-pagan naturalism of the Revolution.

The nineteenth century was certainly familiar with that impulse, although in a form which had clearly been very much reworked. Renan's contemporaries even included one man who took this matter extremely seriously both in his writings and in his personal life. He was Louis Ménard (1822–1901), who graduated from the École normale in 1842 and who maintained a number of connections with Renan. Ménard's works contain plenty of Renanian themes, such as the contrast between the Gothic Church and the sun-drenched Acropolis.[96] However, he differed from Renan on three main counts. In the first place, Ménard was a true revolutionary, whose account of the June Days in 1848 even today remains of major importance.[97] Secondly, he took ancient paganism as one of his principal subjects of study and in 1863 even published a book entitled *Du polythéisme hellénique*, which testifies to both his scholarship and his faith. Finally, like Renan at the time of *The Future of Science*, but in a far more enduring fashion, he associated the French Revolution, both that of 1789 and that of his own times, with a return to Antiquity. In that earlier Revolution he was torn between the Girondins and the Dantonists: 'Greece is the Gironde of Antiquity, Rome is its Mountain',[98] and he was in sympathy with the Athenian Camille Desmoulins. It was in all seriousness that he sought in Antiquity for both a religious and a political model, that of a government which cost the community virtually nothing.[99] Nor was he alone in the nineteenth century in following such a line of reasoning, witness Edgar Quinet. To be sure, Renan, for his part, did not fall for that temptation, but that does not mean to say that he was indifferent to the problem of founding a new cult. However, traces of that temptation would obviously be unlikely to surface in his historical writings.

I shall take as my evidence the first of the *Philosophical Dialogues*, written in Versailles in 1871, so contemporary with the Paris Commune and the *Réforme intellectuelle et morale*, published in 1876, the same year as the writing and publication of the *Prayer*.[100] All the characters in this dialogue are in agreement on three rules: 'the cult of the ideal, the negation of the supernatural and experimental research into reality'.[101] And they all bear Greek names: Philalethes, Euthyphron, Eudoxus, Theophrastus. The first dialogue is called 'Certitudes', the second 'Probabilities' and the third, which astounded Péguy and is entitled 'Dreams', introduces an interlocutor by the name of Theoctistes, that is to say 'the founder of God'.

Theoctistes is an opponent of democracy who proposes 'an oligarchic solution to the problem of the universe', involving the creation of a superior race of gods and even

> a state in which everything might likewise culminate in a single conscious centre, in which the universe might be reduced to a single existence, in which the conception of personal monotheism might become a truth . . . A single being summing up the fruition of the universe and an infinite number of individuals joyful in contributing to it: no contradiction is involved here, save to our superficial individualism.

And once again, an appeal is made to Antiquity: 'In the good olden times, the immolation of an animal intended to be eaten was justly regarded as a religious action. Such slaughter committed under pressure of an absolute necessity should be disguised, it was thought, by garlands and some religious ceremony . . . The majority has to think and live by proxy.'[102] That was the supreme form of the cult that Renan addressed to the gods of Greece. But was it really to the gods of Greece? Is it not clear that the ultimate beneficiary of the sacrifice of all, the mind that was to glory alone in beauty and immortality, was really himself, Renan?

Appendix

Thanks to François Hartog, I am now in a position to produce an unpublished letter from Ernest Renan to Fustel de Coulanges, which has been preserved in the family archives. Renan was about to set off on his travels in the East, which were eventually to lead him to Athens. The letter amounts to no more than a somewhat grandiose acknowledgement, and a reader not aware of this would not necessarily realize that the book in question was Fustel de Coulanges's *La Cité antique*.

Paris, 30 October 1864

Sir,

If my comments on provincial universities have been scathing, I have generally made an exception of that of Strasbourg.[103] Your book, for which I thank you, therefore does not prove me wrong, and I should be happy indeed to receive many of its kind. This book in the first place sets you amongst the best representatives of the school that is seeking to expand history and, by making it more philosophical and more general, to render it more truthful. The profundity and accuracy of some of your perceptions impressed me greatly. Alongside comparative philology, introduced fifty years ago, and comparative mythology, introduced fifteen years ago, we should also have comparative law, the science of origins illuminated by the comparison of laws and customs. Once such studies are created, you will certainly find a place there. Your book has arrived in the midst of my preparations for quite a long journey; but whatever I have not been able to read yet I shall certainly read later. Monsieur Taine and Monsieur Perrot[104] have both spoken of you in the warmest of terms. Please excuse the brevity of these lines written on the eve of my departure and accept the expression of my most sincere respects.

E. Renan

Notes

1 L. Gernet, *Les Grecs sans miracle*, ed. R. di Donato, Preface by J.-P. Vernant, La Découverte, Paris, 1983.

2 Ibid., p. 12 (Preface).

3 Henriette Psichari, *La Prière sur l'Acropole*, CNRS, 1956; Henri Peyre, *Renan et la Grèce*, Nizet, Paris, 1973; Simone Fraisse, *Renan au pied de l'Acropole: du nouveau sur la prière*, Nizet, Paris, 1979; Bianca M. Calabresi Finzi Contini, *Ernest Renan et Émile Egger: une amitié de quarante ans*, Nizet, Paris, 1979. So much did the *Prayer* come to be regarded as symbolic of the whole of Renan's *oeuvre* that the monument erected to him close to the cathedral of Tréguier in 1903 (not without provoking something of a scandal) displays an Athena wearing a helmet-cum-halo, watching over the worthy bourgeois leaning on his cane; a photograph of this monument may be found in M. Agulhon, *Marianne au pouvoir*, Flammarion, Paris, 1989.

4 In the present paper, except in the case of works which do not appear in its text, most quotations from the works of Renan are from the *Oeuvres complètes*, 10 vols, Henriette Psichari (ed.), Calmann-Lévy, 1947–61. I shall cite *OC*, I, etc. However, where English translations are available, the references given will be to them.

5 M. Barrès, *Huit jours chez M. Renan*, Paris, 1888, republished with complementary texts, Pauvert, Paris, 1965.

6 G. Sorel, *Le Système historique de Renan*, Jacques, 1906, pp. 24–5, 29; see D. Lindenberg, 'Mouvement prolétarien et révolution religieuse: Georges Sorel critique de Renan' in J. Julliard and S. Sand (eds), *Georges Sorel en son temps*, Seuil, Paris, 1985, pp. 189–201; on this aesthetic aspect, see T. Todorov, *Nous et les autres: la réflexion française sur la diversité humaine*, Seuil, Paris, 1989, p. 73, in which a comparison with Baudelaire is drawn.

7 For the original version of this text, see H. Psichari, op. cit., pp. 50–1; it reappears in *OC*, II, p. 760.

8 This declaration is, of course, contradicted elsewhere in Renan's own writings: see *The Future of Science*, tr. Albert D. Vandam, Chapman and Hall, London, 1891, p. 205 (*OC* III, p. 904), the famous passage in which he recalls a chance visit to a Breton cemetery: 'I am going to tell you about the most charming recollection of my early youth . . .'.

9 I allude to the famous passage in the *Critique of Political economy*, Introduction (1857), tr. N. I. Stone, Chicago, 1904, p. 312; on this text, see J.-P. Vernant in J.-P. Vernant and P. Vidal-Naquet, *Myth and Tragedy*, tr. J. Lloyd, Zone Books, New York, 1988, pp. 237–9.

10 J. Pommier, *La Jeunesse cléricale d'Ernest Renan*, Publications de l'université de Strasbourg, Les Belles-Lettres, Paris, 1923.

11 Op. cit. above, n. 3.

12 H. Psichari, op. cit., p. 110.

13 'What a miracle that these marvels have come down to us? When one thinks that a whim on the part of an *aga* might have destroyed all that' (letter dated 5 March 1865 to Dr. Gaillardot, *OC*, X, p. 420); Renan was forgetting that it was the cannon of the Venetian Morosini that had destroyed the Parthenon in 1687.

14 In 1851 C. Guigniaut completed his vast synthesis in ten volumes, adapted from Creuzer, *Les Religions de l'Antiquité considérées dans leurs formes symbolique et mythologique*; Beulé's *L'Acropole d'Athènes*, 2 vols, Didot, Paris, 1853, appeared soon after.

15 M. Peyre, op. cit. above, n. 3, p. 67, cites this expression without giving its source.

16 *Confessions*, X, 27, 8; see M. Peyre, op. cit., p. 64.

17 See Herodotus, II, 104.

18 The reference given is quite imprecise. The exact reference is P. Le Bas and W. H. Waddington, *Voyage archéologique: inscriptions*, I, 5th fascicle, n° 32A, p. 17. The inscription discovered in 1836 has since disappeared.

19 There is a similar comparison in an article of 1862 on 'L'Art du Moyen Age et les causes de la décadence', *OC*, II, pp. 487–8; see also *Mission de Phénicie 1864–1874*, pp. 820–1; this allusion to the 'narrowness' of Athena was to irritate C.

Maurras: 'Renan adds: "if your *cella* were large enough to accommodate a crowd, it would collapse". To be sure, but why accommodate a crowd there?', *Anthinea*, Juven, Paris, 1901, p. 92.

20 See *OC*, II, p. 334: 'In everything we aim for nuance, delicacy instead of dogmatism, the relative instead of the absolute'.

21 J. Psichari, *Ernest Renan, jugements et souvenirs*, Éd. du Monde moderne, Paris, 1925, p. 288.

22 Ibid., p. 295.

23 Ibid., p. 325.

24 J. Pommier, *La vie de Jésus et ses mystères*, Nizet, Paris, 1973, pp. 119–27.

25 See *OC*, II, p. 624, n. 1 (1848), on the subject of *John*, XVIII, 36; the whole text is cited in Latin.

26 See H. Peyre, *Bibliographie critique de l'hellénisme en France de 1843 à 1870*, Yale University Press, New Haven, 1932, and more recently the contributions of P. Judet de La Combe, P. Petitmangin and M. Jacob to the volume edited by M. Bollack, H. Wisman and T. Lindken, *Philologie und Hermeneutik in Jahrhundert XIX*, Vandenhoeck & Ruprecht, Göttingen, 1983.

27 See below, in the appendix, the text of an unpublished letter from Renan to Fustel; on Fustel, see the book by F. Hartog, *Le XIXe Siècle et l'histoire. Le Cas Fustel de Coulanges*.

28 M. Peyre, *Renan et la Grèce*, p. 15.

29 *Memoirs of Ernest Renan*, tr. J. Lewis May, Geoffrey Bles, London, 1935, p. 168 (*OC*, II, p. 847).

30 *Cahiers de Jeunesse*, *OC*, IX, pp. 70, 103–10.

31 Ibid., p. 110.

32 See *Averroes*, *OC*, III; Renan writes as follows: 'Philosophy for the Semites was never any more than a purely external borrowing of little fertility, an imitation of Greek philosophy.'

33 On Renan and Egger, see the little book cited above, n. 3, by Calabresi Finzi Contini.

34 Cornélie Renan restored this manuscript to the library of the Institut in 1893; its catalogue number is Mscr 2208; a number of notes on Renan's reading are included in the file.

35 J. Psichari considered publishing it, then gave up the idea (see op. cit., pp. 59–60); J. Irigoin, who at my suggestion was good enough to examine it to assess its philological value, pronounced it remarkable but obviously 'old-fashioned'. It is my belief that it would be worth publishing as a sample of nineteenth-century philology and an example of Renan's own intellectual development. In the course of its composition, the 1848 Revolution took place and the 'Bibliothèque royale' became the 'Bibliothèque nationale'. A young scholar, Perrine Simon, has recently decided to publish a critical edition of Renan's manuscript.

36 See J. Seznec, 'Renan et la philologie classique', R. R. Bolgar (ed.), *Classical Influence*, pp. 349–62, and, above all, in the above-cited volume edited by M. Bollack, H. Wisman and T. Lindken: G. Pflug, 'Ernest Renan und die deutsche Philologie', pp. 156–77, 182–5, and the critical remarks of A. B. Neschke-Hentschke, pp. 178–81.

37 See his 1848 and 1849 articles, *OC*, I, pp. 189–205 and II, pp. 620–31. In the

conclusion to the second of these two texts, Renan remarks: 'The literatures of the East and the second-rank works of classical literature sometimes offer more philological interest and teach us more about the history of the human mind than do the accomplished monuments of the periods of perfection.'

38 'Nothing will be found here that is not simple and obvious, nothing that does not conform with the rules of Greek and Latin epigraphy', Preface to the *Corpus Inscriptionum Semiticarum*, 1881, p. xii; Boeckh is mentioned on p. xiii. See also the above-cited essay by G. Pflug and A. Dupont-Sommer's essay in the form of a *pro domo* apology, 'Ernest Renan et le "Corpus des inscriptions semitiques"', Académie des inscriptions et belles-lettres, meeting of 22 November 1968, which cites the following remark: 'Of all that I have done, what I like the best is the *Corpus*.' On the lack of success of this undertaking, see A. Caquot's contribution to the 'Centenaire de "l'Année épigraphique"', 21 October 1988, *Comptes rendus de l'Académie des inscriptions*, 3, 1988, pp. 10–15.

39 See for example his 1848 and 1854 articles on 'l'histoire de la philologie classique dans l'Antiquité' and 'les grammairiens grecs', *OC*, II, pp. 603–19, 632–42; see also his 'reply to M. de Lesseps', 1885, *OC*, I, p. 800.

40 Letter to Julie Bonaparte dated 16 March 1865: 'Assuredly, if I were not committed, as a kind of duty, to continue my *Origins of Christianity*, I would devote myself entirely to the study of Athens, created year by year, month by month, almost day by day. I am still hoping to persuade Monsieur Taine to undertake a work of this kind', *OC*, X, p. 433.

41 *History of the People of Israel*, tr. C. B. Pitman and D. Bingham, Chapman and Hall, London, 1888, vol. I, pp. x–xi (*OC*, VI, p. 14); see also *The Apostles*, Trübner & Co., London, n.d., pp. 33–4 (*OC*, IV, pp. 463–4), and the lecture of 27 January 1883 on 'Judaism as race and as religion', *OC*, I, p. 937: 'If I were granted a second life, I would devote it to Greek history which is in some respects even finer than Jewish history.'

42 *Revue des études grecques (REG)*, 1892, pp. iii–vii.

43 See his article on ancient Egypt (1865), *OC*, II, p. 369.

44 *The Future of Science*, tr. A. D. Vandam, Chapman and Hall, London, 1891, p. 434 (*OC*, III, p. 1098).

45 Ibid., p. 393 (ibid., p. 1062).

46 Ibid., p. 395 (ibid., pp. 1063–4).

47 Ibid., p. 399 (ibid., p. 1067).

48 *OC*, I, p. 922.

49 *History of the People of Israel*, vol. 2, p. 273 (*OC*, VI, p. 515).

50 *Saint Paul*, 1869, *OC*, IV, p. 832.

51 *History of the People of Israel*, vol. 1, p. x (*OC*, VI, pp. 13–14).

52 Ibid., vol. 2, p. 233 (*OC*, VI, pp. 487–8).

53 *The Apostles*, p. 32 (*OC*, IV, p. 462).

54 *History of the People of Israel*, vol. 2, p. 414 (*OC*, VI, p. 613).

55 *REG*, 1892, p. iii.

56 I am here citing the beginning of the 'letter to M. Marcellin Berthelot', 1863, *OC*, I, p. 633. I was referred to this text by E. Saïd, 'Renan's Philological Laboratory' in M. Bollack, H. Wisman, T. Lindken, op. cit., pp. 186–212. The

essential argument is repeated in *Orientalism*, Pantheon Books, New York, 1978. Saïd is an author who should be read with a certain amount of circumspection; see B. Lewis, 'The question of orientalism', *The New York Review of Books*, 24 June 1982, who makes a number of justifiable criticisms of Saïd but does not quite see the importance of the problem raised by this author. More qualified criticisms of Saïd appear in M. Rodinson, *La Fascination de l'Islam*, Maspéro, Paris, 1980, pp. 12–16.

57 Thus *REG*, 1982, p. v: 'A selection was made from among the thick crowd of humanity'; it is above all to Geoffroy Saint-Hilaire that he is referring; see for example *Histoire générale des langues sémitiques*, 1855, *OC*, VIII, p. 515.

58 See the text cited above, n. 9.

59 *The Future of Science*, p. 153 (*OC*, III, p. 858).

60 *OC*, II, pp. 328–9.

61 *OC*, II, pp. 336–73.

62 Ibid., p. 350, n. 1.

63 On these questions I owe much to T. Todorov's book *Nous et les autres*, cited above, n. 6. I also read and benefited greatly from the manuscript of Maurice Olender's *Les Langues du paradis*, Gallimard, Seuil, Paris, 1989, which contains a substantial chapter on Renan. An unpublished paper by Isabelle Rozenbaumas on Renan and Derenbourg also provided me with some useful references. See also Laudyce Rétat's Introduction to the lectures delivered at the Collège de France in 1888–9, entitled *Légendes patriarcales des Juifs et des Arabes*, Hermann, Paris, 1989.

64 Renan's two letters to Gobineau are to be found in *OC*, X, pp. 159–61, 203–5; the quotation is from p. 204. Todorov cites and correctly comments upon the second letter (op. cit., p. 166); the same cannot be said for Saïd (*Orientalism*, p. 150). The idea that some races are doomed to remain forever inferior was a dismally common one in the nineteenth century.

65 Pausanias, I, 14, 6. γλαυκός was then translated as 'blue', and still is on occasion today (*sic* in the Loeb Classical Library). H. Psichari notes (*La Prière*, p. 85) that Renan's copy of Pausanias was not annotated and many of its pages remained uncut.

66 *Essai*, III, p. 438.

67 Hugo is a relative exception. 'Les sept merveilles du monde', 1862, compared the masterpieces of various cultures without depreciating any of them, Massin (ed.), *OC*, XII, Club français du livre, 1969, pp. 905–20; admittedly however, five of those 'marvels' were Greek.

68 See G. Haupt and C. Weill, 'L'eredità di Marx ed Engels e la questione nazionale', *Studi storici*, XV, 1, 1974, pp. 270–324; see in particular pp. 283–97.

69 See H. Psichari, *La Prière*, p. 111, who bases her remarks on a letter from Renan to Berthelot dated 29 March 1865.

70 J. Michelet, op. cit., pp. 192–3. Greece lacked a sense of love and death, see p. 275.

71 In the Preface (1890) to *The Future of Science* (*OC*, III, p. 724), Renan declared: 'The inequality of the races is established.' 'Racialist' is a neologism for which T. Todorov is responsible.

72 *OC*, VIII, p. 137; see ibid., pp. 513, 527–8.

73 *OC*, VIII, p. 145, 1855; the italics are mine.

74 The most perfect expression of the theory is to be found in the lecture delivered in the Sorbonne on 2 March 1878, 'Des services rendus aux sciences historiques par la philologie', *OC*, VIII, pp. 1213–31; however, the reservations expressed in the conclusion should be underlined.

75 *Saint Paul, OC*, IV, p. 830.

76 Renan the scholar knew of the existence of Semitic polytheism, for which his own *Corpus* provided abundant evidence, but Renan the ideologue ignored it; see J. Darmesteter, the 'Annual Report' of the *Journal asiatique*, July–December 1893, p. 57, a text to which M. Olender drew my attention.

77 *History of the People of Israel*, vol. 3, p. 37 (*OC*, VI, pp. 802–9, 1891).

78 All statements that were commonplace; see M. Olender, *Les Langues du paradis*, for example pp. 82–9.

79 *History of the People of Israel*, vol. 3, p. 37 (*OC*, VI, pp. 685–6, 1891).

80 Ibid., vol. 3, p. 78 (*OC*, VI, p. 7155). 'Thus was the will of Zeus done', a Homeric expression.

81 Ibid.

82 See *Caliban*, 1888, *OC*, III, p. 382: 'Prospero taught you the language of the Aryas. With that divine language, the amount of reason that is inseparable from it entered into you.'

83 *Histoire du peuple d'Israël*, IV, 1893, *OC*, VI, p. 1129.

84 *OC*, IV, pp. 849–50.

85 *OC*, VI, p. 1128.

86 Ibid., p. 1129.

87 *Marc-Aurèle*, 1889, *OC*, VI, p. 1143.

88 *OC*, VI, p. 1145.

89 E. Bickerman, 'The Historical Foundation of Post-Biblical Jerusalem', in L. Finkelstein (ed.), *The Jews: Their History, Culture and Religion*, 3rd ed., Harper, New York, 1960, p. 101.

90 *The Apostles*, p. 189 (*OC*, IV, pp. 601–4).

91 *The Life of Jesus*, tr. William G. Hutchison, Walter Scott Publishing Company, London and Newcastle upon Tyne, 1905, pp. 285–7 (*OC*, IV, pp. 368–9).

92 *REG*, 1892, p. iii.

93 Cited by H. Psichari, *Renan d'après lui-même*, Plon, 1937, p. 276.

94 Peter Gay, *The Enlightenment: An Interpretation*, I. See also F. E. Manuel, *The Eighteenth Century Confronts the Gods*, Harvard University Press, Cambridge, Mass., 1959; *The Changing of the Gods*, University Press of New England, Hanover and London, 1983.

95 See H. Peyre, *Louis Ménard 1822–1901*, Yale University Press, New Haven, 1931.

96 H. Peyre, op. cit., pp. 57–8.

97 *Prologue d'une révolution*, Paris, 1849, reprinted in *Cahiers de la quinzaine*, Paris, 1904.

98 For example, *Opinions d'un païen sur la société moderne*, Dutenay St Amand, Librairie de l'art indépendant, 1895, vol. III, reproducing a text of 1858.

99 H. Peyre, op. cit., pp. 178–9.
100 Péguy commented upon these *Dialogues* in *Zangwill*, 1904, *Oeuvres en prose*, Pléiade, pp. 705–22: 'There are sentences in those texts that would turn you into a democrat.'
101 *Philosophical Dialogues and Fragments*, tr. Râs Bihâri Mukharjî, Trübner and Co., London, 1883, pp. 1–29 (*OC*, p. 559).
102 Ibid., pp. 59–72 (*OC*, I, pp. 611–23).
103 In an article in *La Revue des deux mondes* (1 May 1864, reprinted in *OC*, I, pp. 69–110), Renan had indeed deplored the lamentable standards of provincial universities: 'The provincial universities produce nothing original, nothing first-hand' (p. 88); but it is true that he had made an exception of Strasbourg, where Fustel was teaching: 'Only Strasbourg, thanks to its Protestant institutions, has maintained a strong tradition of study and solid methods.'
104 The archaeologist Georges Perrot, born in 1832, who was to become the Director of the École normale supérieure, was in 1864 a professor of rhetoric at the Lycée Louis-le-Grand. In that same year he published a *Mémoire sur l'île de Thasos*, to mark the beginning of the exploration of the island.

Index